AFTER THE CREDIT CRUNCH

AFTER THE CREDIT CRUNCH

No More Boom and Bust

John Redwood

Middlesex
University
PRESS

First published in 2009 by Middlesex University Press

ISBN 978 1 904750 65 9

Cover design by Helen Taylor
Typesetting by Keyline Consultancy
Printed in the UK by Ashford Colour Press

Middlesex University Press
The Burroughs
London NW4 4BT
Tel: +44 (0)20 8411 4162   Fax: +44 (0)20 8411 4167

www.mupress.co.uk

CONTENTS

ABOUT THE AUTHOR

John Redwood has been a businessman, an academic, a government adviser and a Cabinet Minister. He is currently Member of Parliament for Wokingham, a Visiting Professor at Middlesex University Business School and a Distinguished Fellow of All Souls College Oxford.

He predicted the dangers in the financial system before the crash, forecast the recession and has been contributing to the debate about how to handle the crisis. His daily blog on **www.johnredwood.com** has become a 'must-read' for many wishing to follow the twists and turns of the credit crunch, where he seeks to expose events by drawing on his blend of experience as a former City analyst, businessman, government expert and Minister.

Preface

We now know what a credit crunch is. In the summer of 2007, the world flipped from easy credit – where people and companies could lend large sums to buy properties, commodities, shares and companies that always seemed to increase in value – to the opposite. Suddenly, credit dried up, asset values fell, commodity prices plummeted and the banks wobbled.

October and November, 2008, witnessed a helter-skelter of events affecting banks, economies and governments worldwide. The credit crunch, which first showed itself in late summer 2007 – in the run on Northern Rock in the UK and the collapse of Bear Stearns in the USA – has intensified. Governments, central bankers and regulators have striven to try to catch up with the frightening pace of losses, write-offs, broken credit lines and recessionary forces.

At the beginning of October 2008, it was becoming clear that the combined forces of over-expansion in the good years, coupled with tighter money in recent months, was jeopardising many banks in many different jurisdictions. On 2 October, the Irish were so worried about the state of their banks that their government became the first to announce a comprehensive guarantee for bank deposits. Other competitor countries within the EU fretted that this was unfair: in these uncertain times, this move seemed to pose the threat that more people would transfer their deposits from banks in one location to another where they could benefit from a sovereign guarantee for their funds.

On 3 October, the world was shaken by the huge announcement by Mr Paulson, the US Treasury Secretary, of $700 billion of assistance to US banks. Although the Irish were guaranteeing 400 billion euros, it was altogether different to hear Uncle Sam, in the centre of free enterprise, announce that the US government would make so much money available to buy so-called toxic assets from the banks, to help them establish values for their loans and to give them access to more ready cash. The package proved politically contentious but was, in the end, passed by Congress and the Senate after the addition of money for various causes made it palatable to more politicians. This represented a watershed in thinking. At one and the same time it confirmed people's worst fears about the magnitude and importance of the crisis – and led to false hope that such a large gesture was bound to settle things and lead to early recovery.

By 8 October, the world's authorities had grasped that interest rate reductions were also needed, on a new scale, to seek to reassure broken markets and to ease the cost of credit to all those people and companies who had borrowed too much. The coordinated lowering of rates made an impact on markets, confirming that governments now were firmly in recession-fighting mode and had woken up to the severity of the outlook.

In Iceland, the Prime Minister warned of national bankruptcy and, on 9 October, took a major bank, Kaupthing, into nationalised control. Iceland had an extreme version of a common ailment – large, over-extended banks backed by a state with insufficient revenues to handle the crisis convincingly. The decision to nationalise the banks added to the pressure on state finances and on the local currency.

On 10 October, the G7 Finance Ministers met, agreed to support the banking systems, and formulated a loose general agenda for how to do so. Their meeting was followed, over the weekend of 11-12 October, by a rushed Paris summit of certain of the European leaders, which confirmed European versions of this support.

On 13 October, the UK announced its complex £487 billion package. It offered £200 billion of additional short-term loans to banks, £250 billion of guarantees for inter-bank lending, and £37 billion of new equity and preference capital for three leading banks. The UK banking regulator had increased the capital required of the banks which, given the time constraints and problems with getting access to share markets, necessitated government funding for some of them. The following day, the Japanese government announced that it would inject money into regional banks. The Icelandic Stock Exchange reopened and plunged by three-quarters, as people did their sums as to how much the Icelandic state would need in order to prop up the banks. The US decided to add the purchase of stakes in its top nine banks to its shopping list of uses for the $700 billion Paulson fund.

On 19 October, South Korea proposed a $130 billion package for its banks. By 27 October, a run on Icelandic shares and the currency forced their authorities to hike interest rates by 600 basis points to 18 per cent and to appeal for international help. On 29 October, the IMF offered a $25 billion loan to Hungary, which was also struggling with a run on its currency and was short of reserves to pay the bills. The USA, China and Norway made further cuts in rates.

On 30 October, Japan offered a $51 billion boost to its economy, to be followed later by China, Germany and others. On 6 November, the UK made a further emergency cut in interest rates, taking them down by 150 basis points to 3 per cent. The European Central Bank cut its rates by 50 basis points to 3.25 per cent. On 23 November, Citigroup was bailed out by the US authorities, who offered assistance on a portfolio of $306 billion of loans; they also injected $20 billion of new capital. On 24 November, the UK government announced an £8.5 billion budgetary stimulus by cutting VAT for 13 months; on the following day, the US said it would add an $800 billion support fund for US banks to the original $700 Paulson plan. On 26 November, the EU announced a 200-billion-euro stimulus, primarily coming from individual member state decisions.

As the month of November drew to a close in the UK, two leading retailers, Woolworths and MFI, went into liquidation, and another smaller Scottish bank had to close its doors. In early December, the Bank of England cut interest rates again to just 2 per cent, and the European Central Bank lowered its rates by an unusually large 75 basis points. On 8 December, French and British leaders met in Paris to discuss the crisis and to seek more coordinated reflationary action. Germany declined to attend, preferring a more prudent fiscal stance. The UK government, in its pre-Budget report, revealed that it would borrow £157 billion in 2008-9, more than 10 per cent of GDP, in order to buy bank shares and finance the growing deficit.

Over the weekend of 6-7 December, in the United States, the President-elect, Mr Obama, announced a public works stimulatory programme designed to create an additional 2.5 million jobs. The UK government announced a 'stimulatory' package of a temporary cut in VAT and various increases in public spending. This was to be financed by extra borrowing.

The US Congress agreed a package of support for the three main US car makers, who had been forced to seek financial assistance because of their large losses and balance sheet woes. The Senate was less convinced, and negotiations dragged on with the leading car makers, as President Bush attempted to use bank bail-out money to finance the automotive industry through the route of assisting with auto finance.

While many countries and banks are involved in this crisis, it is most intense in those countries which, consistently, have borrowed too much and are running balance-of-payments deficits. The crisis has brought Iceland, Hungary and the Baltic republics low, as they have been the most overextended. At the other end of the spectrum, countries such as China and Japan, with healthy trade surpluses and large foreign exchange reserves, are in much better shape to try to reflate their economies through the conventional mechanisms of spending more, taxing less, and slashing interest rates.

The two largest Anglo-Saxon economies, the USA and the UK, are at the centre of the storm. They each have their own crisis. There is a family resemblance, since their authorities made similar mistakes at similar times. Both have decided to try to limit the length and depth of the downturns by active responses, slashing interest rates, borrowing huge sums to lend to and through the banks, and underpinning their precarious financial institutions. Both have seen a huge increase in their indebtedness through nationalisations and through the loss of revenues and the increases in spending which come about naturally as an advanced economy slumps. The US authorities took into public ownership their two large mortgage banks, Freddie Mac and Fannie Mae. The UK nationalised Northern Rock, the assets of Bradford and Bingley and a majority of the shares of the Royal Bank of Scotland.

Both governments are now moving onto offering financial support to non-financial sectors, as they see the damage that falling demand and a shortage of bank finance is doing to other parts of their economies.

Many governments adopted a crude Keynesianism, believing that expanding public spending and borrowing would increase activity and help to reflate the economy. They encountered two short-term problems with this approach: the banks were unable to function properly, limiting the impact of any extra spending; and the money had to be borrowed, which meant that money that could otherwise have been spent had to be taken from savers, in order to pay for the government programmes, limiting the reflationary effects.

The US dollar has rallied during this period, apparently reflecting two differing pressures. Many US savers and companies have repatriated investment money from outside the US, wishing to reduce their risk in foreign markets. At the same time, many banks have had to pay losses on contracts and loans that are denominated in dollars, and have had to buy dollars to settle the accounts. Conversely, sterling has weakened badly over the last year. The international community has revised its view of Britain, no longer buying into the government's view of a well-run and lightly borrowed country. The UK authorities have made no attempt to protect the pound, seeing in its fall the advantage that it will help the commercial sector become more competitive in world markets.

In this book, we look at how the authorities handled the early manifestations of the credit crunch on both sides of the Atlantic. We show how their first responses made problems worse, and how they were slow to grasp the magnitude and significance of what was happening. Nationalisation was an expensive way of helping banks which needed more capital, when central banks have powers to tide banks over a difficult period in share markets through lending and guaranteeing against security. Ordering banks to raise more capital when markets were reluctant to help was a strange decision, especially so soon after a long period when regulators had sought too little capital and thus allowed banks to overextend.

We look at how the UK has experienced a particularly vicious version of the credit crunch. An economy which depended heavily on financial sector business borrowed liberally in the good times, to sustain substantial private consumption and to finance public spending in excess of revenue. When the downturn hit the UK, authorities had much less fiscal flexibility than did other countries. At the same time, the country's revenues were bound to drop off more sharply than elsewhere, given the dependence on financial companies badly exposed to the storm. The structural weaknesses of the UK economy were cruelly exposed by a recession brought on by collapses in the financial sector.

The book examines the immediate crisis and takes a longer look at what the UK needs to do to restore a more competitive economy, with a better balance of activities. For too long, the UK has relied on borrowing, on migrant labour and artificially high consumption. For too long, the economy has moved forward – based, primarily, on its successful financial sector. As a result, more than five million people of working age have no job before the recession bites, a figure determined from the number of people of working age on benefits in 2007.

The British economy, in the good years, grew much faster in London and the south east, where the financial sector was concentrated. In the early years of the new century, the gaps grew very stark between London house prices and the rest; London incomes and the rest; and London commercial property and the rest. Now, there is a long and painful process of adjustment.

If the UK wishes to be more successful in the future, with a better-balanced economy capable of spreading prosperity more widely than London and parts of the south east, action needs to be taken in several areas. During this period of downturn, when there will be men and machines idle, the country needs to build the new power stations, roads, railways, reservoirs and other infrastructure it will need for recovery. The country needs to try again to improve and reform its education and training – and remodel its welfare system, so there are more incentives for people to equip themselves for work and get a job. It would be good if the next recovery included many more people in its success than the last one, which spanned the period 1992 to 2007 – and if it were accomplished less on borrowed money and more on earnings from hard work. The danger today is that the government has overextended the credit of the nation by buying such large positions in big banks. I hope the government will turn to cutting the taxpayers' risk and returning many of the banking assets to the private sector quickly, before more damage is done.

I post a daily commentary on my website, **www.johnredwood.com**, much of which is currently given to charting the course of the credit crunch and the responses of the authorities. It may be useful to help readers stay up to date, as events unfold.

1 | The credit crunch

INTRODUCTION

Credit makes the world go round. Taken in moderation, it has a benign effect. People need to be able to borrow to pay to get their business off the ground, to finance their offices and homes, to pay for their work in progress. If credit is taken to excess, a great deal of damage can be done. Like alcohol, a little helps the party along; a lot means it ends in tears or worse.

I first became aware of the seriousness of the world's banking and financial problems in May of 2007. I came across a paper produced by Henry Maxey of Ruffer LLP, called *Cracking The Credit Market Code*. He opened his interesting account of what had been happening with the following words:

> *Anyone with a cautious disposition has a sense that there is a fragility within the US-centric and financial world: too much debt, excess consumption, record deficits, carry trades, ubiquitous hedge funds, monstrous derivatives markets ... but now the sub-prime mortgage pot has knocked the lid from this black box and we've had our first opportunity to observe the mechanics of history's most excessive credit binge. It is our contention that the magic of the mechanism is nothing more than fallacy of composition, wrapped in moral hazard, inside myopia hedge fund partners LLC.*

Arresting language like that made me think. I read more, I studied more. I looked up more details on the hedge funds, the derivatives, the market for securitised assets and banking balance sheets. I soon came to realise that Henry Maxey was right to sound such a strong warning in such exciting language.

In a way it is a story of gross regulatory misjudgment. In the UK, banks are regulated by the Financial Services Authority (FSA) although bank regulation also has an international dimension, with regulations being standardised through the activities of the Basel Committee on Banking Supervision. Regulators at Basel had solemnly set out how banks and other financial institutions were to keep substantial capital. This would mean that they would tend to and grow their businesses prudently. But the rules the Committee adopted were an open incitement to banks to find ways other than keeping loans and advances on their own balance sheets. After the so-called 'Basel I' guidelines were introduced, if you owned the loan and honestly stated it in your accounts, you needed more capital. If you sold the loan on, or financed it through a market-oriented mechanism, you needed less capital. Not surprisingly, banks decided to do just that on a huge scale, lending money to people and then finding others in the market prepared to buy all or part of the loan from them.

In parallel to the banking system there grew up a huge marketplace in different types of paper, as banks sought to lay off their risks and advance yet more money. There were asset-backed securities, collateralised bond obligations (CBOs), credit default swaps, collateralised debt obligations (CDOs), collateralised loan obligations (CLOs), commercial mortgage-backed securities, other mortgage-backed securities and structured finance CDOs, amongst others. All of these were ways of repackaging the loans which banks had made, so that they could be sold onto other participants in the market. Once they had sold the loans on, the banks could advance some more money to others. It created a perpetual credit machine.

These 'other participants' might turn out to be other banks, who took in each other's debt obligations in packaged form. They might be hedge funds, who themselves geared up their balance sheets, buying huge quantities of these things, constructing a careful cat's cradle of asset-backed paper on the one hand and their own borrowings or short positions on the other. They might be conventional investment funds, using more exotic types of paper to increase their yield and returns. One of the joys of the system was its enormous flexibility. Many bright people devoted their energies to slicing and dicing the original loans and debts in ever-more exact and exotic packages and tranches, capable of meeting the individual yield and capital requirements of the individual investors.

Effectively, we saw the manufacture of a parallel system of credit creation. Everyone knew that the main banks had credit-creating powers. Any bank keeps a certain amount of cash in its tills in case depositors turn up wanting to withdraw their funds, but it is allowed by the regulators to lend many times this amount. In a sense the bank 'borrows short' from its depositors and 'lends long' to those wanting a mortgage or a company loan from it. Whenever banks get into trouble, people express shock and horror that they should behave in such an irresponsible way – but that is what they have always done, and have to do, in order to make a profit.

BANKING – A BUSINESS LIKE ANY OTHER

The main way banks make a profit is by taking the risk of venturing their money for longer periods than they are borrowing it, enabling them – in normal times – to charge a higher rate of interest on the money they are lending than they pay on the money they are borrowing. Their profitability is also greatly enhanced by the fact that they can create credit, increasing the amount of lending they can offer for any given amount of share capital and cash in their tills.

Banks are able to do this for two main reasons. The first is that the main credit-creating banks are large and well-established institutions. For so long as people have confidence in them, there is no problem. I know, trusting my clearing bank, that if I did wish to get all my money out tomorrow I could do so. They would have quite enough money in their tills to satisfy me; normally, I would not be faced with the position where all the other depositors also turned up on the same day, wanting their money back. The second reason is that my confidence, and the confidence of others, is further increased by the fact that the central bank will stand behind a large clearing bank. If too many depositors turned up on the same day wanting their money back, requiring more than the bank had in banknotes at that time, it could always get more banknotes from the Bank of England, its 'lender of last resort'.

In parallel with this well-established credit creation system, other financial institutions in the market started to do something similar – but without recourse to the Bank of England should they get into difficulties. Some of the investment funds which decided to invest in the exotic paper developed by the marketplace were able to invest many times the initial starting capital placed in the fund, by borrowing and gearing themselves. They did so, not because they were long-established and much-trusted institutions. They did so, because they reckoned that the securities they were buying would maintain their value, so enabling them to earn big fees from the small margins involved in the very large purchases they were making. In many cases these funds were new and little-known, and were relatively secretive in the way they went about their task.

For example, UBS calculated that a package of what came to be called 'sub-prime' mortgages could be assembled and split up in a way which separated the risks with the resulting assets to different types of buyers. UBS thought that 75 per cent of the total lent on mortgage could be put into an instrument rated 'AAA', 14 per cent could be put into an instrument rated 'A minus' to 'AA plus', 3 per cent could be rated 'BB minus' to 'BBB plus', 2 per cent below 'BBB minus' and 6 per cent in an unrated tranche. The markets believed that UBS's new skills at segregating risk and cash flows could take the 'toxic' elements of the sub-prime mortgage portfolio – the bits that were unlikely to be repaid – away from most of the asset, leaving a package of acceptable paper with all the characteristics of high-grade lending.

Such was the demand for these different types of paper generated by packaging up groups of sub-prime mortgages, the mortgage brokers were able to write more and more of them, relaxing their standards for the mortgages and lowering the interest rate offer to the people queuing up for them. It appeared that markets had created a perpetual money machine, capable of taking credit to the people on low incomes with most uncertain job prospects, in a way which the market could handle.

These developments took place against the background of a general looseness of monetary policy around the world, lasting from September 2001 until the end of 2005. On 3 January 2001 the Federal Reserve Fund of America ('the Fed') was able to cut its rate by 50 base points (i.e. 0.5 per cent) to 6 per cent. The rate fell quite rapidly throughout most of that year, hitting only 1.75 per cent on 11 December. It remained below 2 per cent throughout 2002, 2003 and most of 2004, finally being hoisted to 2 per cent on 10 November 2004, and to 2.25 per cent on 14 December that year. The rate then climbed steadily in 2005 and 2006, reaching 5.2 per cent on 29 June 2006. What the Fed did, so other central banks around the world tended to do as well. We lived through a remarkable few years, where interest rates were extremely low by historical standards. This made it possible for people in markets to lend ever more money to low-income individuals, offering them the benefit of these very low rates and so making the loans affordable for them. People in the United States, the United Kingdom and elsewhere were able to buy homes which would have been out of their grasp at any more normal interest rates.

Why did the Fed and other monetary authorities around the world keep interest rates so low? In their policies, they were tending to target price inflation. From 2001 to late 2004 we lived through a benign era, in which the favourable impact of Indian and Chinese competition was keeping prices down. The more goods and services the Indians and Chinese provided, the more they exerted downward pressure on prices around the world. The central banks' monetary authorities could say to themselves "We are doing a great job keeping prices down. We do not need to increase interest rates to deter lending because, no matter how much people borrow, prices remain under good control thanks to the massive expansion of Asian economic capacity and their willingness to export."

In addition, in the western world, the digital revolution was generating some efficiencies and increases in productivity, further adding to the argument that there was no problem with price inflation. The world economy appeared to have a remarkable ability to respond to the rising demand created by increased credit without causing inflation.

In the UK, used to interest rates between 5 per cent and 7 per cent in the 1990s, rates also fell. From 6 per cent on 10 February 2000 they tumbled to 3.5 per cent by 10 July 2003 and did not go above 4 per cent again until 6 May 2004.

The credit rating agencies (CRAs) played an important part in the development of the market in so-called structured credits. If a US bank, in conjunction with mortgage brokers, lent substantial sums of money to a whole range of new property purchases on mortgage, to begin with it did so out of its own money, placing those mortgages on its own balance sheet. When it wanted to expand this business further, the bank concerned would package up a large number of the existing mortgages and create several different financial products based upon different parts of the mortgage portfolio it had assembled. It would then take these financial products to a rating agency and ask them to decide how risky the different packages were. The main package would have reasonable guarantees about the interest payments and repayments going into it. The most risky package would be in line to take the predicted early defaults on mortgages and so, in order to make it attractive, it would need more income relative to the so-called safer package.

The rating agency would make an assessment of just how risky the different packages were, based upon the typical experience of loan defaults at the time, and give each a rating. Anything getting a rating in the 'As' was a high-quality instrument, which pension funds, banks and others could buy safe in the knowledge that they were likely to be looked after and get their money back. The hedge funds, higher-risks funds and market traders could take the low-rated paper, which the rating agencies accepted might result in default and substantial losses. The various funds were attracted to do this because the income and potential reward on it was so much higher than on the highly credit-rated packages.

When the sub-prime bubble burst, there was considerable criticism of the rating agencies. People said that the agencies had wrongly assessed the risks and they should have realised that many of these packages of sub-prime mortgages were 'toxic'. Blessed with the wonders of 20/20 hindsight, it became popular amongst the wags to say that anyone must have realised that taking 200 high-risk mortgages and putting them together did not suddenly make a low-risk product. At first sight it seemed an obvious jibe, but further analysis shows that this is unfair. The people who undertook this process did so successfully for several years, and they did so for good reasons.

Firstly, there is less risk in having a one-hundredth share in 100 risky mortgages than owning one risky mortgage. The law of averages applies. If having a 'risky' mortgage means there is a 1 in 10 chance of the person holding it being unable to repay it, then if you hold a 10 per cent share in 100 mortgages you know you are likely to get 90 per cent of your money back. However, if you hold just one mortgage you face a 10 per cent chance of losing all your money. On this simple theory of 'portfolio averaging', many people in the market thought it was a good idea to take a group of mortgages – each of which they knew to be riskier than the average mortgage – and package them together to reduce the risk.

Secondly, both the rating agencies and the underlying investors carried out extensive tests on the packages and mortgages put into these instruments. They used figures for the then-likely rate at which people would default on the mortgage or repay the mortgage, in order to do some elaborate sums on just how risky the packages were. This was all fine until the predicted default rate escalated.

The decisive change came when the monetary authorities of the world moved from a period of ultra-low interest rates to a period of considerably higher rates. Moving the Fed fund's rate up to 5.25 per cent at its peak might not have seemed a dramatic move if you look at the long run of interest rates that have applied in the United States of America. However, the Fed was moving the rate up from a low figure of only 1 per cent, which meant a quintupling of the rate of interest governing the American banking and credit system. This was a massive hike, and it had a very big impact upon people on low incomes who had been lent money to buy a house. They had been led to believe that all would be well, as long as they could afford the first year or two of mortgage interest payments, which were carefully protected at the starting low interest rate level. Instead, when their protected year or two came to an end, they were faced with the most enormous increases in their mortgage bills because the general level of market interest rates had shot upwards so much. Some mortgage payers faced a trebling or worse in their interest payments, which was simply too much for them to accept.

As a result of the very large increase in interest rates from a very low base, enormous pressures were exerted on the bottom end of the mortgage market. People who had been persuaded to take on mortgages in the boom times now faced the prospect that far too much of their income would be eaten up in trying to meet the mortgage payments. Many left it to the mortgage company to resell the property. Others decided to sell their properties for themselves and repay the mortgage as best they could.

The more that interest rates rose, the more sub-prime mortgages the central bank created. A reasonable quality mortgage to someone who had every intention of meeting the payments could suddenly become a dodgy mortgage. The more interest rates soared, the more that many people suddenly became priced out of the market into which they had been tempted by the easy-money conditions of a year or two earlier. As the selling pressures in the housing market built up, so house prices started to tumble. When market conditions get tough, American house prices have a tradition of adjusting downwards further and more rapidly than in a heavily planned market, such as the United Kingdom, and so it proved again in 2007. The more house prices fell, the more that people owning houses wondered whether it was a good idea to carry on owning. Some thought it would be a good idea to try and sell their properties before they had lost even more of their money. Another wave of sellers emerged in the marketplace, driving the price of property ever downwards.

This, too, had an immediate impact on the value of all the securitised debt instruments being owned by the hedge funds, the investment funds, the banks and others in the financial markets. To have a successful investment in a package of mortgages two conditions needed to be met. Firstly, most of the mortgage holders needed to be able to continue to afford the mortgages so that they could pay the interest which remunerated everybody else in the financial system. Secondly, investors needed the reassurance that, if a mortgage holder could no longer carry on paying the mortgage, the house could be repossessed and sold for at least the value of that mortgage, thus protecting the capital of the investor. By the middle of 2007, on a whole range of what came to be called 'sub-prime mortgages', neither of these conditions could be met. The investing community was faced with the awful problem that many more people could no longer afford to pay their mortgage and that, in these extreme circumstances, their houses were no longer worth the amount of money advanced against them.

At this point people naturally became very critical of the rating agencies. They claimed that the rating agencies should have foreseen the situation and should not have given such high ratings to the fancy paper that had been created on the back of the mortgage portfolios. In response, the rating agencies pointed out that they did carry out their 'back tests' at the time they performed the evaluations. Unfortunately, these 'back tests' happened to have been based upon a different level of market interest rates, and a different level of house prices, from the ones that came to rule in 2007.

Critics of the system blamed the rating agencies, on the grounds that the rating agency earned its income from approving new financial products. The architects of the products obviously wanted good ratings so that they could sell their products more widely in the marketplace. Critics argued that the rating agencies effectively allowed riskier lending to be packaged and sold on, in order to increase the amount of money they were supervising and on which they were gaining fees. I think this is an unfair criticism of the rating agencies. They followed perfectly intelligent approaches but, by definition, their rating was backward-looking. It was not geared to forecasting higher delinquency rates or higher interest rates, the investment factors which brought some of this lending to an unfortunate end. Investors had become too ready to assume that, because it had a favourable rating on day one, an instrument would always maintain that rating and would prove to be a good long-term investment. Sensible investors have always known that, sometimes, markets move more quickly than do rating agencies in changing their ratings, and that ratings anyway are subject to amendment in the light of market circumstances and changes in the conditions underlying investment.

Critics of the system also claimed that 'securitisation' made the banks and mortgage brokers less prudent in the advances they made. They argued that a bank would pay more attention to limiting the amount someone could borrow if those borrowings would have to stay on the bank's balance sheet as an asset. Conversely, critics said, knowing that it could sell a loan on meant that a bank was inclined to lend more than it should have done. The bank earned fees for making the advance, and more fees on selling the loans on, enabling it to generate ever-more revenue from acting effectively as a broker and arranger rather than having to take the risk of the loan itself. In many cases this, too, could be an unfair criticism, as banks presumably wanted a continuing relationship with the persons they were lending to, and might well be running their current and deposit accounts as well as offering them a mortgage. It would be very short-sighted banking policy knowingly to advance more money to someone than they are likely to be able to repay, just in order to earn a fee for doing so.

Henry Maxey did some general figures on the role the hedge funds played in increasing the amount of borrowing in the system. His worked example, which he took from a 2005 Fitch report, was of a $10 million unlevered hedge fund. He felt that such a hedge fund could lever up its balance sheet, by borrowing and other means, to achieve $60 million of purchasing power. If the hedge fund specialised in buying the lowest two grades of residential mortgage-backed securities with all of its $60 million leveraged fund, it could gain exposure to a residential mortgage portfolio of $850 million. Therefore, by buying just the last 7 per cent of the mortgage-backed security structure – the 7 per cent most likely to result in default – the hedge fund had used the cheap funding of senior tranches to acquire residual cash flows on a huge pool of loans. The leverage multiple to the total package of loans is 14.3 times the original capital.

During the boom years it is certain that far more securities were issued than there were savings in the world economy, implying that many investment funds were deploying a considerable leverage to buy more than the underlying cash flows would normally have suggested. The interest being paid on the underlying mortgages funds the whole business. Out of the interest payments, the trustee and administrators draw their fees on the packaged vehicle. Then there is a management fee to those involved in the 'senior' debt. Next, the interest on the senior debt is paid. Then – if all is still in order – interest is paid upon the 'mezzanine' securities and, finally, anything left over is paid to the lowest grade and equity grade risk at the bottom. If things start to go wrong, then the senior notes get repaid in full. After they have been fully redeemed, anything left over is made available to try and redeem the mezzanine securities. In such a situation, the high-risk obligations are usually wiped out.

As this brief description implies, things are extremely complicated. The whole idea of the CDO structure is to divide and distribute the risk of the underlying loans in different ways. Those investors who want a higher return have to accept great risk than those who want a lower and more reliable return, and who take less risk. Not surprisingly, trying to analyse in advance how these things were going to turn out proved to be difficult. Constructing the complex model to work out value was difficult, because different rules over who got what in terms of interest and repayment, and on what conditions repayment was triggered, applied to different parts of the investment package. As Morgan Stanley explained, in somewhat complex language, in their primer on CDOs:

The complex waterfall structures and the potential for diversion of cash flows because of structural protections and coverage triggers imply that analytical models have to take into account default probabilities, as well as the determinants that the different coverage ratios in a mutually consistent fashion. This, coupled with the optional redemption feature of most CDOs, calls for the modelling of interest rate risk in conjunction with the default risks of assets. Since the underlying collateral pools are managed, albeit according to predefined guidelines, the impact of future trading activities and collateral managers is difficult to model. Some analysts model the trading provisions assuming that the managers are traded to the extremes of all possible trading constraints, which has the effect of painting all managers with the same brush, constraining relative value judgement. Trading further complicates the already difficult problem of modelling and parameterisation of correlation.

An adequate summary of this would be that no one really knows what an investment is worth, and the values can shift dramatically when market conditions change in a way which most models could not hope to capture.

When the crash began, people soon discovered that their valuation systems were wrong. Investments thought to be of good quality traded at prices close to their issue price, with little variation. As soon as people thought their quality was poorer, they fell in price, and the gap between buying and selling prices became bigger. The market dried up in these instruments and there was a panic rush to the exit. It did not matter that an AAA-rated piece of paper had an average default rate of zero within one year of the rating, and anything rated A or above had an average default rate of 0.02 per cent within one year of the rating. It did not matter that a B-rated piece of paper only had an average default rating of less than 6.5 per cent within one year of the rating. The numbers were changing rapidly but, more importantly, people's willingness to buy and hold this paper had changed dramatically as well. In a desperate attempt to clean up their balance sheets and to create more cash, banks had to dump their investments in this paper. Hedge funds, used to trading on fine margins, had to close down their positions rapidly before their losses went out of control. It didn't matter what the valuation model said; across the board, the paper was suddenly deemed to be toxic and to have little value. At exactly the point where the market needed to take the strain, the market in these CDOs and CLOs froze.

The interaction between the investment funds, the hedge funds and the conventional banks became worse as 2007 limped into 2008. Because the markets had frozen, far less new business could be written. Because the markets no longer had a huge appetite for risk and for taking the segregated paper that had been built on the underlying loans, a large number of people in banks were no longer gainfully employed. Fewer mortgages were being written, default rates were up, banks were short of cash – and many people were trying to sell, rather than buy, paper that had fuelled the money-go-round over the previous five years. The greater the cost of people in the banks twiddling their thumbs, the bigger the losses the banks incurred. The bigger the banks' losses, the less confidence there was in them, and the less cash they had to repair their losses on their paper. The money-go-round which had propelled the banks to more turnover, more profit, and thus to even more turnover, was suddenly pulled into reverse. The regulators at the gates were demanding more capital, not less, for any given amount of business. The marketplace was demanding from the bankers a more prudent approach at exactly the point where they were forced into less prudence because they were losing money instead of making it.

THE RISE AND FALL OF BEAR STEARNS

The crisis can be seen in the rise and fall of Bear Stearns. In 2005-7, Bear Stearns was recognised in the Fortune survey of America's most admired companies. First opened as an equity trading house in 1923 by Joseph Bear and Robert Stearns, it went public in 1985. It handled mergers and acquisitions, equity and fixed income activity, as well as providing the normal range of investment banking services. On 2 June 2007, the first rumblings that things were not well occurred when Bear Stearns had to go to the support of one of its funds, the Bear Stearns High Grade Structured Credit Fund, offering to it a collateralised loan of up to $3.2 billion. It also sought banking assistance for the Bear Stearns High Grade Structured Credit Enhanced Leverage Fund. Both these funds had been trading on slim margins in the products involved, and the company suddenly discovered that they were not worth anything like the original estimates of their value. On 16 July 2007, Bear Stearns had to tell the market that, given the collapse of the sub-prime mortgage market, two sub-prime hedge funds had lost nearly all their value. This led to a report in September that Bear Stearns profits were down 61 per cent owing to hedge fund losses.

Unfortunately Bear Stearns had too much of this difficult paper on its own books for comfort. Confidence in the company continued to wane, leading people to cancel business with it or not to seek business through it. In March 2008, the Federal Reserve Bank of New York provided an emergency loan to try to avert a collapse of the company. As of 30 November 2007, Bear Stearns had contract amounts of approximately $13.4 trillion in derivatives and financial instruments. It had $28 billion in assets of dubious value, against a net equity position of only $11.7 billion.

On 14 March 2008, JP Morgan Chase provided a 28-day emergency loan to Bear Stearns at the same time as the Federal Reserve Bank's action. Two days later, Bear Stearns entered a merger agreement with JP Morgan Chase, valuing its shares at only $2 a share. This compared with a price of over $150 a share at the beginning of 2007. On 24 March, the shareholders of Bear Stearns challenged JP Morgan's acquisition of the firm at the knockdown price of $2 a share; a new agreement was thrashed out, raising JP Morgan Chase's offer to $10 a share, to which shareholders agreed on 29 May.

It was an amazing fall from grace for one of Wall Street's most prestigious and finest houses. The talented and commercial people at Bear Stearns had pushed the prevailing market models of the time to the limit, only to discover too late that, if the underlying security started to deteriorate, as the mortgages did, it had big implications for the value of all their securitised paper. Bear Stearns was left holding too much securitised paper after the market had decided it was worth much less than original estimates of its value. Once it was known that Bear Stearns was in trouble it appeared as a wounded (forced) seller in a difficult market and was ultimately prey to cancellation of business, to pressure to raise more cash, and was forced into a deal to save some of its jobs, assets and activities.

As it turned out, although the actions of the Federal Reserve Bank and JP Morgan were not without their critics, it was a very smooth rescue compared with what was going on on the other side of the Atlantic in Britain with Northern Rock, the subject of the next chapter. Once the crisis was clear to see, the Fed and Morgan moved very swiftly. What could be rescued was rescued. The Bear Stearns saga was just part of a much bigger drama as the market struggled to find new values for CDOs, CLOs and the other structured products, and as the market adjusted to the underlying reality in the US housing market.

Out on the streets of middle America, house and flat prices continued to fall. Although unemployment remained low and earnings held up reasonably, the impact of the much higher mortgage interest rates which came through as the easy terms of the early months and years terminated, forced more and more sellers onto the market. The higher rates were also putting more and more people off entering the market in the first place. The US construction industry had to start laying people off and the banks had to count their losses.

Meanwhile, elsewhere around the world, substantial pools of cash and liquidity were being built up. At exactly the time that the US financial system was entering a credit crunch, with banks short of cash and asset values falling, the reverse was happening in the winning economies of the commodity producers and the industrial success stories. China was building her mighty cash pile out of exporting to the world. In the Middle East the oil producers were on a bonanza, with the oil price rising month by month, giving them windfall profits and revenues which – in the first instance – built their reserves. Saudi Arabia, Abu Dhabi, Dubai and the other main oil producers in the Middle East accumulated large surpluses. The same bonanza helped Russia, and the big rise in metals prices meant that a commodity-producing economy such as Australia also prospered. The world was not short of liquidity overall, but there was a substantial redistribution of cash holdings going on at exactly the same time as America and Europe were in credit crunch meltdown.

It meant that as the European and American banks grew weaker by the day, so there was money available from the Middle East and Asia to help refinance them. One way or another, money had to be directed from the very liquid parts of the world to the credit crunch areas of the world, to keep the economic system going. American and European banks clearly needed a lot of new capital in a hurry. They had managed to destroy substantial wealth by putting so much money into risky instruments that were now worth a fraction of the values of a couple of years earlier. The banks were also struggling for profitability against the background of collapsing commercial and residential property markets on both sides of the Atlantic. Traditionally, European and American banks had relied upon property values as one of the main forms of security for their lending, so were exposed to the sharp falls in property markets they experienced in the second half of 2007 and during 2008.

Many of the large banks in America and Europe decided they had to raise more money from the market, often egged on by their regulators. Sovereign wealth funds and cash-rich investors in the Middle East and Asia saw the opportunity to buy into the big western banks, on terms that looked cheap compared with their share prices just a year or two earlier. Banks made new shares available in order to put more cash into their tills and balance sheets.

The credit crunch was made deeper throughout the western world. It was not just in America where banks were too easy with their money, lending it to people who would find it difficult to meet the interest charges, let alone the repayments. The whole system was based upon ever-escalating property values. In the effervescent economies of Ireland and Spain, two countries within the Eurozone itself, the relatively low interest rates within the Zone were much below those that were really required; this led to a substantial increase in lending against property. House prices soared in both countries. Banks, mortgage brokers, estate agents and investors enjoyed the bonanza while it lasted. Subsequently, as in America and Britain, the tightening of money in the middle of the decade led to the predictable retrenchment in both Ireland and Spain and house prices started to tumble. The European Central Bank was deaf to pleas for lower interest rates; they were trying to temper the overall rate of inflation throughout the Eurozone area, and were naturally more guided by the needs and wishes of Germany, the biggest economy within the zone.

The Eurozone was always bound to be unstable for the peripheral economies because they had not been brought into line with the inflation and economic performance of the centre. The wild peripheries of Iberia and Ireland enjoyed a wonderful bonanza while they could, but then faced exactly the same property crunch that the Anglo Saxon economies were experiencing.

The credit crunch which developed in the West had, ironically, been fuelled by the success of the East, which sent ever-increasing values of goods and services, which the West was always prepared to purchase – by borrowing more. The magical money-go-round, while it lasted, enriched the East by putting money into their coffers for goods and services supplied, and enriched the West by buttressing their asset values and allowing people to live beyond their means. At the end of seven years of massive credit expansion, the West had huge debts and the East had huge reserves: Western consumers owned (overvalued) properties, better cars, better consumer durables and had enjoyed many a good holiday. This was balanced by higher incomes and some acquisition of personal effects in the Asian economies, where saving remained higher. National saving, in the form of accumulating reserves, became the principle pursuit of these developing nations.

The world economy was now very much out of balance. Western and Asian economies were mutually dependent: if the West deflated too fast, it would mean redundancies and lower incomes in the East – which had grown accustomed to exporting to it. It would also mean job losses in the West itself. Throughout much of the easy-money period, the dollar continued to fall on the exchanges. Because the Chinese refused to accept much of the adjustment, by managing or controlling their exchange rate, the pressure fell on currencies such as the yen and the euro, which rose consistently against the dollar. By 2007, the dollar had fallen so far that it had priced America back into export markets, and this started to correct the big imbalance in the American trade accounts that had been a feature of the mid-part of the opening decade of the 21st century. Periodically, China gave in to pressure and allowed some upward movement of its currency and this, combined with the inflation now unleashed in China itself, started to erode Chinese competitiveness at the same time.

The seeds of adjustment started to emerge from the weeds of the credit explosion. America had to turn her hand to exporting to earn some more money and to reduce her trade deficit. Consumers in America, Britain and some Eurozone countries had to rein back their private debt and restrain their consumption. Eastern economies, if they wished to keep their growth going, had to consume more of their own and had to be less dependent upon the credit raised in America and Europe.

In the short term, the recessions in many economies are steep and deep. As I write, these imbalances are gradually being corrected by the strong market movements they have unleashed. We can look forward to quite a long period of slower growth – or even recession – in the western economies, as people seek to bring their spending into line with their earnings, and seek to repay some of their debt. We are living through a period of sharp retrenchment in commercial and residential property prices in America and Europe, as reality sinks home and as the credit-creating, property-boosting, money machine is switched off. It was heady and exciting while it lasted. The people who were involved in it were neither as stupid nor as venal as some people now wish us to believe. They all did it for the best of reasons, and they did it primarily because the central banks made it all possible by setting interest rates at very low levels. They were encouraged by the regulators, whose regulatory system was an inducement to have less money on a bank's balance sheet and more money zinging around the securitised markets. People had no reason to expect the music to stop so suddenly, and it took the central banks a considerable length of time, and some very tough actions, to get the merry-go-round to stop. Just as the credit explosion was created by the central banks and the regulators, so the credit crunch was created by them as well.

In September 2008, the US story became a gripping drama. The pressures were so great on the two large mortgage providers, colloquially known as Fannie Mae and Freddie Mac, that the US authorities were forced into offering guarantees, effectively nationalising them and committing taxpayers' money to keep the mortgages flowing for the next couple of years. When Lehman Brothers announced it was having difficulties, it was allowed to file for bankruptcy protection. Merrill Lynch was bought by Bank of America, at a low share price compared to its previous history, to give it the support of a larger group. September was meltdown time in the markets, as financial institutions strove to sort out the mess of all those traded instruments which were no longer worth what, in better times, businesses had thought they were worth.

For anyone who had lived through previous cycles, this one was not so different – even though the extent of the credit excess was greater, and some of the financial technology was even cleverer and more strangely-named than in previous cycles. In the end, it was very similar to all other cycles. Low interest rates set by central banks lead to too much borrowing. High interest rates set by the same central banks stop the process, and cause a fall in asset prices. That is the story of the last decade, just as it was the story of many previous decades.

How a bank is regulated to ensure it has enough capital

Currently, banks and the scale of their lending are controlled by regulation. Among the requirements the Regulator places on them are those relating to capital. Clearly the Regulator has confidence in our banks, and believes all the main UK banks have sufficient capital to trade – if he did not, he would have to withdraw the licence and require an orderly run off of the particular business concerned.

Because there is such an intense de-leveraging underway – stemming from a wish by the authorities to cut overall lending and borrowing – many now think banks should have more capital than the minimum the Regulator requires, and more than some of them currently have above that minimum. Also, fear within the banking sector is forcing banks to raise more capital than the Regulator requires, and more than they have been used to employing in recent years for a given level of lending.

The principal requirement is to have sufficient 'Tier 1' capital. Basically, this consists of funds provided by shareholders to their bank when the shares are first issued, and the accumulated profits left in the bank after all payments of bonuses to staff, dividends to shareholders and other payments have been made. Typically a bank will have at least £5 or £6 of Tier 1 capital for every £100 of advances made to customers and other investments made by the bank. The idea is that if the bank proved a bad judge of these loans, then the shareholders' funds can cover the losses. Usually, it would be unheard of for a bank to lose more than 5-6 per cent on all the advances it made, either due to failure of customers to repay, or failure to raise enough money from the security lodged to repay the loan when a customer does give up payments. Bad debts on most quality lending would normally run at less than 1 per cent overall, after taking into account money released from security where payments are not met.

There is a further 'back up' requirement, which is to have some 'Tier 2' capital as well. This consists of money held as provisions against losses, surpluses on the bank's assets such as its directly owned property, and long-term money borrowed from others. In the unlikely event of the bank having to go into administration this money also could be drawn down or released by asset sales, to pay off the depositors and other creditors. Tier 1 and Tier 2 capital together might amount to, say, £10 for every £100 of loans.

A bank does not have to provide the same shareholder cover for any assets such as Treasury bills and government bonds, since the Regulator assumes that these can easily be turned into cash. It is just the 'risk assets' – the mortgages and company overdrafts – that need the full shareholder cover.

The effect of the requirements is that a bank may be 'ten-times geared' – that is, it can lend 10 times its combined Tier 1 and Tier 2 capital. It raises the money to make loans by taking in deposits from the public and companies, and borrowing in the markets. Those banks that have relied heavily on shorter-term borrowing in money markets are the ones which have faced the most difficulties – Northern Rock being the worst example. When the money markets dried up, the Rock was left short of borrowing to finance its substantial mortgage lending.

The authorities have to decide how much extra capital cover they think banks should now be required to hold. The more they request, the less lending there will be to British individuals and businesses. In addition, the banks themselves may decide to hold more capital, to reassure fellow banks that it is safe to do business with them in current conditions. Banks also have to raise more capital if they make substantial losses, as the shareholders have to make good any funds their managers have lost.

2 | Northern Rock

INTRODUCTION

By August 2007, it was clear to many participants of the financial and banking markets in the United Kingdom that something was going horribly wrong. On both sides of the Atlantic the authorities had decided that they needed to rein in the credit explosion which had taken place in recent years, against the background of relatively low interest rates and a regulatory system which encouraged a wide variety of off-balance sheet financing. The authorities in Britain decided to bring the party to an end.

The decision of the Monetary Policy Committee (MPC) to keep interest rates at relatively high levels, compared to the low inflation rate, was reinforced by the general wishes of the regulatory authorities to reduce bank lending. A virtuous circle of more lending, more profit, more capital and reserves, and more lending, was to be turned, almost overnight, into a vicious circle of less lending, less profit, less capital and reserves, and less lending. In August, the British money markets started to freeze. Banks became very suspicious of each other, worrying that other financial institutions might be in such financial difficulty that they might not get their money back. Market interest rates – the rates which banks and other borrowers have to pay – drifted above the recommended MPC rate. The MPC rate leads or controls those market rates in normal times, but in recent months it has failed to do so. On 7 September 2007, following the MPC solemnly announcing no change in their base rate of 5.75 per cent, market rates hit 6.9 per cent.

The growing suspicion of the banks, and the growing shortage of cash, had driven market rates more than 1 per cent (or 100 basis points) above the preferred rate of the Bank of England and above the levels of early August. It made the Monetary Policy Committee of the Bank of England look irrelevant, and left both the Bank and the Treasury bemused by what to say and do.

The media and public mood in late August and early September was almost one of enjoyment. There was a feeling that, at last, reality had caught up with the bankers, brokers and dealers who had apparently made so much money, so effortlessly, in recent years. There was a strange feeling that, if a crisis came, it would be confined to those in the financial sector who had high earnings, and would in some ways 'serve them right'. People looked on in fascination as markets tumbled, as financial experts became more worried in their looks and more dramatic in their statements, and as the authorities of the world responded in rather different ways. The US, at first, moved to be more accommodating. The European Central Bank managed behind the scenes to keep financial institutions going, whereas in Britain the authorities, probably sensing the public mood, decided to dig in. The British Chancellor of the Exchequer, Alistair Darling, was reluctant to be interviewed on the subject of the credit crunch in August and early September; it was not until 13 September that an interview with the Chancellor, on the crucial subject of the collapse of the banking system, appeared.

In a most extraordinary and ill-judged interview, the Chancellor told us:

One of the things that happens with low interest rates is that banks look around for better returns.

This statement of the blindingly obvious neatly sidestepped the question of who created the low interest rate, easy credit, environment in the first place? The Chancellor had decided in December 2003 to switch the inflation target from the Retail Price Index (RPI) to the Consumer Price Index (CPI); this led the Bank to keep interest rates lower, as the CPI measure of inflation was going up more slowly than the RPI. There appeared to be no understanding from the Chancellor that it was this decision to change its inflation target from the RPI to CPI which stimulated the Bank of England's Monetary Policy Committee to keep interest rates much lower than would otherwise have been the case. This, in turn, stimulated the banks to make large sums available in mortgages and other loans. Nor did it seem to occur to the Chancellor that it was the regulatory structure governing how much a bank could lend that lay behind much of the credit boom.

The Chancellor went on to say:

Institutions have, in some cases, been prepared to lend to people without checking if they're ever going to repay it.

This was a most bizarre statement, out of line with any reality. No self-respecting bank, and certainly no bank regulated by the UK regulatory authorities, would ever dream of lending money without looking into the individual or company's financial circumstances to see whether they could afford the interest and how they might make the repayment. As the Chancellor should have appreciated, many of the offending loans were made at times of low interest rates, when the authorities, through their low interest rate policy, were sending out a clear signal to markets that they wanted more credit to be extended. At the then-lower interest rates, many of the loans looked eminently affordable, and all were checked. Furthermore, the self-reinforcing boom conditions allowed by the creation of 'easy money' meant that more jobs and better pay became available, again reinforcing the ability of the borrowers to meet their interest payments and in due course to repay their capital.

The Chancellor continued:

Institutions themselves need to open their own eyes and be more honest.

This began a consistent theme of the government that more transparency, fuller declarations of how much banks had lent and how much they might have lost on the lending, would deal with the mutual suspicion in the marketplace between one bank and another, and miraculously cure the problem of inadequate credit and high interest rates. This again betrayed a woeful ignorance of how markets work. In general terms, more information is a good thing. However, when markets are spooked and have lost confidence, forcing a sudden 'mark-to-market exercise' for all of their assets (an accounting methodology of assigning a value to a position held in a financial instrument based on the current market price for the instrument or similar instruments), at a time when asset prices were falling through the floor and when there was no good market for a sensible price, could merely undermine confidence further.

Typical of this UK government, based upon an assessment of the public mood, the Chancellor had made a judgment that he could get away with doing nothing. Indeed, he could enjoy grandstanding, giving a stern lecture to the banks about how they needed to live within their own means and sort out their own problems. He clearly bought into the notion that the credit crunch was a crisis affecting just a few rich people and a few big institutions in the City. He made the miscalculation that none of the institutions was so seriously damaged that he had a crisis on his hands, and seemed to believe that a good stern lecture from the Chancellor of the Exchequer (delivered a long time after the actions of the government, the regulators and the banks had created the real problem) would suddenly put everything right. There can rarely have been such an insouciant speech by a finance minister that was so ill-judged and so ill-timed. My blog on the day tore into the Chancellor's crazy decision to blame the banks and wash his hands of it all, and sought to bring out the connections between government policy, Bank of England policy, the credit explosion and the impact of the high interest rate, and their impact on the ecomomy. Among other things, I said then:

> *At the moment the system of monthly interest rate meetings at the Bank, which this government confirmed as their principal macroeconomic policy, is marginalised when it comes to the rates people pay for their borrowings and the availability of credit. A policy of lecturing banks on how to lend is not going to work. The Chancellor is the elected politician responsible for this problem. He has at last taken a step to acknowledge his responsibility by his statements yesterday. Now he needs to think again, realise his statements were unhelpful and try, behind the scenes, to sort out the mess in the money markets which arises from the boom-and-bust approach to lending which has characterised the last few years.*
>
> **www.johnredwoodsdiary.com/2007/09/page/2**

It turned out that, in less than 48 hours, the Chancellor's interview was superseded by events. The man who, one day, had bravely lectured the banks that they needed to be more honest and control their own problems, had, the next day, to endorse a decision by the Bank of England (as the lender of last resort) to make money available to any bank that needed cash. What is surprising about the Chancellor's antics is that, had he done any homework at all before the 13 September interview, he would have known that several mortgage banks were rumoured to be in difficulties. He should have known that Northern Rock, in particular, was very exposed to the sudden drying-up of the money markets.

THE RUN ON NORTHERN ROCK

Worse than the U-turn which the Chancellor had to perform was the fact that someone leaked to the press the fact that the institution in need of 'lender of last resort money' from the Bank of England was Northern Rock. Once this information was out it triggered a run on the deposits held in that institution. Queues formed outside branches, television cameras arrived to record them for the nation – and thus encouraged *more* people to do exactly the same. Savers who had deposited their money with Northern Rock realised that the bank was under such pressure that the only sensible thing for any individual to do was to try and get his or her money out before a possible collapse. By his carelessness over the developing crisis in August and early September, the Chancellor had allowed this to happen. By his ill-chosen words on 13 September, the Chancellor told people that all was not well with the banks in London, further undermining confidence. Two days later, the Chancellor had to make reassuring noises that banks were not as bad as he had implied in his interview and that he and the Bank of England were prepared to stand behind institutions in trouble. Suddenly, a government pledge to non-intervention and letting the banks stew in their own juice had changed to the most expensive and comprehensive guarantee to the banking sector ever made by a UK administration.

Meanwhile, across the Atlantic, the Fed was deciding upon a different approach to stabilise its own under-pressure banking system. In mid-September, it cut interest rates by 50 basis points (or 0.5 per cent), to show markets how serious it was about wanting to ease credit conditions. The UK authorities remained mesmerised by their own previous rhetoric of non-intervention, while deciding to go the route of propping up an institution in trouble. On 19 September, the UK authorities at last realised that the chronic shortage of money in money markets was causing considerable damage, and they decided to make £10 billion available to markets to ease the squeeze. It was too little, too late – but better than nothing.

On 20 September, the Governor of the Bank of England told us that he had wanted to lend money to Northern Rock without making it public, but had been unable to do so, owing to the legal position established by the European Union's *Market Abuses Directive*. In all previous potential banking crises, the Bank of England had moved positively, swiftly and behind closed doors to make money available, to act as lender of last resort or to arrange a takeover bid or merger, and so avoid the damage and embarrassment of an institution actually failing. By the time of the Northern Rock problems, the Bank of England was no longer in charge of its own house. Gordon Brown, in his reforms of 1997, had removed the day-to-day supervision of the banks from the Bank of England and transferred it to the FSA (the Financial Services Authority). He had also removed the supervision and management of government debt from the Bank of England, taking it into the Treasury and the Office of Debt Management.

These two big changes meant that when a crisis hit, as it did in August and September 2007, the Bank of England had a much less clear view of what was going on in money markets. When money markets froze in that August, it was not just due to the fact that banks became mutually suspicious of each other and stopped a lot of the interbank lending. It was also the case that there was not enough cash made available to the markets. Prior to 1997, the Bank of England would have known instinctively, and from its day-to-day transactions, when the markets were starved of cash. It could have seen from its daily position statements that the banks needed more cash, which it could have made available through its open market operations, and through its management of government cash requirements and the government debt system. Now, however, the Bank did not have the same day-to-day information about just how severe the cash squeeze on the banks was in August 2007, nor did it have the day-to-day movements and management of the government's debt. Without these two things it was much less able to understand and respond, hour by hour, to the crisis as it developed.

All of this was eminently foreseeable. In the Economic Policy Review that colleagues and I wrote for the Conservative Party in July 2007 (*Freeing Britain to compete: Equipping the UK for globalisation*, Conservative Party Economic Competitiveness Policy Group, August 2007, p.14) and which was published just before the Northern Rock crisis unfolded, we drew attention to this great weakness of the restructured money system in Britain. We said that, should a crisis arrive, this weakness would make it much more difficult for the Bank and the other authorities to handle it successfully. We recommended, very strongly and clearly, that the Bank be given back its powers to undertake day-to-day supervision of the commercial banks, and its power to run government borrowing. The Bank needed the full range of information and the full range of dealing powers in the money markets, in order to keep them sufficiently liquid, or to tighten them when there was a danger of too much credit and consequent inflation.

It was clear from the conduct of monetary policy from 2003 to early 2006 that things had been far too lax. It was understandable why the Monetary Policy Committee eventually got round to raising interest rates, to try and rein in credit. What was not understandable was why, in August 2007, the authorities collectively were so blind and deaf to the goings-on in the money markets that they allowed a crisis to build up and then burst for Northern Rock: the most aggressive mortgage bank in the British market, and the biggest new lender prior to the crisis.

The failure of the 'lender of last resort' operation is directly attributable to the leaking of the name of Northern Rock to the markets. If the Bank had lent the money quietly, and no one in public had known, we would not have seen the queues of depositors the following morning outside Northern Rock branches.

For a number of years, Northern Rock had been run profitably and aggressively, building a huge position in the British mortgage market. Contrary to rumour and spin at the time, the collapse of the bank was absolutely nothing to do with the parallel collapse of some mortgage institution lending in the United States of America, the so-called 'sub-prime crisis'. The Northern Rock crisis was a British crisis, made in Britain by a lethal mixture of aggressive directors of a financial institution, relaxed regulators as the business was built up, and incompetent authorities as the business ran down. Practically all of Northern Rock's assets were UK mortgages. Northern Rock was entirely regulated by the UK authorities. Its business model was approved by the UK regulatory authorities and in the easy credit years would have been approved by most sensible business people sitting on its Board. Northern Rock decided that it could make a bigger impact, advancing more money, growing its business more rapidly, if it tapped three different sources of funds.

NORTHERN ROCK'S SOURCES OF FUNDS
Like most building societies and traditional mortgage banks, Northern Rock initially collected retail deposits from its customer base and lent on the money it had so received. At the time, this was thought to be the only safe way of raising money for mortgages. Paradoxically, it was this source of funds which actually brought Northern Rock down, because it was the queue of small depositors outside the branches wanting their money back that necessitated the request for a Bank of England loan. It meant that, without further financial assistance – which was given, eventually, in the form of nationalisation – Northern Rock could not carry on trading.

The second source of funds was to rely upon the money markets. About a quarter of Northern Rock's finance came from 'rolling over' borrowings in the banking market itself. Northern Rock borrowed large sums from the money markets for short periods, assuming it would always be able to do this when it needed to. This turned out to be a risky way of financing, but no more risky than financing by customer deposits if those customers were going to lose confidence in the institution.

The third and biggest amount of money, representing about half the total, came in the form of securitised financing. When Northern Rock had written a certain number of mortgages, representing a decent sum of money, it would package them up into a company or fund and sell them all off to market purchasers. In the demonology of the day, on both sides of the Atlantic, 'securitisation' got quite a lot of the blame for the crisis. However, for Northern

Rock this was by far and away its most stable form of financing, which caused absolutely no problems during the crash. It was a fact that half of Northern Rock's money had been put up by institutions and individual investors who had bought into packages of mortgages. They had to hold these for the duration, and could not suddenly demand their money back.

In retrospect, there were two weaknesses in the Northern Rock business model. The first was the directors' assumption that they would be able to carry on borrowing substantial sums of money in the inter-bank market. The conditions that broke out in August, thanks to high interest rates, monetary tightening and the lack of confidence, were most unusual. These started the collapse when Northern Rock could no longer roll its borrowings over. It would be a fair criticism of the directors to say that, maybe, they should have done more to borrow longer, and to securitise more of the short-term borrowings at an early stage, once others in the market were becoming wary of market conditions. By then everyone, including the directors of Northern Rock, could see credit growth being strangled by the higher interest rates and the moves the government was making. The second weakness in the Northern Rock funding model was its reliance on customer deposits for a quarter of its money. But, although it was this which brought the bank down, it would be difficult to criticise the directors in this area.

MORTGAGE PERILS

There have also been criticisms of the bank's conduct on the asset side. Mortgage bank assets, of course, are mortgages – loans to people to buy homes. These are normally most reliable assets. There are only two prime dangers to anyone owning a portfolio of mortgages. The first arises where a large number of people have taken out the mortgages but lose their jobs and no longer have the income to pay the interest and repay the debt. This can prove expensive and disruptive in the short term – but should not result in overall losses to the mortgage bank because, in extremis, they can always sell the house and repay the loan. The second threat to a mortgage bank is that the value of the properties will fall so much that, in the event the property has to be sold to repay the debt, there is not enough value in the property to cover the debt.

Mortgage banks traditionally handle both these two risks. The danger that, through loss of job or earnings, people will no longer be able to afford the mortgage, can usually be taken care of by the 'portfolio' principle. If a mortgage bank has a spread of individuals, with a range of occupations and incomes, even in the most adverse economic conditions it is unlikely that more than 1 in 10 of them will be out of work. Even then, it is by no means certain that someone will necessarily cease paying the mortgage just because they lose their job. Some will have savings or family money on which they can draw to carry on paying the mortgage; some will reach agreements with the mortgage bank about reduced payment systems, which will see them through a difficult period; some will get jobs again in a relatively short space of time; and some will succeed in selling their houses, moving into cheaper accommodation, and thus repaying the loan.

Normally, mortgage banks also provide some protection against a fall in the property market by lending less than the full value of the home. Again, they will tend to look at this on a portfolio basis. After years of rising property prices, such as the UK had experienced prior to the middle of 2007, a mortgage bank tends to have a large number of mortgages on properties that are worth a great deal more than the value of the mortgage. This means that, on average, the portfolio or 'mortgage book' looks very good. This enables the mortgage bank to lend 90 per cent or 95 per cent of the value of a home for a new mortgage while, overall, still having a very cautious book.

LEVELS OF LENDING
The Northern Rock directors went one stage further. They added a facility to allow an unsecured loan *on top of* the mortgage so that, when people moved home, they could afford moving costs, purchase new carpets, cover building and decorating changes, or whatever. This meant that some Northern Rock total loan packages represented 125 per cent of the property's value. The unsecured part of the loan book was separately identified very clearly in the Northern Rock accounts, and the directors always made bigger provisions against possible losses on the unsecured loan element. In a way they were in the consumer credit business as well as the mortgage business, and their actions were no more risky than those lending money to people on credit cards. But because their model was so successful it did mean that, when problems struck in 2007, Northern Rock had a higher proportion of loan value to property value (LTV) overall. This was because so much of their new business had been written at much higher price levels than of the property market and offered very high percentages of the value of the property concerned.

Northern Rock had been part of the inflationary phenomenon which the low interest rates and the easy-credit environment of the middle of the first decade of the 21st century had encouraged. Banks, generally, started lending much higher multiples of earnings to people to buy a home than had been customary in the 1970s and 1980s. In the 1970s a bank would typically look at an individual's income and lend, maybe, three times the annual income as a mortgage. For a married couple of child-bearing age, the bank would normally take just once the wife's salary in addition to three times the husband's salary, reasoning that they may well have children and that this would interrupt the wife's earning potential.

In the last decade, banks have looked at lending rather differently. They have not made a distinction between the husband and wife, or male and female earnings where people live together. They have assumed, as is often the case these days, that a couple could have a child with the wife returning to work.

They have also been prepared to lend up to five or six times a couple's combined salaries, compared with the much more modest three times or so 20 or 30 years earlier. They arrived at this because, instead of doing the calculation as a multiple on salary, they looked at the proportion of the couple's income that would be taken up in paying the interest. Because many of the calculations were done at a time of very low interest rates, this produced some very large sums for potential loans, and meant that large mortgages looked eminently affordable. The rise in interest rates did a lot of damage to these calculations, and placed many people under great financial pressure in a way that, foolishly, they had neither anticipated nor planned for.

The dog days of September 2007 revealed the dangers of the tripartite arrangements put in place in 1997, splitting responsibilities for banking regulation and monetary supervision. The Chancellor became critical of the Bank of England's failure to find a buyer for Northern Rock over a fateful weekend that predated the final run on the bank. He backed away from any idea that he could alter EU law and regulation or ignore the *Directive on Market Abuse*. If this directive prevents secret deals over the weekend to prop up an ailing bank, the obvious thing to do would be to change the directive. Instead, the Chancellor decided a better answer was to make many banks borrow from the Bank of England from time to time, and thus to take away the stigma of any particular bank doing so when it really needed to. This extraordinary artificial device was the best he could come up with, given his impotence to change Brussels law.

THE FSA V THE BANK OF ENGLAND

The division of responsibilities between the FSA and the Bank of England was always contentious. It is rumoured that the incumbent Bank of England Governor in 1997 considered resigning, in view of the number of powers which the government had decided to take away from the Bank. As late as the summer of 2007, there were strong rumours of a continuing turf war between the FSA and the Bank of England over exactly what their respective functions in banking regulation were. While most of the day-to-day functions of the old Bank of England were transferred to the FSA, the Bank was left with general responsibilities for liquidity and solvency in the banking market, and clearly had some role in discussions of any systemic risk. The FSA tested bank balance sheets and business models and gave the necessary licensing approvals. I see nothing wrong with the fact that they did allow the Northern Rock model, as the tripartite approach to raising cash made a great deal of sense. I can further understand how the directors continued to believe that they could base their business on the assumption that there would be reasonable liquidity in the money market. I can also see why the regulators at the FSA would take a similar line.

However, the problem arose with the Bank of England's responsibility for keeping the system liquid if the Bank itself was not in daily or hourly contact with the banks and money markets, in a way which told it how grave the situation was. Apparently, contact between the Bank of England and the FSA was limited to a formal meeting once a month. Of course, the regulators must have exchanged intelligence and information about Northern Rock and other banks which were finding the going tough. Maybe the Bank of England did not believe how tough Northern Rock was finding it, which would explain the extraordinary joint statements of the Governor of the Bank of England and the Chancellor of the Exchequer on the eve of the run on the Rock. Maybe there was a mood at the top that it was time to teach the banks a lesson – and maybe Northern Rock was, to some extent, a casualty of the continuing battle between the Bank of England and the FSA over the whole issue of banking regulation. It was inevitable that the question of who did banking regulation, and how they did it, would be raised again following the disaster that hit in the middle of September.

The disputes between the two main regulators were well known and were talked about in the City and beyond. In *Freeing Britain to Compete*, the Opposition's economic policy review, we stated:

> *We are concerned about the division of responsibility between the FSA and the Bank over banking and market regulation. Fortunately conditions in the last decade have been benign internationally, with no threats to banking liquidity. We think it would be safer if the Bank of England had responsibility for solvency regulation of UK-based banks, as well as having the overall duty to keep the system solvent. Otherwise there could be dangerous delays if a banking crisis did hit, with information having to be exchanged between the two regulators; and there might be gaps in each regulator's view of the banking sector at a crucial time when early regulatory action might have spared a worse problem.*

Freeing Britain to compete, *op. cit., p.14*

If this much was obvious for an Opposition, it makes it even more incomprehensible that the government, with access to all the information being supplied by both the FSA and the Bank of England about the state of the markets and the state of Northern Rock, was not more speedy in seeing off the problems that were emerging.

By the end of October, when Alistair Darling reported to the Treasury Select Committee, it emerged that he did know all about the problems at Northern Rock in advance of the final crisis. He stood at the head of the tripartite system of regulation, but seemed unaware of just how short of cash the markets were and what damage that was doing. He did not ask why the Federal Reserve Board and the European Central Bank made their markets more liquid during the early days of the credit crunch, whereas the Bank of England stood by and watched banks struggle even more. It was also clear that, in the early days, the Chancellor was unable or unwilling to help the private sector rescue of Northern Rock before the run became public. In his testimony to the Committee he made an attack upon banks for hiding debts off balance sheet. This came from the leading financial minister in a government that had specialised in hiding its *own* debts off balance sheet, including the debts relating to Northern Rock following the nationalisation that came next.

SAVING NORTHERN ROCK

By early November 2007, the Bank of England and the government's decision to refinance Northern Rock's loan book to the extent necessary to preserve confidence in the institution – and to back up the Chancellor's offer to guarantee all deposits – had cost the taxpayer some £22 billion of advances to Northern Rock. The scale of this financial intervention was amazing. The government regularly lectured the Opposition that any spending suggestion or proposal of a few hundred million pounds would create an impossible black hole in the public finances. The government was already planning substantial borrowings in 2007-8, yet suddenly it was able to find colossal sums of money to refinance a mortgage bank in trouble. Worse still, the troubles at the mortgage bank had been greatly exacerbated by the Bank of England's own lack of action to make money markets sufficiently liquid, to allow the bank to carry on financing itself in the normal way – and then by the authority's careless remarks which helped undermine confidence and led to the run on the bank.

So large were the bale-out operations for Northern Rock in the autumn of 2007 that the Bank of England needed to seek a letter of comfort from the Treasury. There had to be discussions about how much of the cost could be borne on the Bank of England's own balance sheet. The Bank of England is a relatively small bank, with a balance sheet, when the crisis struck, of only some £40 billion; it was attempting to refinance a mortgage bank with a total balance sheet of over £100 billion. Presumably, when the Chancellor of the Exchequer first authorised such action, he had no idea of the relative scale of the Bank of England compared with Northern Rock and, subsequently, officials had to sort out the muddle that the scale of the guarantees and the market operations created.

During November, a big debate started about what to do with the ailing Northern Rock bank and the very substantial lifeline of cash injected into it by the government and Bank of England. Vincent Cable, for the Liberal Democrats, set out a stark and misleading choice. To him there were only two options. On the one hand, the government could put Northern Rock into administration. Such an action would stop all new lending by the mortgage bank, would trigger a sale of the mortgages and other assets of the institution, and lead to the repayment of the £25 billion or so of money advanced by the government to the bank as and when the assets were sold (assuming, of course, that the Bank of England and the Treasury had taken sufficient claims on those assets when making the advances). The likely outcome of such a proposal would have been mass redundancies in the north east, the termination of Northern Rock's business, and maybe the return of all the taxpayers' cash in due course. But receivership would not have been easy, given the complex web of guarantees offered by Northern Rock to other organisations which had helped finance its business.

Dr Cable's second option was the nationalisation of Northern Rock. When he first raised this, the Labour government sought to resist it, saying that they were seeking a private sector buyer for the bank in conjunction with Northern Rock's existing shareholders, and did not favour nationalisation themselves. The Cable argument was a simple-minded one. Vincent Cable said that, effectively, the taxpayer owned the bank already, because the bank had only been able to continue in the difficult days of September and October because of taxpayer funding being made available on such a lavish scale. He regarded this as tantamount to nationalisation – and therefore felt that the shareholders of Northern Rock should lose their future rights to any business profits and eventual recovery, with the shares being forfeit to the taxpayer following suitable legislation. This argument evoked a lot of sympathy on the Left and also appealed to some of the Northern Rock depositors and mortgage holders, who felt that it might offer them greater security. It also revealed a great misunderstanding of how nationalised businesses operate and the likely financial outcomes to the taxpayer.

In practice, there were two other options available for the future of Northern Rock that were much more inviting than either immediate transfer into administration or the assumption by the taxpayer of full responsibility for the bank. The first, more sensible, option was the one that was followed by the government. It was to seek a private sector buyer of the bank, one likely to be able to repay the taxpayer debt and to trade Northern Rock out of its difficulties. Clearly, the government needed to find a buyer or buyers for the whole or parts of the mortgage bank: someone who had enough money, to be able to inject enough capital into the bank to see it through the difficult times of the credit crunch, and enough skill in financial services, to be able to continue making mortgage advances likely, in due course, to turn a profit for the new shareholders.

There were always problems with this scheme. Firstly, the most likely buyers were all other banks, since they had the necessary skills. Unfortunately, the credit crunch and their own mistakes in the advances they had made at home or abroad were limiting their financial capability to take on anything as large as Northern Rock. It was a less than ideal time to be seeking to sell a mortgage bank! Secondly, the government refused to set out clearly how much public money would continue to be available to the new owners, or even to specify a clear schedule for repayments of the monies already advanced. In the credit crunch conditions it was obvious that anyone seeking to take on Northern

Rock would need some or all of the public money already advanced, in order to be able to continue with the business. The reluctance of the authorities to make it very clear how much would be available undoubtedly put off some potential bidders.

Thirdly, the government was not the vendor of the bank. Throughout the period when a private sector buyer for Northern Rock was being sought, it was the independent shareholders of the Rock who remained its owner and had the power to sell. Yes, the government was an important participant as, through its role as lender of last resort, it had become one of the prime sources of finance for the ailing business. However, this did not entitle the government to dictate terms to the independent shareholders about which party they should (or should not) have as a bidder and what price they should accept. It might be in the government's interest for them to accept a bid at any price, including zero, just to get the bank into new hands, under new management and with stronger promises on the repayment of the debt. In contrast, many of the shareholders felt their bank should have considerable value and were still reeling from the huge decline in share price that they had experienced from the spring of 2007 (just over £10 a share), to the very low price it reached by the end of that year (around 80 pence). In addition, some newer shareholders who had bought into Northern Rock during its time of troubles, including some influential hedge funds, were taking an aggressive or bullish view of the prospects of the bank and were not minded to give their shares away or to take a loss on their recent purchase prices.

This background made it extremely difficult to attract a wide range of interested parties, to select one or two that were likely to make a decent bid and to negotiate a satisfactory outcome. The government thought that a bid from Richard Branson was the most likely to succeed, and announced that he was the preferred bidder. This caused some problems with other potential bidders – and with the existing shareholders – and negotiations dragged on.

There was always the fourth option which, for some reason, the government, the Liberal Democrats and many of the media commentators ignored altogether: to continue with the existing shareholder structure and ownership of Northern Rock, with the government and Bank of England acting as firm and strong bank managers of the troubled business.

This was, in fact, the legal position the government had put itself into by its antics in the autumn of 2007. The taxpayer was now an important lender to Northern Rock, providing about a quarter of the total finance needed to support the £100 billion-plus book of mortgages the bank had built up. While, clearly, there was more detail than was ever revealed to Parliament and the public as a result of the negotiations between the Treasury, the Bank and Northern Rock, there did not seem to be proper banking controls and supervision of the loans; there was also a marked absence of anyone prepared to act as an intelligent bank manager. It would have been possible to say that there was a ceiling of £25 or £30 billion on the amount of money that the Bank of England and the Treasury were making available, once they had stabilised the deposit base. Half of the Northern Rock mortgage book was soundly financed by securitisation, so the maximum total that the taxpayer might have had to finance was around £50 billion – not the full £100 billion of the total bank.

More importantly, the government and Bank of England had spelt out terms and conditions about the duration and repayment of the loans. As an intelligent bank manager, they could have been in the driving seat, dictating terms of the business over husbanding cash, selling mortgages and reducing the scale of its operations in order to meet tough repayment schedules. The shareholders would still have owned the bank, and the new management appointed by those shareholders would still have been directing the bank. However, they would have had to have managed the business with a tough eye on generating cash – which they could have done by making more profit, by selling assets, or by a combination of the two. Given the scale of the repayments the taxpayer and government would need, there would have to have been substantial asset sales as and when markets picked up, as well as payments out of profits and cash flow.

It is one of the remarkable parts of the saga of Northern Rock that the most obvious, practical measure to avoid the taxpayer having to take full responsibility for the bank, its employees, its customers and its losses, was for the Bank of England to carry on doing what it had been forced into doing in that fateful September – but to do it better, and over a longer time period. Despite this, the media, Parliament and all those responsible for the overall conduct of public debate, decided that the one sensible option was not a feasible option at all, and that people had to carry on arguing about whether Richard Branson would buy it or whether it had to be nationalised.

The government's premature announcement that Richard Branson was the preferred bidder implied that a proper evaluation of all potential bidders had been made, and therefore the government had something about which to negotiate with him. By 7 December another bid, the Olivant bid, had arrived. The Chancellor then changed his tune and said he favoured a competitive auction for Northern Rock, to see which was the best bid out there.

On 6 December, the Monetary Policy Committee of the Bank of England made its first hesitant steps to ease the credit crunch that they had helped create. They took 25 basis points off their recommended interest rate, lowering it from 5.75 per cent to 5.5 per cent. The Bank of England itself was still unable to deliver anything like this interest rate to the marketplace, because it was still not supplying enough cash to the hard-pressed banking system. Too much of its money had been directed simply to Northern Rock for its partial rescue, instead of making cash generally available to money markets to ease the overall crunch. On 18 December, the Bank of England accepted that it needed to make more money generally available and sought to ease markets in this way.

Behind the credit crunch of 2007 lay not just the incompetence of the British monetary authorities, but also the dubious decisions of the world regulators in their Basel I system of banking regulation. As discussed in Chapter 1, this system laid down rules for regulators around the world to deploy, to work out how much capital any given bank or financial institution needed in order to carry out its functions. Under the Basel I rules, mortgages were regarded as higher-quality loans than other kinds of advances, because they were pledged against property. This encouraged the British banking system in general, and Northern Rock in particular, to increase their mortgage books significantly, skewing the total amount of debt in the country towards the purchase of property – especially residential property. In addition, the Basel I rules encouraged banks to put their assets or loans to individuals and companies off balance sheet; the more they did this, the less capital they needed to sustain the growth in their loan book. This also lay behind the Northern Rock decisions to securitise the finance for a lot of their lending, as this naturally reduced the amount of capital the bank needed to carry out its functions.

In such a highly regulated world, where regulators take responsibility for telling bank directors how much capital they must have to sustain any given level of business, directors of aggressive banks will naturally seek to minimise the amount of capital they have to have in order to increase the returns on that capital. They will, therefore, study very carefully the rules laid down by the regulators and seek to minimise the capital by, for example, increasing the amount of mortgage lending they are doing and by putting a lot of the lending off balance sheet – in exactly the way Northern Rock did. It is difficult to criticise the Northern Rock directors for lacking any business nous when they were clearly following the requirements and permitted strategies laid down by global regulators. One of the interesting paradoxes of the Northern Rock crisis is that, in the last report and accounts prior to the crisis hitting, Northern Rock directors discuss with their shareholders the possibility that Northern Rock needed *less* capital to carry out its business, owing to their good management under the then-pertaining regulatory rules. The more mortgages they advanced and the more they securitised, the more they created a favourable position in terms of the ratio of the amount of revenue-generating lending they were doing, to the amount of shareholders'capital they needed to have in order to carry out the business at all.

Throughout the crisis, of course, the regulators either kept quiet or made out that somehow Northern Rock was an aberration that lay outside the normal parameters of, and the capital requirements laid down by, the regulatory system. There was no willingness to own up to the fact that the skewing of capital requirements and styles of business in Basel I was a part of the problem.

Indeed, to this day, there is a danger that the regulatory system reinforces the boom-and-bust tendencies of the markets. In the good times, when banks are advancing more capital and making more money as a result of expanding their businesses, the regulatory rules allow them to carry on doing so in a virtuous circle. In the bad times, usually triggered by the authorities seeking to rein in the amount of credit and raising interest rates to do so, the reverse happens. The regulatory rules bite with growing ferocity. The more losses the banks record, the less capital they have. The worse the loan experience turns out to be, the more capital the regulatory rules require them to have. So the banking system lurches from having too little capital (but with its loans being assessed favourably by the regulators) in the boom times, to having too much capital (with its loans assessed very unfavourably) in the bust times. We are today seeing a period of massive recapitalisation of the banks required by the regulatory rules; in the process we are probably creating the conditions for the next subsequent boom in lending, as the banks stock up with capital which will look excessive under the regulatory rules once lending conditions improve.

THE UK'S HOUSING MARKET

The British government compounded these international regulatory difficulties with its own uncertain views that touch on the whole question of house prices. Fundamental to the long-term solvency and success of a business such as Northern Rock is the trend in UK house prices: practically all the assets of Northern Rock took the form of lending to people who had bought residential accommodation in Britain. A lot of it was concentrated in the north-east of England, where Northern Rock had its head office and its principal operating branches. In the run up to the credit crunch, and in its early weeks, the government's view was that there were not enough affordable properties in Britain for people to purchase to live in. The government had commissioned a report by Kate Barker on how to make housing more affordable (*Review of housing supply. Delivering stability: securing our future housing needs*, HM Treasury 2004). In an economically illiterate piece of work, Barker and her team set out the proposition that house prices were too high in Britain, and that this had come about because not enough new properties were being built. They seemed unaware that new construction accounts for only around 2 per cent of the total market supply in any given year, as most of the homes which are bought are 'second-hand'– existing homes. The first review ignored the crucial role of mortgage finance in determining prices in the market. As we have been living through a thirty-year period when financial institutions moved from lending around three times one income to lending as much as five or six times two incomes for people buying their first homes, it was not surprising that house prices had boomed, rising substantially faster than prices generally. This was a financial phenomenon to which even a doubling in the new construction rate would have made very little difference, given the high volume of transactions involving second-hand homes.

The government had a single policy towards bringing house prices down. This was based on exhorting the house-building industry to build more homes, insisting on more space being made available for house building in local plans, overriding the views of councils that did not wish to see this and granting substantial planning permissions to those seeking the right to construct homes in all sorts of places. Despite all this activity, the rate of new house building did not respond very positively; until the middle of 2007, house prices continued to soar, thanks to the ready availability of credit and the impact of ever-larger mortgages upon the sales of second-hand homes.

The credit crunch changed all that. Suddenly, ministerial pleas for more affordable housing were going to come true. The cessation of large amounts of new mortgage credit, and the withdrawal of the biggest new mortgage provider, Northern Rock, had a sudden and dramatic impact. House prices started to fall. When I asked ministers by how much they would like house prices to fall to make them 'affordable', they declined to tell me. Ministers immediately realised the political sensitivity of arguing for a specific decline in house prices, although they carried on with their rhetoric that they wanted to make houses more affordable. They seemed to argue the absurd proposition that, if they encouraged enough new building, builders would be able to make available those new houses and flats below the current prevailing market prices, without having some wash-on effect on the prices of all the second-hand homes – where people who had already paid high sums for them would take exception to recording losses.

The credit crunch brought about an immediate refutation of the government's nonsensical view that more house building would lower house prices. Once the credit crunch started to bite, two things happened which, given the government's theory, should have been contradictory. House prices started to fall, in some places very rapidly, whilst the supply of new homes dried up (as builders withdrew from the market and property developers had to cancel their plans to undertake new construction). Because the supply of new mortgages was greatly restricted it would be much more difficult to sell the new homes once constructed. Because the supply of new finance to property and construction companies was also being damaged by the credit crunch, and by the fears about saleability of properties they might build, the builders and property developers had to withdraw their plans because they could not afford them. Instead of fewer new houses being built, creating higher house prices, as the government theory stated, we started to live in the nightmare world for most people of a cessation of much building activity and a plunge in the value of most people's principal asset, the family home.

This process further weakened the position of Northern Rock. The government prefaced every statement about the credit crunch and the financial difficulties with a word or phrase implying that this was a credit crunch made in the United States of America and was part of the US sub-prime crisis. Despite this, it rapidly became obvious to all sensible observers that the Northern Rock crisis was very much a British crisis, made of the peculiar British circumstances in the residential property market, exacerbated by mishandling of money markets and the regulatory mistakes made in London.

By 10 January 2008, the government was worried that it was not going to be able to negotiate a private-sector purchase of the whole of Northern Rock. Their advisers, Goldman Sachs, were rumoured to be looking at the possibility of selling on the taxpayers' loans to Northern Rock, in what seemed like an enterprising proposal. In addition, rumours spread that, maybe, the government would buy a minority stake instead of taking on ownership of the whole. Despite this, the BBC continued to give great coverage to Vincent Cable leading the charge in favour of complete nationalisation; the government's response to the Cable proposal implied that they were very happy for him to be making these waves. Many in the Labour Party, and particularly on the Labour benches in the Commons, were secretly enthusiastic about nationalising their very own mortgage bank. They foolishly thought that nationalisation would enable them to maintain the jobs and the businesses of the north east, and to treat it as another taxpayer-financed 'make work' scheme.

All of the work resulted, on 21 January, in a new position adopted by the government. It decided to avoid nationalisation, to get some cash back more quickly by selling bonds to replace the loans it had advanced in Northern Rock, and by seeking a new private-sector owner. The taxpayers' position was to be further protected by granting warrants, so that they would have some participation in any increase in value of the shares – should the new private owner succeed in turning the business round. This was a very sensible set of proposals but unfortunately, as it turned out, there was no one of sufficient skill and energy who was capable of delivering it.

Instead of positive action in running credit markets to make things easier, the government came up with a review of the regulatory arrangements for banks. The review made suggestions in five areas. It recommended strengthening of the financial system, by introducing better risk management of banks, and better supervision and rating of securitised loans. (The stable door clanged shut long after the horse had bolted.) The review recommended reducing the likelihood of banks failing, by asking for more information and changing the arrangements for providing liquidity for banks. It would have been more positive to have injected enough cash into markets to prevent otherwise perfectly solvent banks going under for lack of funds. It was proposed, as a third recommendation, to reduce the impact of failing banks by introducing a special resolution regime, which would allow the authorities to take action with a failing bank to achieve a rescue or an orderly run off. There was no explanation of how this would be legal under European rules, when it had been felt that – when Lloyds Bank had expressed an interest in Northern

Rock – similar action was against the *Market Abuses Directive*. The fourth recommendation was for effective compensation arrangements, including faster and bigger payments to anyone who did have a deposit with a bank that went under, as a way of reassuring depositors to keep their money in banks that were in difficult circumstances. The review also recommended strengthening the Bank of England and improving coordination between authorities.

It was typical of the government's response to a major crisis that it should go off and study it and then, long after the crisis had developed, come up with a mixture of good and bad proposals. It was a containment exercise to handle the media – rather than a serious set of proposals awaiting early and full implementation. Most of the proposals were to tackle some future banking crisis, rather than to deal with the more important and immediate task of sorting out Northern Rock. On 7 February 2008, the Chancellor decided to give us all the benefit of his mortgage advice. He told us that more people should take up long-term mortgages at fixed rates. It was another one of his foolish interventions in the debate over housing finance. He seemed unaware that mortgage advice on broking is a regulated activity, and that the first thing anyone has to do before offering advice is to find out more details on the individual's circumstances. Even in the general terms in which his advice was couched, he made no comment on the fact that we were entering a period when interest rates were going to be falling. (By the end of 2008, of course, interest rates have collapsed across the world, as governments try to prevent recession, or at least ameliorate its effects.) Locking yourself in to a long-term fixed rate of interest was a crazy thing to be doing at such a time. It was a further reflection of the muddle the government found itself in over housing finance, panicking that there could be further increases in interest rates in the future that would mean yet more people would be unable to repay the very large mortgages they had been sucked into obtaining.

On 17 February, Alistair Darling decided that he had to nationalise Northern Rock. A man in a big hole decided to make it considerably bigger. We moved from a position where the government was guaranteeing underwriting or lending around £50 billion to a position whereby the taxpayer would be responsible for the whole £100 billion of Northern Rock liabilities. We moved from a position where the government and taxpayer, as banker and bank manager, could look forward to repayment of their lending over a period of time (as either the business was run down and the mortgages matured, or as the business recovered and revived) to a position where the government and the taxpayer was responsible for all the costs of the staff, the offices and servicing the business. We had previously been told that the government and the Bank of England had taken sensible collateral against the loans to Northern Rock, and that they had not taken as collateral a group of loans likely to perform badly – thus resulting in protection from losses for the taxpayer. Suddenly the taxpayer was the proud owner of *all* of the loans advanced by

Northern Rock, some of which were bound to go wrong. On 19 February, Parliament was invited to improve the transaction.

As a businessman by background, I have occasionally bought or sold companies. Never have I been asked to buy a company with so little information available on its assets, liabilities, and past and future performance, as I was when the government sought my vote to approve the purchase of Northern Rock by taxpayers. I was asked to put the taxpayer at risk for £110 billion – when the government would not even tell me how much they wished to pay for the shares. That was to be decided after the government had announced the purchase, as part of the legislation. The government did not spell out how much risk taxpayers might face from eventual legal actions, or share with us their legal advice about why they thought they could take this extraordinary action.

We were not told the true state of the mortgages that were the bank's main assets and we were not given a schedule of either assets or liabilities. Parliament did not receive an accountant's report, nor assessment of the term structure of the loan and assets, nor commentary on the likely movement in the bad debts. We did not see the management accounts for the last year, and we did not have budgets for the next couple of years. We were not given the basic outlines of the business plan because clearance from Brussels was still awaited on how much new trading could be undertaken. However, we were aware, from other sources, that the bank would be able to offer very little in the marketplace as its privileged access to public money left it open to allegations of anti-competitive trading.

We were not given a report on the size of the pension scheme deficit nor how it had been calculated; nor were we warned that the pension deficit might be about to get larger, in the light of recent regulatory actuarial comments on the fact that people are living longer and that this had to be provided for in many pension calculations. There was no environmental report on the properties and assessment of risk under environmental legislation, which any normal purchaser would require. There was no property report about leases and freeholds and the lease and maintenance obligations. We did not see the main contracts for the senior staff or the bonus arrangements. We saw no human resources report on pay and morale and efficiency of the workforce. There was no survey of customer attitudes or study of the value of the brand, no report on the relationship to the Northern Rock Trust, or on the ability of a public enterprise to continue sponsoring a local football team.

In summary, Parliament had none of the usual information that, as a matter of course, directors would require from a management team acquiring a business and from their advisers before agreeing to an acquisition. Parliament was railroaded and sidelined by the government as, of course, they had enough votes from Labour MPs to push the legislation through. Only one busy parliamentary day was allowed to consider all stages of the Commons' procedures for the nationalisation bill. Never had so much taxpayers' money been placed at risk with so little time to debate it. A piece of legislation made the taxpayer liable for every broken window in every branch; every severance and pension payment; every mortgage and every loan.

On 23 February, the legislation returned from the House of Lords. The Lords had dared to pass three amendments to Labour's bank nationalisation bill. One wanted the Freedom of Information Act to apply to Northern Rock, just as it applies to the rest of the public sector. The second wanted a proper audit report on what the country was buying, and the third wanted more detail on the competition arrangements. All three were perfectly reasonable requests. The Lords did not seek to prevent the nationalisation of Northern Rock or some other bank, and they were well within the spirit of the majority decision in the Commons to press ahead with nationalisation.

These amendments required several hours of debate. Each one raised very different issues, worthy indeed of a separate debate. Instead, the government gave us just one hour, grouping all three amendments together along with some government amendments. The Opposition offered to sit through the night, as urgency was part of the government's agenda. Alternatively, the House could have met the following day on the Friday, transferring Friday's business to the following week. The government refused to cooperate.

In the single hour's cursory debate, the Chief Secretary to the Treasury occupied half of the time with her comments. The shadow spokesman kept his remarks much shorter, allowing Sir Stuart Bell to speak from the Labour backbenches and a few minutes of the Liberal Democrats' spokesman. No Conservative backbencher could make a full speech. It was a disgrace. We were not even told why the government would not demand a full audit report before they were buying it, would not give us a proper statement on the very important competition issues, and why we were denied public information under their legislation.

The wider crisis continued despite the action to nationalise Northern Rock. Indeed, in some cases, the nationalisation made the problem worse. As expected, but not debated properly in Parliament, European Union competition rules prevented Northern Rock making new advances. New management was brought in, who decided that the only way to repay the government debt over any sensible period of time was to undertake a rapid rundown of the Northern Rock business. Over half the staff were to lose their jobs under the plans, reflecting the reality that if Northern Rock was not to write new mortgages it did not need all the staff who had been recruited in the heady boom days of 2006 and early 2007 to write and handle that business.

In the first half of 2008, substantial fundraising took place, as all the main banks showed they needed more liquidity and, in some cases under the regulatory rules, more capital. On 19 April, the government and the Bank of England made another £50 billion available to get the mortgage market going again. The government made the money available by offering government debt in exchange for mortgages.

It was extraordinary that £50 billion was available in April 2008 when nothing had been available in August 2007. If £50 billion had been made available to the markets then, Northern Rock could have raised the money it needed from the money markets and we would not have had the run on the Rock or its nationalisation.

As the year 2008 unfolded, so it became obvious that Northern Rock was going to suffer badly as a nationalised institution. The new management decided it needed to make substantial provisions to tackle future losses on loans. It was not happy with the level of prudence by the previous Northern Rock management, and reported losses of £585 million in the first half-year of 2008. It also requested £3 billion of new equity to shore up its balance sheet. The government decided to convert £3 billion of its outstanding debt into equity so that the bank would have better ratios to satisfy the regulator. We can look forward to further big losses and further difficulty in running the business down. This contributed greatly to the freezing of the mortgage market in Britain and to the delayed response of residential house prices. By the summer of 2008, house and flat prices were falling rapidly and noticeably throughout most of the United Kingdom and the mortgage famine was very pronounced.

Britain demonstrated that it was possible to create a domestic credit crunch out of the difficult circumstances of 2007. The British banking crisis began with the run on the Rock. Subsequently Bradford and Bingley, another mortgage bank, needed government rescue. In September 2008, the regulators asked all banks to raise more capital. These discussions were leaked to markets, pushing bank shares down. The government decided to offer public capital to three of them which thought it might be difficult to raise all the money they needed from the private sector. The subsequent decision to buy a large stake in RBS forced the government to think again about its strategy towards nationalised banks. They decided RBS was too big to put into effective wind up, so they determined to pursue a policy of allowing it to run as before with arms-length management. Subsequent events, including a row over the payment of bonuses, forced them to intervene more than they planned in the decisions of the management – just as they did at Northern Rock.

3 | Globalisation: hero or villain?

INTRODUCTION

From the turn of the millennium, the first few years were great years for the world economy. Trends that gathered pace in the latter half of the 20th century became prominent and dramatic in the early years of the current century. The main themes of recent years have been globalisation, the rise of Asia, the digital revolution and the commodities rush.

GLOBALISATION

Globalisation is the overarching development which has facilitated substantial growth in advanced Western economies; it has also provided the surge in living standards and economic activity in many of the emerging countries. The rise of Asia is based upon the dominance of the Asian peoples in the world population, and on the application of new and better management techniques to their economies. Together, these have enabled them to join the world party. We are moving into a 'Pacific century', away from the Atlantic bias of the successful economies of the 19th and 20th centuries.

Technology is a major driver of change. The advent of the Internet and web-based technology has reinforced the process of globalisation, enabling people to see, at the click of the mouse, offers of products and services around the world. This has facilitated the development of global brands. As more and more people come to the world party, so more and more basic resources – oil, energy generally, metals and agricultural commodities – are demanded to feed, clothe, amuse and maintain the lifestyles of an ever-increasing number of people.

Globalisation means trading goods and services over national borders and between continents. Freer movement of people, goods, ideas and money lies behind the phenomenal success of the world economy after 1945. Successive rounds of trade liberalisation through what is now the World Trade Organisation have helped to power this success, which is visible in the rise in living standards of so many in the advanced world, now complemented by the increase in living standards, from very low levels, of many in the developing world.

Globalisation has offered choices to people in poor countries that did not exist before. Some people are able to use the educational and travel opportunities that present themselves to travel to rich Western countries, where they can earn far more than at home, and can improve their skill and experience levels – which, in turn, enhance their earning power. Some stay in the West and send remittances back to family and friends. Some learn what they need to learn from their Western exposure, then return to their home countries, more confident and better able to earn a good living in businesses that already exist. Some set up new businesses, based on things they have learnt in advanced countries. All of these methods contribute to faster growth and better lifestyles in their home country.

CENTRES OF EXCELLENCE

Globalisation entails the pursuit of specialisation – by cities, regions or even whole countries – and the development of a relative advantage in supplying particular goods and services. London and New York have developed dominant positions in the growth and development of world financial services: their big markets trade the overwhelming amount of currencies, shares, bonds and other financial instruments. These great markets attract an ever-increasing and stunning array of talent from around the world. They are centres of excellence and innovation, the new products and services cascading down from their expensive streets and now being shown around the world by letter, fax, email and personal travel.

The Chinese have developed great expertise and a dominant position in textile production, taking over from previous dominant areas such as Yorkshire and Lancashire in 19th-century Britain, and the textile lands of Italy and France in 20th-century Europe. Now, it is to China that people turn for quality, inexpensive cloth and ready-made garments.

In Germany, its traditional excellence in engineering still underpins one of the world's most successful and important motor vehicle industries. Germany reinforces her position of strength by employing substantial amounts of engineering talent to refine, innovate and improve her motor vehicles to respond to the rising tide of regulation – over matters as diverse as safety and fuel economy. Germany has built the great brands of Mercedes, BMW and Audi, which are now ubiquitous marks, offering value and prestige worldwide.

Globalisation also entails the manufacture of complex products, for which components and subassemblies are made in different countries – or even different continents – before final assembly. While the German automobile may be based on the excellence of German engineering and design, with the brand founded in German values and concepts, the German company making the cars will now consider manufacturing in a range of places around the world. They will purchase the components and services necessary to make the car from wherever they are cheapest and best on a global basis. The Airbus project in Europe was a very public, politically supported, version of what is now common practice in modern manufacturing: it was decided that different parts of the Airbus plane would be made in the different countries participating in the project, with the components taken to Toulouse in France for final assembly. Some British firms have outsourced their customer handling and call centres to places such as India, where able English-speaking people are available at cheaper rates than locally in Britain. 'Back office' functions can be carried out anywhere in the world, sometimes thousands of miles away from the founding business. Products and components for a manufactured good may travel halfway around the world to reach final assembly.

Modern businesses are truly citizens of the global village, constantly looking worldwide to see where they can buy the best goods, where they can hire the best services and where they can employ the best labour.

The third important aspect of globalisation is the homogenisation of goods and services beneath well-known global brands. Sometimes the brand and the product become interchangeable or indistinguishable. In marketing, it is regarded as a great success if you can persuade the world to call the underlying product or good by the name of your company. Hoover achieved this with its electrical cleaner. Coke and Pepsi are still battling it out for world dominance, but both have become wider words for the fizzy soft drink, whilst McDonald's is now a ubiquitous way of describing a hamburger. Some companies are remarkably successful at persuading the world that their particular variant of a good or service is the universal answer; in some cases, the more people who adopt the given system, the easier it is for them to use it. Microsoft has developed a dominant position in worldwide software, facilitating communication between millions of computers around the world, running on the same or similar programs. Even the protesters against globalisation are usually drafting their press releases and sending out their messages on Microsoft software!

CRITICISMS

Globalisation has received a very bad press: its left-wing critics have been extremely successful in getting across the idea that globalisation is a means for powerful companies and individuals to exploit the rest of us. Its critics see, in globalisation, a new form of imperialism led by the United States of America. They are right in identifying the important presence of large American corporations among the world's leaders when it comes to developing world brands and selling large quantities of product and service around the world – but they are wrong in thinking that, somehow, this is an enforced or evil process, which the world ought to resist. It is the arrival of the large multinational corporation in a poor developing country which so often offers some hope of new investment, new jobs and higher standards. The companies arrive in countries beyond their own, not on the back of armed force, but because people in the receiving countries are keen to buy the goods and services if they can afford them, and are enthusiastic about welcoming the jobs, the skills and the technology that the large corporations can bring.

Critics also claim that large multinationals damage the environment. You might as well argue that having children damages the environment, because it is the *demand* created by people to which the environmentalists object. It is true that, if people live to a higher living standard, it will drive up the amount of waste material and the amount of carbon dioxide emitted to permit them to maintain their lifestyle. However, it is not a straight-line graph, with higher living standards automatically leading to more degradation of the environment. There is considerable evidence to show that the richest countries in the world have done the most to contain the impact of their economic activity upon the air we breathe and the waters we bathe in or drink. It is often the fast-growing, lower- or middle-income countries that pollute most – certainly relative to the amount of their output. Most people, when asked, would prefer that everyone in the world had the chance of a decent lifestyle, and that efforts were redoubled to solve any environmental degradation by technology and other means.

Critics claim that globalisation increases the gap between the rich and the poor. This is, of course, partially true: globalisation enables some people to become so much richer. However, the implication behind much of the criticism is that the rich become rich only by exploiting and driving down the incomes of the poor rather more. This is not borne out by the evidence, which is that, as globalisation influences more and more countries, the average level of income rises at the same time as the most successful and the richest people become substantially richer and better off.

The global market really allows some people to become fabulously rich in a way which national or local markets would not. Football stars are now paid many multiples of the salaries their predecessors received just 30 or 40 years ago. A Manchester United footballer in the 1960s could draw only a limited salary because the bulk of it had to be paid for by the Mancunian audience that would turn up on Saturday afternoon to watch the game, buy a ticket and programme. Today, the fabulous salaries of Manchester United players are supported by millions of people around the world buying videos, buying Manchester United shirts and tuning into television programmes to watch the games, for which the television companies have to pay substantial royalties.

Similarly, the chief executive of a large business serving the British market in 1960 was paid a salary which, even when adjusted for inflation, was a small fraction of the sums now paid for a chief executive of a British-based multinational. The reason, again, is that his or her salary can be paid for out of the purchases of millions of people around the world who want to have access to the goods and services of the multinational – whereas his or her predecessor 50 years ago was dependent, mainly, upon the purchases of a more limited (and poorer) British community. Wherever multinationals go to create jobs and hire people, they usually bid wages up. There is no known case of a multinational arriving in a new country and undercutting or driving market wages down. The critics are, therefore, wrong to imply that the growing gap between rich and poor under globalisation occurs at the expense of the poor. It occurs to the benefit of both the rich and the poor. However, it is true to say that the super-rich are the biggest winners of all, because they are best able to exploit their talent and their market access, collecting tiny sums from each of millions of new subscribers and consumers.

An allied criticism of multinationals is that they exploit local labour. The more mature critics, on production of the evidence, might be forced to accept that multinationals arriving in a new country do not bid wages down. However, critics still argue that it is morally wrong for a multinational to arrive in, say, a poor African country and offer wages only a little above the going market rate in that country, rather than offering people the kind of wages the multinational would be paying if they employed similar staff in the advanced West. This is the economics of the madhouse. If the multinational had to pay the same wages in a poor African country as it pays in New York it would be far less inclined to employ the people in the African country, and more inclined to have more New Yorkers with higher educational standards and a better immediate understanding of what the company needs and wants. Paying 'home market' rates would also be pretty damaging within the new territory concerned. The very few individuals who got the jobs with the multinational would attract enormous jealousy from all those who could not get such jobs and would have disproportionate spending power in the local community, giving them a potential lifestyle out of kilter with the goods and services available locally at the prevailing average income level.

Most multinationals conclude that it makes sense to offer good salaries or wages by local market standards, but not to seek a globally agreed wage or salary at advanced country standards and apply it everywhere. Most multinationals are flexible about the remuneration of middle-ranking and senior executives and there are cases where individual executives recruited in low-income countries achieve extremely good deals for themselves: they are potentially 'footloose' and their skill and achievement is recognised appropriately by the hiring multinational. In other words, as people from the poor African country are able to add substantial value, so the multinational will reflect this in its wage levels when they offer transfers to other countries, which can be attractive to the individual staff member. Rather than being a case of *exploitation*, the arrival of the multinational offers *opportunity* to the bright and talented, and offers fair wages appropriate to local skill levels and market conditions.

Some critics also fret that globalisation is too materialistic, inviting people to substitute material for spiritual values. Again, the evidence from around the world does not bear out this hypothesis. The United States of America remains one of the richest countries in the world – but it also has very active and vocal Christian communities, capable of attracting large numbers of people and funding their own viewpoint, so becoming an important force in American politics as well as in spiritual life. If you are very poor, your main focus is on how to get a little more money and how to get enough to eat and sufficient shelter. When you are better off, you have more time to think about spiritual and moral issues. There is no necessary conflict between global capitalism and the great religions, and no necessary conflict between global capitalism and individual spirituality and morality.

Instead of constantly going on about what is bad about globalisation, maybe it would be better if some of its critics or students also spent a little time realising what is so good about it. There must, after all, be something very good about globalisation, because it has been so widely adopted: it is not adopted just because America forces a country to adopt it. It is not adopted because its greed is backed up by American rocketry or enforced at the point of the submachine gun of a visiting American marine. Some of the most dramatic adoptions of global capitalism in recent years have taken place in former communist countries, where no American soldier has stepped foot in anger since 1945. Global capitalism swept through the Eastern European lands as soon as the Berlin Wall came down and the communist regimes were shaken off. The joyous rebels of Eastern Germany or Hungary or Poland wanted access to world markets and world brands. They had caught a glimpse of them through travelling westerners or through covert study of western magazines and broadcasts. Once the communist hold was broken, people were queuing up to buy into western material success. They were keen to invite large western corporations into their countries to make the goods they wanted locally, and to use them to the higher employment and skill standards of the West.

In communist China, still a single-party tyranny, the regime decided that Marxist-planned production was not working. There were many years when thousands of Chinese died of starvation owing to the failure of the agricultural system; even as late as 1990, most Chinese could scarcely aspire to owning a bicycle, let alone thinking about having a fridge, a television, a washing machine or a car. Today, in China, it is all so different, thanks to their 'one country, two systems' approach. China now has that combination of political autocracy and economic freedom that Asia has made its own in more than one territory. Their talented people now go into business and economic activity, where they are free to express themselves and make themselves rich, wisely keeping out of the political sphere – where what they say and think is closely controlled, and where no choice or competition is permitted. It is globalisation which is giving hope to the Chinese peasant moving into the nearest city to find an industrial job; hope to the burgeoning Indian middle classes, as they join the consumer world of the West; hope to the Brazilians, to the Russians and to all the others who, one way or another, now have joined the global marketplace and who, when it comes to economic decisions, understand the need for lower taxes and reasonable economic freedom.

The more that people specialise and trade with each other, the higher that average incomes will become. This underlying truth, taught in the early lessons of economics in most schools and universities around the world, so often gets forgotten in political debate. If I own a fishing rod, but have no access to a lake, I cannot use my asset (the rod) or my skill at fishing and I starve. If I own a fishing lake, but have no rod and no ability to fish, I also cannot use my asset (the lake) and would starve. 'Trading' makes it possible for the person with the rod and the fishing skill to reach an agreement with the person with the fishing lake, so that both can enjoy some fish and both can make a return on their assets. In practice, the world is full of many different skills, accumulated capital and assets. It is far more complicated than my simple model: one person with a fishing rod and one with a lake. But all of free trade rests upon the simple proposition that, if you put two or more people together, and two or more assets together, they can be so much more valuable than if you have to do everything for yourself. If I choose to do all my own cooking, I can eat tolerably well. If I want to enjoy a really fine meal, it makes sense for me to pay a great chef in a good restaurant for the privilege of enjoying his skill. If that chef needs representation of his political view in Parliament, but he himself is not a good student of law or a good orator, it makes sense for him to pool with many others to elect a single representative for his area in Parliament and to pay that representative a salary.

Aggregate all of these decisions and choices, and the economists will rightly tell you that the more that people specialise, the richer that society becomes. Specialists get better at doing something. Their skill or better product will command a premium. Once they can charge a premium price, they have more income to spend on their own welfare – which in turn creates more income for all those who are providing the goods and services they need. It is a simple money-go-round: the more money that circulates – and the faster it circulates to people with skills and with products – the richer society becomes. Globalisation extends the theory of specialisation from the national to the international level. The more countries and people that participate in world athletics at the Olympics, the faster the times and the higher the jumps become. The more people and nations that participate in global capitalism, the better the products and services become.

Globalisation spreads best practice and new ideas very rapidly. Prior to the globalised digital age, the spread of new technology took time. People tended to be protective and defensive of their inventions; information about them was often not shared widely through the printed word and only a few people travelled around to see what was happening. An enormous breakthrough was made with industrial technology in England in the 18th century, with the development of factory-based production of textiles, backed up by steam power and automated spinning and weaving machines. It took a long time to spread this around the world. In the digital age, new technology spreads far more rapidly since borders are porous and people are mobile, taking the ideas to the four corners of the free economic world as quickly as possible.

In the Cold War era, the communists in the Eastern bloc tried to invent everything for themselves. They spent an ever-larger and disproportionate amount of their national income on defence innovation, desperately trying to keep up with the more successful American system. As a result, they fell further and further behind in the art of peace. By the time communism finally collapsed under its own contradictions, the typical eastern car, mill machine, power station and all the rest were way behind their western equivalents, where the free market and free enterprise had driven change and innovation and where income levels were so much higher, sustaining much bigger investment activities across the whole range of human activity.

BENEFITS OF GLOBALISATION

It is this pursuit of *scale* which can combine with better innovation and excellence. Large companies can put much more money into research, innovation, sales and service than smaller companies. As the mighty multinationals reach out around the world from New York, London, Amsterdam and Frankfurt, so they collect more money, gain more customers and, in turn, have much more money to spend on improvements and refinements of their products and services. The big global pharmaceutical companies spend huge sums of money on researching new compounds which can combat resistant diseases and conditions. The large automotive engineering companies pour money into improving fuel efficiency, speed, safety and the other important ingredients of a successful vehicle. The breakthroughs become more breathtaking and more exciting, as corporations grow and as more money is put into research.

Globalisation allows the many to enjoy global brands; global brands allow the many to enjoy the luxuries possessed, in past decades, only by the few. In the 1920s you needed to be seriously rich to own a motor car. By the 1990s cars were commonplace. In the 1940s and 1950s you needed to be middle class or better to own a television. Today, in the advanced West, anyone who wants a television owns one – or, indeed, more than one. The large multinationals, spending more on research, sales and service – and through larger sales – have brought down the prices of these 'luxury' goods. Today, a young married couple would expect to have a fridge, a freezer, a television, a washing machine, dishwasher, fitted carpets and a small car. None of these things was present in the typical home of 1950.

A brand is an aspiration and a guarantee of quality and enjoyment. People go for brands because they come to trust them and relate to the values incorporated in the particular brands. Globalisation allows more people to live the Hollywood dream; it creates the potential for footballers, pop and film stars and others to be fabulously rich. It enables the budding entrepreneur, who may have failed at school and been poor at sport, to hit upon a product or service and discover that he or she has millions of potential customers by plugging in to the world market. The poor girl from an African village who practises her running or the poor boy from a West Indian household who practises cricket in the backyard may find they can use their talents on the world sporting stage and so completely transform their lives.

Globalisation can be good for the environment. Contrary to the attacks of its critics, it is in the richer countries that most work has been done to clean the factory chimney, to remove the pollutants and hazardous waste, to recycle materials and now even to cut down on CO_2 emissions. When communism ended in Eastern Europe, it left in its wake an ugly array of polluted lakes and rivers full of dangerous chemicals, large areas of ground laid waste by over-farming, by chemical pollution or by nuclear accidents. The planned society of communism was not good at planning what to do with its waste products and was careless with its natural environment. The more democratic West always placed some greater value on maintaining the natural environment and in recent years has rightly become extremely concerned, wishing to intensify its actions and to increase the spend from its riches to maintain and enhance the natural world we have inherited.

Globalisation is beneficial, because it allows poorer countries to get out of poverty. You do not need to have great natural resources or to start with an extremely skilled and educated workforce: the barren rock of Hong Kong jutting into the mighty Pacific has spawned one of the richest and most thriving communities in the world, building up its riches from hard work and through developing and attracting talent. What Hong Kong did in the 1950s and 60s, Shanghai has done in the 1990s and the first decade of the new century. It is access to the ideas, the investment money and the organisation of skills of the great multinationals that so often produces the best poverty-relief programmes. Critics claim that the multinationals only come in order to extract the minerals, to take advantage of local conditions. Of course, it is true that the commodity-producing companies do want to be where the commodities are, and this may often be a poorer country. However, they are usually welcomed because they have the capital investment, the money and the mining skills that are needed and they will offer training programmes to local people. Sensible developing countries negotiate quite tough deals with incoming companies, so that they participate in the success that the companies enjoy from exploiting local deposits.

There could even be a political benefit from globalisation: the more instant news and communication we have, the more it exposes the tyranny of bad government worldwide. So many poor countries are let down by their own national governments. Corruption, a lack of choice, a refusal to put things to democratic votes, and the reluctance of the tyrants to move on and allow new governments to arise to tackle problems, are still symptomatic of many foreign countries today. The more that we create a global village, and the more the global media can expose these tyrants and their mistakes, the better it is going to be, and the more likely it is that pressure for change will build up. The more exposure that people from poor countries have to the way of thinking and the managerial skills of the West the better, because the more likely it is that they will return to their home countries and start applying these essential truths.

Finally, to those who are still not persuaded that globalisation is a good thing, I have a piece of advice. If you do not like global companies, then stop buying their products. The global multinationals are only as strong as their customers enable them to be. If a global multinational still gives you a bad feeling, and if you still believe that everything can be done locally without specialisation, then I suggest you try it for yourself. In practice, very few people in Britain would maintain anything like their current lifestyle without multinational trade across borders, without goods and services supplied by the multinational corporations. From hat to trainer, from food plate to computer program, from telephone to writing paper, we are dependent upon the enormous, sophisticated, complex, interrelated, global production and trading system. It has served recent generations well, and has made many people much richer. It is curious, indeed, that it still evokes so much hostility when the overwhelming majority of people in the West, and now in Asia, have voted with their feet to join the global marketplace.

THE RISE OF ASIA

When I wrote my book *The Global Marketplace* in 1992, I drew attention to the way that world brands were being established in a range of areas: consumer durables, travel, communications and financial services. I explained why manufacturing was globalising and I looked at the evolution of popular capitalism after the defeat of communism. Writing that, 17 years ago, convinced me about the rise of Asia – but in those days we were talking about Singapore, Taiwan, Japan, Hong Kong: not mainland China. We were talking about world multinationals developing world brands and sourcing wherever it was cheapest – but not on the scale made possible by the advent of the Internet. The cover for that book showed a computer screen with the world linking it, as I and others at the time had a hunch that phones, media and computers were about to come together in an interesting way. The rise of the worldwide web, an Internet base of trading and services, is a very recent phenomenon.

Is there any alternative to globalisation – and would it be one that we would prefer? In the 20th century, communism was meant to be the answer to the world's problems of scarcity and social exchange. Communism became a global creed spread by the enthusiasm of a very limited elite in communist states, allied to propaganda and suppression once communism had a hold. The communists created a world which was poorer, dirtier and less free than the West. Many communists held global ambitions for their ideology and sought to enforce it through infiltration, propaganda and even force. Communism collapsed in the USSR and Europe at the end of the 1980s through a series of popular revolts, and in China today it is being transformed through its enforced alliance with capitalist economics. Communism proved to be an alien creed, even to the proletariat, so-called by the Marxist theorists in their patronising way. The proletariat did not lose their chains through communism – but were placed in new ones. Many of the intelligentsia were locked up or killed for having alternative views. People were shot when trying to leave the communist bloc to seek a better life elsewhere, whilst the many western intellectuals who favoured communism did not favour it sufficiently to choose to go and live in a communist country for themselves. By popular choice, communism was rejected throughout Europe. Today, in the free democratic world, communists can stand for election – but never get elected in sufficient number to govern any country, because people remember how evil their system was.

If you ask the many critics of globalisation today what they would prefer, they single out parts of the communist programme without calling it communism, and try to cobble together a left-of-centre consensus which they think would be preferable. Some of the things they want could make sense. They might like more localism and a gentler kind of society. They often want more redistribution of income between the West and the rest, through action by global institutions such as the World Bank and the United Nations. They seek increased aid budgets and want strongly redistributive taxation and benefit systems within any individual country. They favour much more state involvement in planning – but they fall short of recommending the complete planning of labour movements, capital movements and control of the thoughts of everyone in the society, which was the stock-in-trade of communism at the height of its empire.

STATE INTERVENTION

It may be true that, if you have less communism than that which true communist societies had to endure, you will be less worse off, less dirty, less in chains than if you adopt full communism. However, the extent to which the state interferes *more* will inevitably mean that individuals and families can achieve *less*. The more that is planned, the less the exuberant spirits of individuals and families can expand their talents to the betterment of mankind. The more that the state pre-empts money to spend on what it thinks are the priorities, the less money that talented individuals and companies have to spend on investigating, innovating and changing the world for the better. Capitalism is ultimately democratic; companies which behave badly get punished in the marketplace.

Encouraging local action is currently very popular. Like many, I think it makes sense to support local talent, to encourage organic production and, in order to minimise 'food miles', to buy local food products. However, it would be unrealistic to assume that I or my neighbours could feed ourselves today by relying on local produce alone. We like to eat oranges and lemons, pineapples and mangoes; we like tropical and subtropical produce as well as temperate produce – and that requires international trade. If you go too far in encouraging local action, you lose the many benefits of international specialisation and you slow down the transmission of new ideas.

It is also generous and public spirited to want more aid to go to Third World countries, to try to help them out of poverty. However, pumping in aid at government level all too often fails to motivate and improve developing countries in the way intended. Sometimes it can do the opposite. If the money is passed into the hands of an evil dictator or a corrupt regime, it may be spent on luxury cars, armaments or soldiers, to protect and cosset the ruling classes – rather than on sensible economic projects, which might employ and improve the lifestyles of that country's poor. All attempts at Western aid and assistance to a country can be rendered meaningless if a country persists with evil government, with civil war, with genocide and the denial of human rights.

Whilst most people in a civilised country would agree that a national government should make provision for those who are sick, old, ill or unable to provide for themselves, there also needs to be strong incentives in the system so that the able-bodied and the capable will make the best of their skills, will work hard and industriously, and will seek to improve their talents in the contribution they make to the society. If the balance between incentive and protection is wrong, society will get poorer and weaker as a result.

THREE MODELS FOR WORLD DEVELOPMENT

There are three broad models for world development currently being tried around the world: the European, American and Chinese systems. Each is having some success but, as we will see, the more a system backs economic freedom, the faster the growth and the higher the incomes it will achieve.

The US system is based upon democratic challenge, whereas the European system is based on bureaucratic consensus; the Chinese system is based on political repression, allied to progressive economic liberalism. The United States enjoys lower taxes and more free enterprise. The European Union has higher taxes and more government involvement. China now has lower taxes and some freedom in her lead sectors, which are performing well; however, government planning and intervention is common in the rest.

The United States has lighter regulation – although it does have a culture of heavy expenditure on lawyers and litigation. The EU has stronger and wider-ranging regulation. China has less regulation in lead sectors, allied to strong government control over how far and how fast different areas of the economy are liberalised. The US allows you to do what the law does not prohibit; the European Union allows you to do what they set out in the law, and China allows you to do what suits those in power. The law in China can be capricious and variably enforced, whereas the law in the US and the EU tends to be more fairly enforced. In the case of the EU, there is considerable variation amongst the member states. The US is globally engaged and sees herself as a global power. The EU is more introspective, confining herself in the main to matters affecting Europe.

China invites in the best of the world in selected areas, and has ambitions to be a global power.

THE US SYSTEM

The USA has a settled constitution and is a unified country – following a bitter and expensive civil war, which established the writ of the federal authorities throughout the land. She has a constitution based on separating the powers of the executive, the legislature and the judiciary, and creating a more productive and democratic tension between the three. There is a stable relationship between the 50 member states of the Union and the powerful federal government, largely established following the civil war – but subject to amendment through long and complex procedures to amend the constitution by plebiscite. The USA is the most powerful country in the world, capable of projecting her power through every ocean and country. She has the technology and the manpower to assert her will almost wherever she wishes. The only serious political risk or threat is that of terrorism: as we have seen in recent years, America can win almost any conventional war she chooses to fight but now has to deal with cleverer and more dangerous opponents who indulge in asymmetric warfare that can reek carnage on the streets of New York or Washington. There is no immediate likelihood of political instability or a major change in the system, as enough Americans buy in to the strength of their democracy and to the desirability of their country remaining a united federation.

THE EUROPEAN SYSTEM

In contrast, the European Union has a troubled and evolving constitution, set up shortly after the end of World War II. It is now looking old fashioned and is the subject of endless wrangling between, and within, the member states over what changes to put through. The EU is a set of divided countries coming together, some of which have a long history of disliking each other and disagreeing with each other – most notably France, Germany, Britain and Italy, but also quite a few of the smaller countries as well.

Not only that, but also *within* several of the countries there are very strong divisive forces at work. The Flemish and Wallonia regions of Belgium dislike each other and don't wish to remain part of the same union; Scotland is in disagreement with England within the UK union; the Catalans and the Basques are not very happy about the Spanish union; the northern and southern Italians do not have a great deal in common.

There is no clear democratic control over the EU's executive or judiciary. A largely impotent Parliament has no power to tax or legislate on its own and little will to bring the Brussels Commission, the Executive and the European Court of Justice to democratic account. There are unstable relationships in the Union. We have no idea how many states will wish to join the Union in the years ahead – nor whether any states will wish to leave. We have no idea what the final resting point of the relationship will be between these member states and the central government. The EU currently has little power outside her own borders and has no established way of supporting her foreign policy outside the EU area, but the federalists are keen to develop common military activities and military institutions.

There is serious political risk of instability, as different countries, peoples and parties want very different degrees of centralisation and government interference in member states' affairs. The only thing we can surely forecast is that, over the next 50 years, there will be massive changes in the relationships and power balances between the member states. Nor is the EU immune to the risk of terrorism and asymmetric warfare, either internal or external. External terrorist threats affect the EU almost as much as the United States of America, because the European Union is perceived by some outside Europe as backing and supporting the American line. There is also the additional risk of nationalist movements arising within the EU, both against the existing member states and against the EU itself as centralised power develops.

THE EASTERN SYSTEM

China, in contrast to the other two territories, is a one-party state. Her main decisions are made by the Committee of the Political Bureau of the Communist Party. The Communist Party does not permit political dissent, it places people in prison or mental institutions if they disagree too much and has a very poor record on human rights. China entered world trade arrangements on 10 October 2000 and has since benefited greatly from the liberalisation of trade that this permitted. Her collective farming system is being gradually dismantled as it failed so miserably and left many people in hunger. There is a rapid movement of people from rural to urban areas, as poor peasants leave the land to seek better incomes in factories in the bigger cities. China is now pursuing the Hong Kong/Singapore model of economic development through liberalisation of sector after sector. They invite in foreign capital and foreign ideas, although this remains allied to a strongly authoritarian political system.

China is already the world's fourth-largest economy at market exchange rates and the second-largest at purchasing power parity rates. In 2006, she had a total output (or income) of $10 trillion when measured on a purchasing power parity basis, and $3.4 trillion when measured at then-current exchange rates. China has been the fastest-growing major nation for the past quarter of a century, with an annual average income growth above 10 per cent. Over the last three decades, individual incomes have grown by an annual average of more than 8 per cent, drastically reducing poverty and catapulting large numbers to riches. China is now the world's third-largest trading nation after the United States and Germany and has foreign exchange reserves in excess of $1.5 trillion as a result of successfully exporting so much more than she has imported.

SOME COMPARISONS

When it comes to military power there is a huge imbalance in the world, in America's favour. Whilst the EU has a bigger military force in terms of numbers of service personnel, it is very poorly armed and ill-equipped to move outside the European territorial area. The same is true of the enormous Chinese army. The US has a near-monopoly of modern troop carriers by sea and air, especially when acting with the UK as its main ally.

The gap between America and the rest has been getting bigger, even during the period of the Asian economic surge. By free-world standards, America has spent a relatively high proportion of her national income on defence research and weapons procurement. She has specialised in developing enormously important technologies for command, control, surveillance and delivery. As a result, she can see a potential battlefield in almost all conditions, with sensors and surveillance that can peer through the mist, the fog, the rain, the trees and even camouflage to find the location of enemy forces. Furthermore, she can now strike powerfully from many thousands of miles away, often not needing to engage individuals in the final delivery of the weaponry to the target. America, in short, can gun, bomb and explode enemy forces before the enemy can see where the threat is coming from. It is the American ability to lift men and material across thousands of miles, by air and by sea, which strikes terror into the hearts of would-be opponents. It is the ability to understand and see the battlefield from a distance, together with the terrifying ability to deliver a huge explosive force to pinpoint targets with considerable accuracy, that means no major power in the world is going to take on America in open battle.

The US is also outperforming the Europeans when it comes to growth and economic activity. The EU's own review of economic prospects for 2002 thought that the EU's share of world output would fall from 18 per cent in 2000 to only 10 per cent in 2050, whereas it was expecting to see the United States rise from 23 per cent to 26 per cent. On the EU's own forecast, the ratio of the US to the EU would double from a modest 1.3 times the size of the EU in 2000 to a whopping 2.6 times by 2050. Nothing that has happened so far leads one to believe that these forecasts might be wrong.

On the other hand, the Asian Pacific century seems well set. The phenomenal rise of India and China continues apace. They are joining the economic success and high growth rates of Hong Kong, Taiwan, Singapore and Korea. The world is shifting rapidly and visibly from an *Atlantic* centre (powered by the economies of Europe and the eastern seaboard of the USA) to a *Pacific* centre (powered by west-coast America, India, China and the smaller successful Asian Tigers of the last few decades). Over the 20 years to 2006, the United States Gross National Product (GNP) grew by an impressive 82.5 per cent – despite starting as the richest of the major countries in 1986. Over the same period, from a much poorer and lower base, India's economy has grown by 236.5 per cent and China's by a stunning 531.6 per cent. China regularly grows at 10 per cent per annum and India regularly achieves around 8 per cent per annum. The performance in the middle of the current decade has been the strongest yet from these emerging giants, with consistent high levels of growth year after year.

Although it is true that both India and China were having to slow their economies in 2008 to deal with inflation, overheating and the wash-back from the big increase in commodity prices worldwide, they will still grow at a far faster rate than the ailing advanced economies.

The Asian century will be dominated by the great Asian powers based upon strengths of population alone. India and China, between them, have 2,500 million people, well in excess of three times the combined populations of the United States and Europe. Their populations are younger, with more in the active working-age bands. Furthermore, huge gains in output and productivity are possible as people leave the low-productivity, subsistence farms of the past and move into the cities to be recruited by the new industrialists to power the factories.

These emerging giants are also well aware of the importance of the service sector as well as manufacturing. They understand that, to attain the lifestyles of the West to which they aspire, they need to take education, training and service activity very seriously. Indian and Chinese students are hardworking and intelligent, learning English to plug themselves into the global marketplace and often seeking employment with a multinational or travelling abroad to get the skills and experience they need before returning home.

The Asian century will develop on the back of western ideas and western multinational company organisation. It is now gathering a momentum of its own. The Asian nations have plenty of their own money for reinvestment, and are rapidly learning the skills and acquiring the talents needed to run their own multinationals very successfully. In the Asian basin they can look across the water to Japan, which followed a similar course of catch-up with the West in the 1960s and 1970s. By the 1980s, Japan had surpassed many western countries in terms of income levels and output per head, and was a world giant in its chosen sectors of consumer electronics and automotive products. Japan succeeded in building global brands and world companies, led by Toyota, Honda, Nissan, Sony and others. We are now witnessing something similar in China and India.

THE DIGITAL REVOLUTION

After globalisation and the rise of Asia, the third big theme that has been playing out in the last two decades is the digital revolution. In some ways this is the underlying motor of American power. It was the US which revived her fortunes in her competitive battle against Japan and Europe, through the excellence of her technology and the brilliance of her Silicon Valley scientist entrepreneurs. By 1990, it was clear that America had won the Cold War: the United States could take her weapons technology onto a new level, using microelectronic controls and digital communications in a way that eluded the Russians. Gorbachev recognised that they were outclassed and outpaced. The Russian economy was groaning under massive defence expenditure relative to the low level of national income, merely to keep up with the mechanical and nuclear weaponry that characterised the 70s and 80s. Gorbachev's understanding of the superiority of American technology is probably one of the most important reasons why he opted for glasnost and a different approach to Russia's relationships with the rest of the world. Russia needed access to western technology and she was not going to get that in Cold War conditions.

By the end of the last century, the American computer and digital revolution was spreading into civvy street. It was the Americans who first managed to pull together the different technologies of the television, the telephone and the computer. It was the Americans who understood that digital communication enabled the rapid transmission of data and pictures around the world. It was the Americans who developed the computing power necessary to handle the huge quantities of information that the information age required: whole libraries were put into computer databanks. Large picture libraries were accumulated, which required enormous computer storage for the digital processing of the images, and the Americans were in the driving seat with the crucial software to power the digital revolution.

Despite an early hiccup in 2000-1, when a large number of hi-tech companies overstretched themselves and when software and digital-age stocks plummeted on the New York Stock Exchange, America carried the revolution onwards and was soon the accepted world leader. Microsoft's software took over in every office and on many a home desk. The world was laced and linked with cables and microwave links carrying messages, the news and the pictures. Soon, everyone with some money wanted to be part of the revolution: buying a home computer, acquiring a state-of-the-art personal telephone for mobile use and expecting, when going to the office, to spend a lot of the day staring at the screen, reading emails and surfing the Internet for information.

The growth of the World Wide Web gave a huge boost to globalisation generally. Whilst it was the American corporations which were in the lead, providing the software and the technology, any company that could afford a desktop computer and a phone line could join in. Companies soon realised that advertising their wares and products on the web was a good way to get access to the world market. 'Mail order' became 'email order'. Shops went online, offering their products for those who wished to make their choices from pictures viewed from the privacy of their home – at any time of the day or night. Companies seeking to source new components or find new services could look on the Internet to see who could provide them, and could use it for getting competitive quotes. It became possible to run a business thousands of miles away from where your customers lived. Some western companies decided that they would send their back offices to India, where the labour was cheaper; they sent the information to them electronically and received the necessary services electronically or over the phone.

Whilst the digital revolution is now well underway, it is probably the case that there are still many applications we have not thought of and many potentialities of the technology not yet being exploited. 20 years ago, few would have thought we would have video and film on demand electronically; that we could bring our television, our phone and our home computer together; that we would have access to a worldwide library, with huge amounts of information easily accessible by means of search engines and Internet links. The world has shrunk decisively, and the consumer is greatly empowered through digital technology. It has fuelled a large increase in cross-border and cross-continental trading, since the best in the world can be offered to those who want it, anywhere in the world, at any time of the day or night.

THE COMMODITY RUSH

The fourth important trend which all this has produced is the surge in commodity prices and the enrichment of the individuals, companies and countries that specialise in commodity production. When Arab oil first went over $10 a barrel in 1973-4 the world economy shook to its very foundations. People suddenly realised that the era of cheap oil was over: profligate use of oil had to stop; new sources and resources had to be found. The successors of the world economy in America, in Europe and in Japan had to understand that they could no longer rely on abundant supplies of cheap oil to fuel their factories, to power their homes and to keep their transport systems moving. In July 2008, oil hit an astonishing $147 a barrel. Whilst this caused some additional inflationary pain in the economies of the West, no one thought the rise in the oil price, on its own, was going to bring the world to a halt; no one argued that we could not adjust. The intervening years had demonstrated to the world that it can handle dearer oil and will continue to have to handle dearer oil.

Similar things have taken place in recent years, with the price of copper, steel, lead and, more recently, with agricultural commodities. The sudden arrival of 2,500 million Indian and Chinese at the global party has created a massive increase in demand for all types of raw materials to feed their factories. In the post-1945 world, the West had got used to the assumption that it could buy metals, foods and fuels relatively cheaply in order to maintain its living standards. A few other nations came to this party, the biggest being the approximately 110 million Japanese, assisted by those living in Singapore, Hong Kong and Taiwan. But it did not make much difference to the overall picture: less than 20 per cent of the world's population was living to a high standard, using the resources of the whole world to maintain that style of living.

As the earlier reactions to the first oil crisis demonstrated, economies do adjust; it is possible to get used to the dearer prices and relative scarcity of any given commodity or fuel. The advent of the $10-12 barrel of oil greatly helped the exploitation of the Norway/UK oil and gas reserves in the North Sea. Later on, further price rises and political changes led to an increase in Russian oil production, new discoveries on the mainland of North America, the exploitation of deposits throughout Asia, and growing consideration of extracting oil from the tar sands in Canada. At the same time, high oil prices spawned alternative technologies for generating electricity, helped the development of a much bigger market in internationally traded gas, and made at least some of the people much more attentive to fuel economy and efficiency – for, at least, some of the time. Whilst there are many more motor vehicles around in the West than 30-40 years ago, they are on average much more fuel-efficient. People have begun to substitute teleconferencing and Internet and email communication for what otherwise would have been trips and visits. Many factory processes have been made more fuel-efficient, and many manufactured items have been made lighter in weight, reducing the material content and reducing the power needed to transport them.

Today, the speculative excesses are being squeezed out of commodity prices. During the credit crunch towards the end of the first decade of the 21st century, and the resulting contraction of the major economies, there will be a reduction in the growth of demand – and in some cases maybe even a fall in demand – for commodities. Although this will affect their prices, it is likely that the trend towards more demand and higher price will be the persistent feature of the next couple of decades, as the economic enfranchisement of India and China continues apace, and as some other developing countries also seek to join the party. Russia has emerged from her period of troubles and is getting richer on the back of the successful exploitation of her oil and gas deposits. She, in turn, will become a bigger consumer of all types of raw material. There are signs that Brazil, the sleeping giant of the last few decades, is making more steady progress in growing her economy. She, too, will make more demands on world resources.

All this means that the West will have to turn its attention to technological ways of limiting its demand for given scarce commodities. It will need to find better ways of travelling, keeping warm, making things and communicating. Digital technology is part of the answer. It can help create a more fuel-efficient and less resource-intensive world. Meanwhile we may well be pleasantly surprised at just how much unexploited resource remains to be found or to be mined and excavated. Price signals are very strong. The higher the prices go for commodities, the more ways will be found to bring unexploited reserves into use. Already, high prices of basic metals have developed a much more robust market for re-smelting and recycling in second-hand metals. People are talking about greater recovery rates from oil fields, and the exploitation of deep water and tar sand oil that, previously, was uneconomic. One way or another, the world will muddle through. However, we need to understand that the balance of power between the commodity producers on the one hand, and the manufacturers and consumers on the other, is tilting more and more in favour of the former, after their experience in the 20th century when they were usually the poor relations.

4 | Why are some places rich and some poor?

INTRODUCTION

Why has the European Union fallen so far behind the United States of America in terms of growth? Why has the UK done slightly better than the European Union – but not as well as the United States? Why do the economies of some parts of the United Kingdom, especially London and the South East, do so much better than those of the more remote locations in the north and the west? Why do some countries stay rich, why do some countries become rich – and why do other countries remain mired in poverty?

You would have thought that, after all the dollars and pounds spent on economic research, after so many economic treatises have been written, after so many Development Agencies have been established, after so many governments have made speeding up the growth rate their prime aim, we would by now have a clear idea of the answer. Instead, there is a ready industry for economists, government officials, policy advisers and others to spend their time (and usually other people's money!) on trying to determine the best recipe for improving a regional or national economy.

The world has been offered three broadly different models for economic progress and development in the last 50 years. Different countries have followed different models at different times in their historical evolution. Governments come and go and change the policy mix but, for the purpose of analysis, it is possible to extract the outlines of very different approaches by considering those things which made America rich and those things which made China and the Soviet Union poor. For much of the second half of the 20th century there was an economic battle going on, alongside the political tension and Cold War exchanges, between the communist countries of the East and the free-enterprise countries of the West.

FREE ENTERPRISE – OR COMMUNISM?

In the free enterprise corner stood the United States of America. In the communist corner stood the Soviet Union and her satellites and, further east on the shores of the Pacific, China. As the decades rolled by, the experiment came to a conclusive answer. If you wanted to be poor, stay poor and grow slowly, adopt the communist model. If you wished to be rich, stay rich and grow more quickly, then adopt the American free-enterprise model. The long experiment ended with the collapse of the Soviet Union, the declarations of independence by a host of her former satellites in Eastern Europe, and by China, in the economic sphere at least, morphing away from a communist state and planning to adopt progressive liberalisation along western lines.

Rarely has anything been as clear as the free-enterprise system's almost total victory over communism, which characterised the period 1945-90. In every field, the more free-enterprise-oriented western economies outperformed the state-planned eastern economies. Many theoreticians in the West could not believe it. They had devoted a great deal of their lives to arguing that state planning – the communist system – was superior to western capitalism in many ways. They argued that state planning could ensure the best use of resources, as it would mean that money did not have to be spent and wasted on 'unnecessary competition'. There did not need to be large expenditure on advertising, different company management structures or competing companies within the same industry. It meant the state could decide where people should best work. There could be labour planning, capital planning and production planning.

As people in the West fell in love with planning, they introduced elements of it into the western system itself. The Europeans adopted it more strongly than the Americans – but even the Americans decided that some planning was necessary, particularly to win wars and to come out of recessions.

A THIRD APPROACH

As communism began to collapse under its own innate contradictions, many in Western Europe decided there was a third way. They argued that a superior method to American free enterprise was a Western European social democratic system, where the government intervened and planned in certain fields, but left other fields freer for enterprise to flourish. This compromise position, this third way between the two extremes, was lauded as being gentler, kinder and – according to some commentators – more successful economically in some periods than either the free-enterprise American system or the communist Soviet Union system.

Yet the figures demonstrate that there is absolutely no truth in the supposition that a little bit of communism, the Western social democratic model, is more successful at growing economies than the American system which involves rather less communism or state planning. Nor, more importantly, is there any evidence that the degree of state planning and state intervention introduced into western economies in Europe has been more successful than the American system at alleviating poverty or creating better social justice.

The European system, with more government planning and involvement, has persistently maintained much higher unemployment than the more free-enterprise American system. As one of the main ways of getting people out of poverty is to allow the creation of new jobs, it is at once apparent that the high unemployment rates on the continent of Europe are a severe impediment to anti-poverty strategists. Furthermore, bureaucratic rationing systems are often delivering more to richer and better-educated families than they are to those in real need, since bureaucratic allocation systems respond better to the articulate and more forceful than they do to the dispossessed; the British National Health Service is a case in point. Overall, the European model has produced lower incomes than the American model, higher unemployment, and has still been faced with persistent areas of high deprivation and low achievement.

The American model is not a pure free-enterprise model; it may be the nearest one gets, in any of the major world economies, but it still has a substantial state sector and big government involvement. The American economy, for example, has to carry the burden of high military expenditure. While there is some technological spin off from the substantial sums spent by the state on new weapon development and procurement, and while US weapons companies are able to export some of their product worldwide, it is nonetheless a distortion that a great deal of talent in the American economy is used in the field of defence.

The American state provides a large and expensive healthcare system for those without health insurance, provides food stamps and other benefits for those out of work and down on their luck, has substantial public involvement in the finance of housing through mortgages, and has substantial federal and state-financed spending programmes for a variety of areas from transport to construction projects.

The Heritage Foundation publishes an annual *Index of Economic Freedom* which attempts to evaluate how economically free different countries are, using both a ranking and a score. In 2008, it estimated that the United States was the 5th-freest country in the world after Hong Kong, Singapore, Ireland and Australia. The United Kingdom was in 10th place, with continental European countries considerably further down the table. North Korea came in at 157th, the bottom place amongst the countries listed. (The *Index of Economic Freedom* is published by The Wall Street Journal and Heritage Foundation, and can be found on **www.heritage.org**.)

The index takes into account the level of tax rates, the degree of regulatory interference, the strength or weakness of the law in favour of free enterprise contracts and private property, and an evaluation of the effectiveness of government and the infrastructure. All the top-ranked countries are 'rich' countries; all the lowest-ranked countries are 'poor' countries. As soon as a country starts to get a higher rating within the *Index of Economic Freedom*, its growth rate usually picks up. There is a good correlation between those countries that follow a path of greater economic *freedom* and the list of countries achieving greater economic *success*.

THE IMPACT OF TAXATION

Tax is one of the big definers of a country's economic performance and of how economically free it is. The higher the average tax rate on individuals and companies, especially taxes on incomes, the slower is their economy's growth. In 2006, Sweden weighed in with a hefty 50 per cent average tax burden, with Denmark close behind at 49 per cent. Belgium, Italy and France were also well over 40 per cent. In contrast, Ireland at 31.7 per cent, the United States at 28.2 per cent and New Zealand at 36.5 per cent had much lower tax rates. Partly as a result of that, they have enjoyed much better economic growth in recent years. The tax burdens in the fastest-growing developing countries are considerably lower than those even in the successful economies within the richer West. The Indian tax burden is 10 per cent, the Russian 15 per cent, the Chinese 17 per cent and the Brazilian 33 per cent. Rich Switzerland enjoys an average tax rate of only 30 per cent and the average OECD American total is only 27 per cent, compared with the much higher average rates on the continent of Europe.

Given how much is now known about the relationship between lower tax rates on enterprise and incomes, and rapid economic growth, it is surprising that more countries have not adopted the low tax rate strategy which has proved so successful for others. It is true that, in recent years, the Germans have woken up to the attractiveness of lower tax rates and have started moving in that direction. The Dutch have moved more vigorously. As a result, since the Dutch rates are now below the British rates, they have attracted companies to set up their head offices, and to expand their operations, in Holland rather than in neighbouring Britain. Thanks to reforms in the 1980s and early 1990s, the UK economy enjoyed considerably lower average tax rates than the continentals for many years and, as a result, attracted much more inward investment and the creation of more private sector jobs than the other EU countries. The competitive advantage of these lower taxes has been gradually eroded in the last decade, as other countries came to see a need to cut their tax rates to attract jobs and stimulate domestic economic activity.

Lower taxes, on business profits or individual incomes, act as a natural stimulus, both to externally and internally generated investment. Clearly, if a business faces the option of investing in country A with a corporation tax rate of 35 per cent and in country B with a corporation tax rate of 20 per cent, it will opt for country B – all other things being equal. Every pound of extra profit generated in country A will only yield 65p of income to spend on new investment or new jobs, or to pay as dividends to shareholders. In country B, in contrast, 80p would be available for every extra pound generated. This acts as a great incentive, for all those contemplating new investment, to establish themselves in the territory or place where, after taxes, they will have the most money left over for pursuing the purposes of the business.

THE IMPACT OF REGULATION

Similarly, businesses seeking new investment opportunities look very carefully at the cost and extent of regulation imposed by host governments. In many respects, regulation is a surrogate form of taxation. If you need to pay a licence fee to operate in a given territory then that, effectively, is an additional 'tax' on profit or turnover. If you need to employ additional staff to monitor compliance with local regulations, and to keep you informed about future and additional local regulations, this too is a 'tax' on doing business in that country, similar to the costs imposed by direct taxation. The European area has been particularly keen on regulation; its politicians and bureaucrats believe that unrestricted business will do damage to its customers, be unfair to its employees, and do damage to the environment. They believe there needs to be a panoply of regulations, including those concerning safety, employment and the environment, to prevent businesses from creating the damage they fear.

No amount of evidence placed before the EU bureaucrats, that good competitive businesses need to take care of their customers and employees and to be good neighbours, will dissuade them from regulating or legislating. This would not matter if the regulation or legislation simply reinforced best practice in successful, profitable, competitive businesses. Of course, no business should mind having to be fair to its employees, deliver a good product at a good price in a timely way to its customers or be a sensible and responsible neighbour wherever it has established its factories. To the extent that businesses would do such things anyway, a formal regulation would not be irksome or impose extra burdens.

However, regulation is not like that. Regulation does not just say to the company 'you should be fair to your employees and should be a good neighbour'. It goes into considerable detail into interpreting what fairness might be or what being a good neighbour entails. In some cases the regulator's interpretation may chime with the popular interpretation and the company view. In other cases it does not.

Indeed, in some cases, following the letter of the regulation or law can take one outside the spirit of it because, so often, the detailed regulations are perverse. There are many cases where regulations often end up achieving the opposite of what they set out to achieve: in their wish to be prescriptive or detailed, regulators lose sight of the impact they have upon individuals running a business. They forget that there are many aspects to fair treatment and good neighbourliness that they cannot summarise in their extensive legal and regulatory codes.

One example of the futility, or perverse consequences, of regulation lies in the European Union's fishing regulations. One of the main aims of fishing regulation is to prevent overfishing of the crowded and much-plundered waters of the North Sea. To try to prevent overfishing, the European Union not only imposes a physical quota on the *quantity* of fish that individual fishermen can catch (in itself a much-disliked intervention in the economic process) but also sets a minimum *size* of fish to be caught. In an ideal world this would be a good approach: it seeks to prevent fishermen from catching smaller fish which need time to develop, so that they in turn can become worthwhile catches that people could eat. Furthermore, the European Union imposes different quotas on different species, reflecting their estimate of how many fish of each kind are left in the North Sea.

Unfortunately, there is no easy way of achieving the aim. Whilst it is sometimes possible to prevent catching too many small fish by adjusting the net size, so that the smaller fish have more chance to swim out before the net is landed, it is an imprecise science and still allows small fish to be caught in the net. There is certainly no way for a trawler owner to know what kinds of fish are being caught until he has landed the net on his deck. Very often trawlermen, seeking to comply with the regulation, discover on opening the trawl net that they have caught large quantities of banned or quota-controlled species which they are not allowed to bring back to port; or they have accidentally caught smaller fish than they are allowed to land. They proceed to weed these out and to throw them back but, of course, by the time they are thrown back, the fish are dead.

As a result, a European rule ostensibly designed to preserve fish stocks actually increases the rate of depredation of the stock. Because the banned species and sizes of fish cannot be landed for human consumption they are thrown back into the ocean dead, requiring the trawler to catch yet more fish to meet the demand for fish consumption back at the home port.

This is not an isolated example of the idiocy of regulation. We will see in subsequent chapters just how big a role bad regulation played in the development of the credit crunch, which has so disfigured financial and economic progress in the latter years of the first decade of the 21st century.

Overall, the European Union – an area of relatively high tax rates – compounds its error by imposing far more regulation than jurisdictions elsewhere. The combined impact of high taxes and high regulatory costs are a major turn-off for businesses looking around the world for the best locations to invest their money in building factories.

Of course, it is true that businesses want an orderly society. They do not wish to set up business in a country with no framework of law, no rules of competition, no ability to preserve and protect private property or to sustain private contracts between parties. They are not after the absence of government – but they are after a government which is controlled, capable of creating and enforcing a sensible volume of law. They want a government capable of avoiding being over-intrusive, not one seeking to specify in its legal codes all types of conduct and activity which are best left to the marketplace and competitive forces to sort out.

POPULATION SHIFTS

The problems for Western Europe in responding to the pressures of globalisation, and the ever-mounting challenge of India and China as well as the United States of America, are greatly compounded when one looks at the demographic background. The biggest single change in world power and economics, occuring over the first half of the 21st century, is the big shift in relative population. The coming dominance of Asia rests very strongly on the large number of people already born and resident in India and China. In addition, according to UN population figures currently available, it is very likely that the population of the 27 member states of the European Union will fall by some 15 million (or 3 per cent) in the years up to 2050. At the same time, the UN expects the US population to expand by over a third, or over 100 million, and for the Chinese population to expand by a little under 100 million. In other words, the increase in populations in the USA and China will be the equivalent of 40 per cent of the current EU population, at a time when the EU's population is falling.

Worse, still, for the European Union is that the modest overall fall in population conceals a far larger fall in the expected working-age population (those aged 15-64) over the coming 40 years. In 2005, the 27 member states of the European Union had a working-age population of 303 million. The UN population division's 2006 forecasts estimate that, by 2050, this will drop by 66 million to only 237 million, a colossal fall of 21.7 per cent. However, they estimate that the falls in Japan and Russia will be bigger, at 38 per cent and 35 per cent respectively. In contrast, the UN reckons that, over the same time period, the US population of working-age people will go up by 48 million, or 24 per cent.

Within the European Union itself, the UN anticipates a very wide range of experiences. Out on its own, with a big increase of more than a half, is Ireland. A combination of a younger population with more live births and anticipated inward migration produces a dynamic increase. A small increase is also expected in the United Kingdom, reflecting its more liberal immigration policies as compared to the other member states. The population of France, traditionally a country that encourages a bigger population, is expected to be static. The big declines are anticipated to be in Germany and Italy, with falls of about 25 per cent, and Greece and Spain, with falls of about 20 per cent.

In countries such as Italy and Spain there has been a big change in social behaviour: the liberation of women, and the decision of many women to take paid employment, has led to far fewer children being born. Many adults now see children as an impediment to a good lifestyle and have them either later or not at all. The traditional large Catholic family is becoming a thing of the past, as the hold of Catholicism on the population weakens and as social behaviour changes.

THE EFFECT OF POPULATION CHANGES

Whilst many people have now noticed these important population changes, there has been surprisingly little comment about just how dramatic they may well be, nor the consequences they are likely to have for economic development. The first, and most obvious, consequence is that the relative power of the European Union, economically and politically, will diminish further. Economic clout does depend upon the level of a country's national income and output. The European Union's output will be much reduced relatively by such a large decline in the number of people available to go to work. Similarly, the European Union's aspiration to political power will be limited, because there will be far fewer people to draw on to design and make weapons and to employ in the armed forces. In international forums, discussing the big issues such as energy, commodity prices and international banking, a European voice will be that much less important – because it will speak for fewer people and less economic activity. The voices of China, America and India will be proportionately greater, with a faster-growing population. Indeed, there is a chance that by 2050 India, rather than China, will be the world's biggest economy, based on size of population alone.

The second consequence for the countries facing a decline in the workforce will be noticeable shifts in the prices of labour and services. The last time Europe experienced anything like this was during the mediaeval period with the Black Death, which rapidly reduced populations, sending shockwaves through the European economy. As workers were killed by the dreadful disease, so the bargaining power improved of those workers who remained. The breakdown of serfdom and the conversion to money wage contracts was a long and complicated process, which did not have a single cause. However, the Black Death and the population contraction was part of the reason why workers moved from serfdom to employment and why, in some cases, they started to get a much better financial deal.

In a complex, modern world some of the reduction in the workforce would be accommodated by technological breakthroughs and improved capital investment. However, as the proportion of the elderly population increases, in need of a wide range of care services, so will the demand grow for these labour-intensive services. The need will increase to find people to staff the care homes, the surgeries, the pharmacies, and the leisure and travel businesses catering for the elderly. It means that service costs are likely to rise, relative to other costs and prices in the economy, as increased demand meets reduced supply. The costs for getting old will get greater, and there will be more intense competition by the elderly to secure the services of the young.

Thirdly, we should expect there to be some impact upon property markets. Attention in Britain in recent years has concentrated on the upward movements in prices – at least until 2007 – the explanations of which have been based upon growing demand both from inward migration and from more individuals and families deciding that they wish to live on their own, rather than as couples or in bigger family units. High divorce rates, high break-up rates of partnerships, and the wish of young people to form their own household at an early age, have all pointed in the direction of more demand for accommodation. Ever-rising prices, and the allied necessity for many young people to live with their parents for much longer, and the likelihood of someone from a broken marriage or partnership forming a new marriage or partnership, have tended to mitigate these pressures. Such trends have often been ignored in the social commentary.

What cannot be ignored, when looking at the German, Italian or Spanish property markets, is the impact that the sharp decline in working-age population will have upon family housing and those more expensive properties that require good work incomes to sustain rents or mortgages. During the Black Death, Europe retreated from whole villages and sections of towns, as there was more property than there were people to occupy it. Today, the effect is unlikely to be as extreme, with the elderly living for longer and with more people wanting more than one home, but there are likely to be areas where the impact on prices (and even upon the number of occupied properties) will become quite obvious. High-quality locations, close to lakes and seaside, close to good shops and in good districts of towns and cities, will continue to attract a premium. The global marketplaces will mean that there are many more potential buyers for the best, tending to drive up the prices of such property, wherever it may be located, and detaching it from the reality of national conditions. However, for many other properties in a population-declining Western Europe, there will be no getting away from the downward impact of fewer people needing such properties, and fewer people having jobs with good enough incomes to afford them.

Migration, of course, will be an important issue in either reinforcing or undermining these predictions. To date, the Anglo Saxon economies – the USA, Australia, the United Kingdom, Ireland and, to a lesser extent, Canada and New Zealand – have welcomed in many more migrants. This has sustained demand for property, provided a ready supply of willing labour and added to the flexibility of those economies. In contrast, countries such as Germany and Italy have been more reluctant to accept so many migrants. It is possible that all countries in the freer West will find it difficult to resist inward migration in the years ahead. The physical controls imposed by the European Union as a whole, and by individual member states, have not been entirely successful. There is a relentless pressure by migrants from the Middle East and from the African continent to arrive in Italy or Spain, pressure which the authorities might find more and more difficult to combat. It may even be that some countries, including Germany, decide to soften their policies against migrants, recognising the help that migrants might bring to their job market and to the provision of services to the growing elderly, indigenous population. However, it still remains likely that the UN population predictions will be broadly right, and that the European Union is going to suffer from its demographic time bomb. The EU would need to take very early and dramatic action to reverse this well-established and now well-predicted trend.

To the Future

So what will the future look like? According to PricewaterhouseCoopers in their 2006 projections, the world in 2050 will be a very different state, economically, compared with the world in 2005. Germany's economy will have shrunk to about the same size as the United Kingdom's. The French economy will be smaller than both those of the UK and Germany. Brazil's economy will have risen to be considerably bigger than each of those three. Russia will be little changed, but India will have moved from having an output around 30 per cent of US levels to being the about the same size; China's output will have moved from around 75 per cent of US levels to over 140 per cent of US output.

All these figures are based upon purchasing power parity (PPP) estimates of domestic product. The difference between purchasing power parity and current price domestic product at the moment is very great. According to the IMF's 2007 figures, China's $4 trillion (measured by current prices) was the equivalent of $13 trillion when measured by PPP, which is a system designed to adjust for the reality of what money can buy in each country. Similarly, India's 2007 economic output of a little over $1 trillion at market prices is the equivalent of over $5 trillion at purchasing power parity. We will expect the gap between PPP and market price values to narrow as these economies accelerate to higher levels of income, bringing their prices and purchasing power more in line with those of the rest of the world.

These figures are borne out by the United Kingdom Treasury's own forecasts for shorter time periods. The IMF consensus forecast, put out by the Treasury, reckons that the European Union's contribution to total global output, which was more than 25 per cent of the world's total in 1980, will be down to only 15 per cent by 2015. The USA's contribution will be well ahead of it, as will China's. There is no one out there saying that the European Union is going to undergo an economic renaissance and suddenly start to match or exceed the growth rates of the United States of America. There is no one predicting that the European Union's population is going to turn round and increase. There is no one suggesting that China or India are going to start to get it wrong, and no longer be the main sources of growth in the worldwide economy. While, quite frequently, the general view may turn out to be wrong, on this occasion I suspect the general view is right. The broad outlines of changing economic power are as described here and by the consensus forecasts.

In more detail, the likely developments over the next 40 years are based on the inherited position and dynamics in each of the main countries and power blocs. In the European Union, population reduction will be a decisive factor. The area is likely to continue with slower and lopsided technology growth as compared with the United States of America. The EU will remain wedded to its model of increasing government involvement. Whilst saying that it does not believe in backing winners, the EU national and federal governments will believe in interfering in the marketplace, offering grants and research contracts for certain types of technologies, and seeking – through regulatory and planning frameworks – to influence what kind of technology the region develops. There is little evidence that this approach will be as successful as that of the US; there is considerable evidence to assume continuation of present trends, where the US technological lead through the digital revolution *increases* rather than *diminishes*.

The European area is likely to have an economic policy remaining in flux. Relative failure will ensure continued tinkering and changes. The battle between the federal power of the Union and the individual national governments may well intensify. The premature currency union, with many countries adopting the euro as their single currency, has left countries struggling to accommodate its disciplined framework. Economies such as Spain and Italy find the interest rates and the exchange rate, settled upon the area through the structure of the euro and its German-centric influences, to be far from suited to their own requirements. Italy is being consigned to slow growth and a strangulation of its export activities, while Spain has been through boom and bust in its property market, as a direct result of these countries linking themselves to the euro area before their economies had come into line. If the Europeans insist on adding yet more countries and currencies to the euro area, without ensuring proper alignment and conformity of economic policies, so will the stresses and strains increase.

The single interest rate, and the single monetary growth target set for the European area as a whole, are never going to suit the complex and divergent European economies. The German view is that it is up to the other economies to adjust themselves to the discipline of the exchange rate and the interest rate set by the European Central Bank (ECB). After all, Germany itself suffered in the early years of the euro because it, too, entered the scheme before it had properly converged with the requirements of the ECB. Germany fought valiantly to get her costs down and to make herself competitive again against the background of a relatively high exchange rate. She did it with great aplomb and is now relatively relaxed about the euro's discipline upon the German economy. She is probably less relaxed about the way in which the ECB has allowed price inflation to take off to considerably higher levels than were traditional in Germany and, if anything, she wishes the discipline to be made more severe.

In contrast, Italy (used to much higher rates of inflation and periodic bouts of devaluation of her currency to relieve the pressure on her export industries) is reeling under the cosh of a high euro, relatively high interest rates and the impact these are having upon her leading export industries. Spain found in the early years the euro exchange rate and the euro interest rate level too low for her condition and enjoyed a credit and property boom. More recently, the tightening of credit and the persistence of relatively high interest rates by world standards has created a bust in the Spanish property market, and considerable gloom throughout the economy as a whole. These manic fluctuations are likely to continue as the economies of Western Europe are still too divergent to enjoy a comfortable single currency interest rate and money growth target.

The euro is likely to continue with substantial government and regulatory interference in certain key sectors. Europeans traditionally like big government involvement in transport, in energy, in communications and even in media. In Britain we have a semi-nationalised railway, a nationalised public broadcasting system and a complex web of regulation for transport, energy and communications. All these things are detracting from British economic performance and from choice and plentiful supply for customers. On the Continent, in many of these crucial sectors, it is even worse with governments believing that they have a right – and a need – to intervene quite substantially in media and communications. The European Union itself is not bold in encouraging liberalisation, save in the area of post. As these are such crucial sectors to the economy, we are likely to continue to see shortages of train capacity, electricity-generating capacity and a restriction on choice in broadcasting and media, compared to freer jurisdictions elsewhere. This will be allied to a more competition- and free-enterprise-driven model in other areas of the economy which will continue to work quite well.

In contrast, China is likely to see continued rapid growth in output and per capita income. We should witness the growth of a large domestic market for cars, household goods and other manufacturing products. Unless the government starts to get it wrong, it will pursue a policy of progressive economic liberalisation. It will encourage more and more talented and bright people to achieve higher educational standards and to move seamlessly into a range of high-performing companies. People will be encouraged to follow Mammon in order to keep them more docile when it comes to politics.

China will continue to dominate in many export areas. Currently accounting for three-quarters of the world's exports of leather goods, China also exports over half of the world's exports of textile products, and around a third of the exports of radio, TV and communications equipment. These sectors will continue to advance, and will soon be joined by Chinese success in vehicle manufacture, in other types of engineering, in chemicals and in pharmaceuticals. These targeted sectors are being opened up to more foreign ideas and capital and are likely to grow very quickly.

This forecast assumes that the Chinese dual system of economic liberalisation and political control will continue successfully. It is, after all, a model that worked very successfully in a different form, under British rule in Hong

Kong. The British colonial power did not offer the locals full democracy, although they did offer a better deal on human rights and the rule of law than the Chinese mainland. As Britain found, so China is finding that such a dual system means that talented people go into economic activity more than into politics, with beneficial results for economic development. It is true that the Chinese growth model is very lopsided: some sectors do extremely well because they are encouraged and liberalised, while others remain very backward. Worse still, some parts of China are still dragging in their agrarian past, whilst other parts of China have already attained first-world, high, modern standards. The growing gap between rich and poor is stark, but the extent to which that is based upon the rising prosperity of the few (rather than the falling incomes of the many) is something that should be manageable. There should be enough growth and development in China for there to be something in it for most people, and for the success of the few to be a spur to the many, rather than a cause of rebellion.

So what do we do anticipate for the world's only current superpower, the USA? Despite all the current gloom based upon credit crunch extrapolation and mistaken interpretations of the extent of the US problems, I forecast a continuing and relatively fast growth in the USA in the decades ahead. This will be based upon the flexibility of her workforce, upon the inward migration of talent from around the world, and from rapid technology growth. Whenever the USA has been written off in my lifetime, as it has regularly by bien savants and so-called liberal thinkers in Europe and the communist world, they have quickly been proved wrong.

By the end of the 1980s, Japan was said to be about to eclipse the United States of America, based upon the diligence of her workforce and the excellence of her consumer electronics and vehicle engineering. Ten years later, America had shown a clean pair of heels to the ailing Japanese economy, which had turned out to be awash with debt and overblown property prices, unable to make the digital breakthroughs that America came up with. Similarly, in the 1960s, people said that the Soviet system was so much better than the American system, because it concentrated national effort through proper planning and did not dissipate it on the waste of competition and free enterprise. The British Prime Minister of the time, Harold Wilson, made a speech on the so-called 'white-hot heat of technology'; this praised the success of the Soviet system, and said that Britain needed to get closer to that and its successive plans for economic growth, rather than to the American model. Fortunately, he did fall short of recommending single-party government and political tyranny, but he liked the economic planning and economic drive of the Soviet system. That, too, proved to be wrong, as America soon surpassed Russia in its space exploration and developed a stunning array of weaponry with which Russia could not compete, leading to the eventual collapse of the Soviet model.

The next couple of decades, of course, will see a growing challenge to American economic dominance by the rising Asian powers. However, it would be a foolish person who not only predicted that China and India would surpass America in terms of total output – something that they will do one day, based on numbers alone – but also suggested that both countries would surpass America in terms of intellectual property, technological dominance and military hardware. In the last 10 years, far from the technological gap between West and East narrowing, actually it has increased.

When America and Britain fought the first Gulf War in 1990, the two armies could fight alongside each other comfortably (although the American contribution was much bigger in scale than the British) because they shared a common technical base. Today joint American-British military cooperation is much more difficult, because the American military machine has made such huge advances in battlefield technology, weapons systems and intelligence capability.

American success and strength will continue to be based on her relatively open society, her passion for competitive activity, whether it be sport or art, service sector or manufacturing. It will be based on the excellence of the American education, upon the quest of government and people alike for things which are bigger, better, faster, stronger. America still has that pioneering spirit of a young country, that get-up-and-go, that belief that problems are there to be surmounted and what you cannot do today you will probably be able to do tomorrow. The country that put the first man on the moon, the country that used the first nuclear weapon in combat, the country that can project her power today to any of the corner of the world, the country that has given us Hollywood and Microsoft and Coca Cola, the country of the digital revolution, is not finished yet and is not about to be eclipsed any time soon.

The US has the advantage of an economic policy geared to the domestic requirements of her large, fast-growing and integrated single market. It sets interest rates and the money growth to facilitate that. As the recent crisis has shown, for all its regulatory mistakes, US regulators still moved further and faster that those elsewhere to bring growth back. The US believes in the free enterprise of a competition-driven model and all the evidence shows that this is the model which has the most favourable impact on world activity. Whilst there will be countries with lower taxes and less regulation than America (and there will definitely be countries with fewer laws and fewer lawyers than America) America remains relatively lean, relatively mean and extremely competitive when taking the package as a whole.

We are going to continue to live in a world where America is the only true superpower. We already live in a world where the challenges of asymmetric warfare, terrorism and world opinion can provide some checks and balances to the American might. We will see the emergence of much stronger economic powers in Asia, which will naturally want a bigger say in the big economic decisions confronting the new world order. We are not about to see a world in which the EU takes on the might of America as the EU will struggle with its own contradictions, its own falling population, and its own lack of economic success. We are entering the Pacific century. America is fully part of that, with its vibrant and vital Californian economy as one of the glittering centres of the Pacific rim.

5 | Energy policy

INTRODUCTION

Part of the crisis in the world economy in 2008 is based upon the shortage of hydrocarbons. Soaring oil and gas prices have created huge trade imbalances, as large sums of money have been transferred from the importing western world to the exporting Middle East, Russia and some other fossil fuel producing countries. It has been a good time to be resource-rich and a bad time to be energy-dependent. Some people see US President Bush's intervention in Iraq and Afghanistan as part of a wider plan to institute friendlier and more democratic regimes in that part of the world – a part which is still dominant in oil and gas production. In Europe, the renewed strength of Russia owes much to her strong position as an oil and gas producer and exporter. Russia is using her new-found wealth from oil and gas exploitation to re-arm and to assert herself both economically and politically. Many of the manoeuvrings in Eastern Europe relate to the routes of gas pipelines and the supply of the precious material from East to West.

The advent of political tensions over access to energy is bringing together two unlikely groups of politicians. The green campaigners are extremely keen to reduce the usage of oil and gas by the rich West. They believe that all oil and gas burning is harmful, generating too much CO_2, and want the West to turn to lower energy usage on the one hand, and renewable energy generation wherever possible on the other. The neo-cons, and those on the Left who favour the West acting as some kind of policeman and democracy enforcer, want to intervene in the oil- and gas-producing areas and endeavour to make these friendlier towards ourselves. They also now talk about the need for the West to move towards greater energy self-sufficiency. On the right terms, they also favour the development of renewable and non-fossil fuel sources of energy production, to reduce the West's dependence upon imports from dangerous and difficult parts of the world.

Both parties want change. Both, for different reasons, want the West to be less dependent on fossil fuels; both find their wishes reinforced by the very strong pricing that is now coming from the marketplace, as a result of the surge in oil and gas prices in the last couple of years. A speculative 'bubble' had built up in oil prices, driving the price to $147 a barrel, before the economic downturn punctured the market.

With oil at over $100 a barrel, the world is a very different place from the one with oil at half that price. Suddenly, new sources of oil and gas, which previously rested unknown or lingered in the ground for want of the investment dollars to bring them out, are discovered or considered ripe for exploitation. At these prices it should be possible to exploit the tar sands, huge reserves in politically safe North America. Big gas finds were reported in Louisiana in 2008. It should be possible to re-enter ageing fields in the North Sea and use enhanced technology to increase the recovery rates. Frontier areas in safe waters are now ripe for exploration. The rush is on to gain access to continental shelves in the more remote parts of the world. The big powers are staking out claims to the land under the Arctic Sea. Others are making sure that they are in a good position should the ban on exploration and drilling in Antarctica ever be lifted. Argentina is once again making noises about the need to gain access to the continental shelf around the Falkland Islands. The search is on, the rigs are fully used and drilling rates have been bid up, as the oil companies see new opportunities and governments gradually come to the view that they need to be encouraged.

At the same time, consumers recognise the need to do something about curbing their appetite for once-cheap oil. The price signals of the market are greatly reinforced, especially in Europe, by greedy governments which choose to impose huge taxes upon petrol, diesel and other energy products. The price of petrol at the pump in the UK of 115p a litre (in early October 2008) comprised 75p a litre of tax and only 40p to be split between the exporting country, the company that explored and developed the oilfield, the company that refines the crude oil into product and transports it to the filling station and the company selling it to the customer. The government has a majority stake in the sale of oil product to the hard-pressed motorists in Britain, and uses its taxation policy to reinforce the signal that motorists should use less of the product. At these prices and tax levels there are strong incentives for people to drive more carefully, to drive less, and to try to afford an upgraded and more fuel-efficient car. The drive is on to find more fuel-efficient solutions for transport, to improve the insulation of people's homes, to exchange outdated and inefficient boilers for modern condenser boilers (which are almost 100 per cent efficient) and to persuade people to switch off appliances when they are not being used.

All of this is commonsense and a natural response to a strong market reaction. The advent of 2,500 million Indian and Chinese at the world party, all demanding rather more oil and gas to back up the manufacture of the products they wish to consume and the lifestyles they wish to enjoy, has made a decisive change to the price of oil and gas. While, in the short term, there is price weakness, as a result of recession and downturn in the western economies, most forecasters believe the long-term trend of oil and gas prices will remain upwards since so many more people around the world will seek their share of the limited resource. This intensifies the pressure on western countries to look for new ways of doing things which require less energy – and to find new ways of generating their own energy beyond oil and gas.

THE UK AS AN ENERGY IMPORTER
You would have thought that the United Kingdom was particularly well-placed to deal with this problem: an island of coal, set in a sea of oil and gas, and with access to good scientists and technology, should not need to be importing any energy at all. Thanks to policy failure and delay in recent years, the UK is now an energy importer. We import electricity from France,

we import oil and gas from many sources around the world, and are now crucially dependent upon imported gas to see us through the winter. We have reached this position for a variety of reasons.

The first has been the way the government has seen the oil and gas industry domestically as a ready source of cash flow and revenue. Tax rates have been increased and tax demands have been brought forward, in order to take more money out of the sector more quickly. Because the North Sea is now a mature oil province, where the easy finds have been exploited, it is now a high-cost area in which to explore and develop. At the margin, the increased tax demands put companies off spending their additional exploration pounds, or their additional development pounds, in the UK. As a result, the North Sea has not been an exciting province in recent years. There have not been enough rigs looking for new oil and there has not been enough expenditure on new technology to exploit and develop the oil that is already there. While it is true that, over the years, oil recovery rates have risen substantially from the low levels forecast when the province first became exciting in the 1970s, it is still the case that, on current plans, around half the oil and gas discovered will remain unexploited beneath the waves.

The UK coal industry

The second reason the UK has become energy-dependent is the treatment of its own domestic coal industry. For years after the 1939-45 war, coal was in nationalised ownership. This meant that it went the usual way of a nationalised industry. In spite of huge subsidies from the taxpayer it was a story of endless closures of pits, with the sacking of their miners. Often, this occurred well before the point it would have happened if the pits concerned had been run by commercial interests. Throughout its nationalised years, the industry was in constant decline, cursed by an incompetent management and a difficult workforce. The combined forces clashed dangerously in the 1980s during the long miners' dispute. The Coal Board was determined to close pits on the grounds that they were not economic when, if run commercially, some of them could have been made economic. Some of the workforce responded in a way designed to do most damage to what remained of the industry, and the inevitable tragedy occurred.

In the early 1990s I was pleased to be involved in the salvation of one of the pits the Coal Board decided to close. As Secretary of State for Wales I was approached by a group of miners from the Tower Colliery in South Wales. They said they thought that, with suitable backing, they could take the pit on and make it economic, long after the Coal Board had sentenced it to premature closure. I was excited by the prospect, as I thought they would be right. I had always thought Coal Board management closed pits too early, and had the wrong cost structure and wrong approach to managing them. The idea that the miners themselves would have a participation in the mine (and the profits it could generate) would transform attitudes, while there was geological evidence to show that substantial coal remained in the seams beneath the earth. After some difficult exchanges I was able to persuade Cabinet colleagues and to require the Coal Board to allow a buyout to proceed. The miners bought out their pit and succeeded in mining coal profitably for more than a decade after the successful purchase, demonstrating just how wrong-headed the Coal Board had been over that particular pit. I fear that many other pits went the way of closure, unrelieved by brave and enterprising miners prepared to take them on and prove the Coal Board wrong.

Opencast mining in Britain is made difficult, if not impossible, by the problems of gaining planning permission. Opencast mining can be a noisy and dirty occupation. People living anywhere near a possible opencast site do not, of course, wish to have the dust blowing into their homes nor the heavy trucks passing their doors. In order to extract more coal by opencast mining we need to be more enterprising in the way we approach the management of such issues. Some combination of greater dust suppression, and the diverting of lorries to suitable large roads away from the general population, would be basic to success in getting through more opencast planning permissions. Offering substantial compensation to people who are too close to the mines would also be a way worthy of exploration.

Britain's coal is her hidden resource, one which could represent an important salvation while energy supplied from renewable and other alternative energy sources built up to serious levels. Coal is still relatively cheap, and at current coal prices it should be quite possible to get more out of the ground if permits are forthcoming in a sensible way. The environmentalists will object to burning more coal, since it does produce substantial CO_2 emissions in normal processes, but there are technologies under development which may provide a partial answer to this problem. These technologies are grouped under the generic heading of 'clean coal' and are receiving substantial support from the miners and related unions who see the advantages in terms of jobs and prosperity of recreating a domestic coal industry. 'Clean coal' technology can include collecting the carbon dioxide produced when the coal is burnt and sending it off to an underground store, the so-called 'carbon storage option'. It is quite possible now to clean, up to much better levels than in the past, the other gases emitted from coal burning at a power station. Handling the waste gases on the way out of the power station with scrubbers, filters and the like can reduce or remove the pollution that was customary with previous generations of coal-fired power stations. The country could also examine more imaginative technologies still, including combustion underground or fluidisation of the coal. In the last war, when oil was very scarce and difficult to transport around, the use of fluidised coal was one of the answers.

GENERATING ELECTRICITY

Much of the debate in Britain relates to how we generate our electricity. There is no single uncontentious way of doing it. One might have thought that all parties would acclaim the use of hydropower: it is clean, green and not that difficult to create, given the quantity of rain, lakes, rivers, tidal estuaries and the like that we enjoy in our country. However, when people come up with particular schemes to create tidal barrages across estuaries, or to dam rivers to create holding reservoirs preparatory to releasing the water across turbines, there are always environmental objections. It seems to me that these environmental objections are from people who are not in the business of making sensible choices: very often, the environmental changes required to create a hydro scheme would *enhance* the environment, creating beautiful lakes and using the water more intelligently. It should be possible to get more agreement about the need for more hydro schemes in wet Britain.

More contentious still, in the list of renewables, is the advent of the 'windmill'. Many hillsides and prominent places now sport one or more modern wind turbines. There are two main objections to them, environmental and practical. Environmentalists often object to them on the grounds that they are ugly and an intrusion into the countryside; they can harm bird life, and they can be noisy. Practical people, concerned about economic growth and development, may also object to them on the grounds that they are expensive and that they can only operate when the wind blows within certain wind speeds: it is not much use, they say, having an energy policy dependent upon wind-generated power in a country where the wind is intermittent and very variable in speed. You need to build back-up power stations for those times when there is strong demand for electricity but no wind is blowing, and this makes it a very costly option.

There is some opportunity for solar-generated power, despite the number of days in Britain when the sky is overcast and the sun's rays are weak, and there is also some scope for tapping the natural heat of the soil. These methods of generating power, or at least supplementing our energy, are best undertaken at a local level, by individuals and communities. At the moment, the technologies are quite expensive for what you get back, but as energy prices rise and the volume of demand for these products grows, so the reward relative to the cost should improve.

In the British debate about electrical energy there is a growing feeling that one of the reasons we are short of capacity and facing serious problems over the renewal of our power stations is that we have gone for the top-down, centralised model. Although we now have competition for supply rather than monopoly provision, the competitors are still mainly generating power by using large, centralised plants left over from the nationalised era. Many people now think that we need to move to a more decentralised model, where many of us become mini-generators at home and at work, tapping into the local energy sources that are available. Individual homes, offices and shops could have a *producer* as well as a *consumer* relationship with the National Grid, sometimes putting energy into it, because their solar panels or the wind turbine on their roof are running well or (more often) extracting electricity from it, because they have a bigger power demand than they can generate themselves. Decentralised and local energy could also take place on a slightly bigger scale, with towns and villages having their own generating plant based on, or supplemented by, local heat and energy sources.

There is need for a lot of change in electricity generation. Britain has an ageing generation of power plants, and big decisions are now required about modernising and changing these. Around one-fifth of British electricity is generated from nuclear power stations. Many of these power stations are at, or near, the end of their planned lives and will have to be retired over the next 10 years. There has been a very active debate amongst political groupings over whether to replace nuclear with nuclear.

The government now claims that this is what it wants to do, and has said it welcomes the debate. However, all attempts to get government involved in the detail, and to get them actually to make some decisions, still prove difficult. Eleven years into the life of this government, we are no nearer to seeing a commitment to a single new nuclear station than at the beginning of the period. We have been treated to endless green and white papers on the energy problem; we have been told periodically that the government wishes to have a major national debate about the nuclear option, which it is minded to recommend. Still, there are no actual plans and projects; still there are no licences being issued; still, there are no decisions about which nuclear technologies are preferred nor where the stations might be constructed.

There is an active debate about the safety and costs of nuclear power. You might have thought that the green movement would welcome nuclear power generation, since practically no CO_2 is produced – unlike generating power from coal, oil or gas. However, many greens are strongly against civil nuclear power. Perhaps their opposition comes from the way that, in the early days, civil nuclear power was an adjunct of a nuclear weapons programme. Perhaps some genuinely do fear that the magnitude of risk in generating power from nuclear sources is something many times bigger than that from other large generating plants, although the safety figures do not demonstrate this. Many people have a special fear of nuclear power because they believe that, if it does go wrong, it is likely to go wrong spectacularly, and it can visit cancer and death on people invisibly.

The issue of cost is difficult to tease out. If you talk to the nuclear industry, they will tell you that they could generate nuclear power in Britain without subsidy. However, they go on to say that this assumes that all carbon is priced sensibly. When you ask what that means, they say that they require a carbon price higher than the current market price of carbon, and this price has to be levied on their competitors generating electricity from coal, oil and gas.

This puts a new perspective on the merits of nuclear power. What most of us want is access to a plentiful supply of realistically priced energy that we can afford and enjoy. We would also like this to be generated in a way which is safe and does little damage to the environment, but the realists amongst us understand that all methods of generating power carry some risk and involve some emissions to the atmosphere. As individuals, most people do not hold a candle for any particular method of generating power. I have no idea whether the power coming out of my power socket this morning has come from a wind turbine, a nuclear power station, or a combined-cycle gas one. I would guess that most of it has come from the latter, simply because that is still the dominant way of generating power in Britain. It makes no difference to me as a user, since power is power. What I want to know, however, is that those taking the overall decisions have come to a sensible balance, in their judgment, to provide me with all the power I need at a price I can afford, while at the same time taking into account the environmental and safety implications.

How then does one proceed? The obvious thing to do would be for the government to say that permits and planning permissions to build a new generation of power stations will be made available. However, if companies need some kind of guaranteed carbon price or some other subsidy, then there will be bidding competitions to establish which is the least-cost, most environmentally friendly way of proceeding. The result may be a mixture of different ways of proceeding with subsidised power in order to gain certain environmental objectives. It would be best to pit nuclear against renewables in such a competition, to establish what would be the least cost to the customer and/or the taxpayer, in order to generate the necessary power to the required specification of low carbon or no carbon. At the moment, there is a lack of clarity about the actual costs of generating power by these different means. We need to have a sensible, diversified balance between different methods of power generation domestically, to cut our dependence on imported oil and gas. This balance may include clean coal, hydro, wind, solar and perhaps some nuclear, depending on costs and safety evaluation. The options have to be judged based upon best bids to minimise the burden on the taxpayer and the consumer.

INTERNATIONAL ENERGY USE

Quite often, when listening to the British debate, one gets the impression that Britain, along with America, is somehow a uniquely large polluter and needs to take particularly stringent action to deal with its emissions. Yet the overall figures for primary energy use show a rather different picture. If we look at the world's use of primary energy in 2007, expressed in millions of tons of oil equivalent, the US leads the pack, burning 2,361 million tons, followed closely by China at 1,863 tons (and growing rapidly year by year). At 311 tons oil equivalent, Germany is a heavy energy user; France's use is 255 million tons. At 216 million tons of oil equivalent the United Kingdom is burning 16 per cent less energy per head of population than France, and 30 per cent less per head than Germany.

The UK generates a lot less electricity than the other majors. In 2007, measured in terawatt hours, the US again headed the list at 4,368 compared with China's 3,278. Both Germany at 637 and France at 567 were massively bigger than the UK at 398, even when Germany's usage is adjusted for her population difference, around a third more than either the UK or France. Part of the usage difference is accounted for by greater industrial use in Germany, but part of it must also be accounted for by the fact that the French, the Germans and the Americans all use more electricity and more primary energy in living to a higher standard in terms of energy use. They have more powered appliances, more air conditioning, and better heating systems than we do in the United Kingdom.

The usage figures also show a big gap between developing countries and the West, which will be narrowed significantly as the developing countries decide to achieve levels of energy use and comfort closer to western levels. China has still not overtaken America in terms of energy use, although she has a population four times as big. India, with a similar population to China, is still well behind the Chinese levels of energy use. It is these overall figures which lead most analysts to conclude that there will be plenty of additional demand for energy as the developing countries become richer.

ENERGY RESERVES

When we look at the pattern of world energy reserves, we see a concentration of riches of oil and gas in the Middle East. Russia does not have especially large oil reserves but does have a very strong position in gas and coal. The *BP Energy Book*, published annually, contains the best western estimates of reserves. The 2007 figures for oil show that known world reserves had risen to 1,238 billion barrels, an increase of 14 per cent over the previous decade, despite increased exploitation and use. This shows the magic of higher oil prices in encouraging additional oil discoveries. North America, including Mexico, at 70 billion barrels of reserves, is in a very similar position as Russia, at 78 billion. At 111 billion barrels, South and Central American totals are second only to the massive total of 758 billion barrels of reserves still located in the Middle East. If the world wishes to carry on burning oil, it is going to need friendly relations with the Middle East, and there needs to be sufficient political stability in the region to continue pumping.

When it comes to gas, BP estimated known reserves at 177 trillion cubic metres, in 2007. Of this, only 8 trillion metres was in North America. An impressive 45 trillion metres, a quarter of the world's total, have been discovered in Russia; there are 73 trillion metres in the Middle East, confirming Middle Eastern dominance in hydrocarbons.

Of the world's coal reserves, which in 2007 were estimated to be around 850,000 million tons, the Middle East accounted for practically none. The United States has a strong position here, with 243,000 million tons, followed by Russia at 157,000 million tons. China has a respectable 114,500 million tons and South Africa an important 48,000 million tons. The UK's 155 million tons of reserves seem small by world standards, but these do give the UK the prospect of 75 years of production and consumption of her own coal reserves, at a rate of 2 million tons a year. This gives it a much stronger position than most countries.

THE POLITICAL IMPERATIVES

All these underlying statistics confirm that Russia is a serious player in energy markets. In order to achieve reasonable world growth, ways have to be found of developing and sustaining friendly relationships with Russia, and in keeping her included in the world trading system. The extraordinary dominance of the Middle East in oil and gas reserves means that world prosperity still rests, in no small measure, upon the principal states, including Saudi Arabia, being friendly enough with the West, as well as with the emerging giants in the East. The figures show that while there is more to be exploited in the safer and more democratic parts of the world, the world energy trading system rests upon satisfactory political outcomes in the Middle East and with Russia, unless there are major technical changes.

From this point of view, the conduct of the United States of America, the world's only superpower following the collapse of the Soviet Union (and the end of the Soviet pretence that she could keep up with American technology) has not been perfect. The United States has felt that she could be an aggressive crusader or champion of democracy and western values, where necessary backing these up by force of arms. The West has undertaken military intervention in both Eastern Europe (close to the borders of Russia) and in the Middle East. Democracy has made considerable natural advances in Eastern Europe, with many of the countries exiting from Soviet control – either taking to democracy with great alacrity or returning to it after a long, dark period of communist totalitarism.

The Middle East has been rather different. There, there is no established tradition of democracy, no golden age to which to appeal. Islamic people have a different view of what the state should do and say. Many of them believe that it is the state's duty to lay down – on an exclusive basis, enforced by law – standards of conduct and morality which would be regarded as unacceptable by people in the freer, democratic West. Many Islamic apologists for their system would argue that it represents a different approach to freedom, since Islamic society aims to give people freedom from lewd, immoral or inappropriate conduct, as judged by the clerical authorities. In contrast, western democracies try to give people freedom of action, which is limited only if they make unreasonable intrusions into the lives and welfare of others. The conflict of civilisations and moral attitudes has been very obvious in recent years. Exponents of Islam resent the crusader approach of the United States hegemony; the Americans resent the way in which Islamist extremism is seeking to redress the imbalance of power in the world, through illegal terrorism against America and her allies.

Oil, gas and politics have become extremely intertwined. The advent of an oilman, President George W. Bush, to the White House in 2000 gave the Pentagon plenty of opportunity to argue the case for a more aggressive interventionist stance in the Middle East. George Bush may have been smarting from the failure of his father to prosecute the 1990-1 war against Iraq to a complete conclusion. At that time, an allied coalition went in to liberate Kuwait, which had been invaded by the Iraqi tyrant and occupied. The West kept the support of a lot of Arab opinion in seeking to free Kuwait. Other smaller states were worried about the possible impact of unchecked Iraqi aggression upon themselves, and were grateful to see America come to right the wrongs and remove the tyranny. However, Arab opinion became more concerned with America and her allies when they were poised to take Baghdad and to throw out the tyrant from power at home as well as abroad. George Bush senior backed off and left Saddam Hussein in charge.

There was a sense of déjà vu and unfinished business when his son, President George W. Bush, decided that the Iraqi dictator's many violations of human rights and United Nations resolutions justified a call to arms. There was some uncertainty or hesitation about whether or not the various United Nations resolutions condemning Iraq gave the United States and her allies the legal right to intervene – but the allies were sure they had this right, and they seized the moment. Moderate Arab opinion found this difficult to accept, and radical Arab opinion decided it amounted to a declaration of war – not just upon Iraq but upon Islamic people generally. The stage was set for bruising and bloody encounters: America showed that she remained the dominant military power, by a fairly quick and easy win against the conventional forces of the dictator. But she then discovered what great colonial powers had discovered in the past, namely that winning the peace is far more difficult than winning the war. Injecting into a foreign country an army that was well trained and better-armed than its opponents was relatively easy for the superpower; getting the people to love it, and then to develop a new sort of government which met the people's aspirations (as well as those of the superpower) were to prove extremely difficult.

In Eastern Europe, NATO, the US and her allies have been more successful in working with the newly emerging democratic states. The West would say that the people of the countries emerging from the Soviet Union spontaneously chose democracy. Without prompting, their elected governments chose to apply to join NATO and, in many cases, the European Union as well. They wanted the safety and security that comes from knowing that the world's only superpower would guarantee their borders and their democratic rights against any future Soviet-style aggression or intervention.

From the Russian point of view, all this seemed rather different. To many in the Kremlin it seemed that the West was deliberately provoking Russia, by seeking to bring more and more of her former satellite countries under NATO control. The West protests that NATO is a defence alliance, with no aggressive wishes and no hostile intent to Russia. But old habits die hard in the former Cold War warriors; their sons and daughters in the modern Kremlin see Russia being encircled by the increasingly successful and popular combination of democracy and NATO membership. This is not a good background against which to negotiate over gas supply and gas prices with one of the world's leading suppliers.

MOVING FORWARDS

The more the world can move towards energy generated from resources other than gas and oil the better it will be from all points of view. The International Energy Agency estimates that, in the next 30 years, the world will need to invest $16 trillion in new energy infrastructure, which equates to $550 billion of investment each year. If one-fifth of this were to be spent on renewable energy technologies, it would mean investment of more than $100 billion going into renewables – each year.

In 2006, estimates of finance for new energy capacity were that $71 billion was spent on renewable power generation, bio fuel and low carbon technology generally. Much of this investment will go into China and India, as they seek to keep pace with the burgeoning demand for energy in their home countries.

China, at the moment, is mainly building coal-fired power stations. These are relatively cheap and easy to construct, and do not come with the scientific and safety complications of nuclear power stations. They play to China's relative strengths, since at home she has more coal than any other natural source of energy, and clearly anticipates mining more of it as the years progress. Such a huge Chinese programme, opening maybe one new power station a week for several years, means that those seeking to battle carbon dioxide emissions and noxious fumes are going to have their work cut out. When the Olympic athletes started to assemble in Beijing, the Chinese authorities had to put a stop to, or enforce a reduction of, all types of polluting activity to try to improve the air quality during the Games. At some point, China must and will want to achieve a similar or bigger improvement in air quality, for the benefit of the people who live there. This is going to require a massive investment in clean-up technology (for existing industrial and energy generation plants) and in the development of newer technologies, which do not produce the pollutants in the first place.

In the UK, over a third of electricity is generated from coal and over a third from gas. As one-third of the UK's total greenhouse gas emissions come from power generation, it shows just how important decisions on the balance of electricity generation will be in the battle to reduce CO_2 output. The Sustainable Development Commission's 2006 report estimated that every 10 gigawatts of nuclear power generation in the UK saves either 6.7 million tons of carbon output (when compared with generating from gas-fired stations) or 17 million tons of carbon (when compared with generation from conventional coal-fired power stations). The UK has huge scope to lower its carbon output in the energy-generation sector – if it is prepared to make substantial investments in a whole generation of new power plants. Instead, the last 11 years have seen practically no movement, and today the only application outstanding for a new power station is for a coal-fired one.

The government has rightly identified that the very slow nature of the planning process is one of the reasons why things move so slowly in the UK; they decided to tackle this by changing the planning legislation in order to create a new structure for the approval of major projects such as power stations. While this might have seemed like a good idea at the time, it has now become another reason for delay. When ministers were asked how this would speed things up and how they would avoid it becoming another cause for indecision, they responded that we are at least two years away from having the new plans outlining where power stations could go, prior to applying for the accelerated planning permissions which would be on offer under the new regime. This seems to be taking two steps backwards to go one step forward, and may well now be creating a new kind of planning blight over the possibility of constructing new electricity-generating stations.

Meanwhile, in the real world, energy-intensive business is moving offshore as quickly as possible. The United Kingdom gas market does not function well, since it is part of the general European gas market which (as far as the UK is concerned) has displayed gross imperfections in recent years. In the winter of 2005-6, the UK ran very short of gas. Technical problems at the Leman field, one of our gas storage areas, revealed how little cushion we now have. Prices went through the roof, but gas did not flow readily through the interconnector from the Continent, which had been put in place to create a proper market. People on the Continent were reluctant to respond to the very strong price signals indicating that the UK market was short of gas and needed supply. The government pressed European partners to produce a more competitive market on the Continent but, so far, progress has been painfully slow. Only the UK has completed deregulation of its gas market. Things are a bit better in the Netherlands, Ireland and Spain. Unfortunately

Germany, Luxembourg, Sweden and Belgium have only taken initial steps and progress in Austria, Belgium, France, Italy and Denmark is also very limited. Unless we have a properly functioning market in gas throughout the Continent, Britain's reliance upon continental imports will continue to become hazardous in times of stress, as we saw three winters ago.

The UK is especially vulnerable as the country depends rather more than most upon natural gas. In 2006, 36 per cent of our electricity came from gas. Natural gas was the fuel of choice for new power generation in the UK during the late 1980s and 1990s, owing to the big steps forward that had been made in the efficiency of gas-fired electricity generation. When the electricity industry was privatised in the 1980s, it was very dependent upon coal-fired power stations. As soon as it was in private ownership, the new owners did the sums and realised that there was much more fuel efficiency – and therefore lower cost – to be had by moving over to combined cycle gas. Whereas a coal-fired power station might only generate as electrical energy 35 per cent of the base energy it burns, wasting a massive two-thirds, a combined cycle gas station could ensure that more than half of the primary energy burned emerges as secondary energy – electricity for our use. This was a big stride forward for green policies, meaning that the UK could hit its Kyoto targets (the Kyoto agreement at the end of the last century tied the signatory countries to cuts of 12.5 per cent in their carbon emissions by 2010); it was also a big stride forward for consumers, who could benefit from cheaper power, since less was wasted.

The great problem with electricity is the multiple levels of waste encountered when converting that energy to something useful. If about two-thirds of the primary energy is wasted to start with (as it is if using coal-fired power stations) it puts you at a considerable disadvantage. When you then supply that electricity to people's homes and factories, there is further loss of power in transmission; finally, you encounter further losses through the inefficiencies of the appliances, engines and motors that burn the electricity. As an example, something like an electric train running on power from a coal-fired station would be doing extremely well if it captured, for propulsion, one-fifth of the primary energy burnt.

HANDLING THE ENERGY PROBLEM

The future of international politics and the prospects for rapid economic growth hinge crucially upon how we handle the energy problem. The advanced West has to spend more time and money to find ways of doing more with less energy. Japan has often shown the way, being a country with practically no indigenous energy production of her own. Awoken cruelly by the big first oil price shock of 1973, Japan systematically set about changing the way she did business to cut her energy requirements for each unit of output. America and the European countries need to do much more to cut the power burnt at home, in factories and above all in the power stations.

Our technologies should be able to move us more towards renewables and non-carbon sources for generating electricity. They should be able to produce far more fuel-efficient breakthroughs in machinery and transport. Prices and technology should encourage many more of us to insulate our homes, run better boilers, buy more fuel-efficient vehicles and make more energy-savvy choices. The green message is a very sensible one, because it reinforces the essential move we must make away from reliance upon imported energy from dangerous and difficult parts of the world.

In the meantime, it would be foolish of the American superpower to pick too many fights with too many large vested interests elsewhere in the world. While America's technological lead in defence and weaponry has grown in recent years, thanks to the digital revolution and the excellence of American science, the countries that disagree with America have grown their economic power without America apparently realising. Even America, with all her stunning brainpower and technology, cannot afford to have, as hostile, Russia, China and the leading Middle Eastern states. America cannot, by force of arms and strength of argument, expect to convert all of the former Soviet Union, all of the Middle East and big chunks of Asia to the causes of liberal democracy and free enterprise capitalism. America is going to have to live in a multipolar world where the Middle East has enormous power, thanks to her oil wells; where Russia has considerable power, partly thanks to commodity-based wealth and partly because she wishes to divert so much of her limited national income into defence; and where, above all, China will have huge power and influence because she is such a highly populated state.

While America has grown stronger in terms of her technological lead and the excellence of her weaponry, she has become much weaker in recent years thanks to her reliance upon foreign energy and, above all, to her reliance on foreign money. While America has borrowed and consumed, China has saved and invested. While America has embarked on difficult military expeditions to the Middle East, Russia has conserved her strength and built up forces capable of defending and extending her borders. While America has concentrated upon military excellence, Russia has concentrated on using the sinews of commerce and the importance of gas to give her more power and influence over her neighbours.

The change of President at the end of George W. Bush's regime is likely to make some changes to the American stance. The rhetoric may well become more conciliatory and more dependent upon diplomacy. However, the reality of the Pentagon and the American war machine is likely to influence Democrat and Republican alike to continue with some military adventurism. If America wishes to reinforce her military power, she should now embark on fewer military adventures and concentrate rather more on getting her strength back by moving towards self-sufficiency in energy. If she did so, it might also change her view of world politics and her ambitions to control and influence governments in faraway places.

6 | UK in a jam

INTRODUCTION

A growing economy needs plenty of good transport. In Britain we have lived through more than a decade when there has been practically no investment in new transport capacity; we have congestion everywhere – and only a congestion charge in sight. In the 1990s the UK was short of public capital to invest. A reduced programme of road and rail investment continued and the railways were privatised in a desperate attempt to break the logjam and to bring in more outside capital. Since 1997 there has been a virtual cessation of all road building and a partial re-nationalisation of the railways. This has led to ever-bigger claims on the public accounts to maintain even the current network of railway activities. Sources for figures in this chapter are mainly from **www.dft.gov.uk/pgr/statistics** and *Freeing Britain to Compete,* my 2007 publication for the Economic Competitiveness Policy Group.

DRIVE TIME – USING YOUR CAR

By 2002, a quarter of all Britain's trunk roads were congested for more than an hour a day and, at over 45 minutes the average commuting time was higher than that in the UK's EU competitor countries. Ever since 1945 there has been continuous growth in the number of motor vehicles on the road, in the number of journeys made and in the distances people wish to travel. Owing to its flexibility and the freedom it brings its users, the motor vehicle has remained the most popular means of travel, despite big increases in the regulatory requirements on vehicle owners and drivers, and substantial increases in taxation.

More than 85 per cent of all passenger miles in the UK are travelled by car. 75 per cent of passenger movements and 66 per cent of freight movements are by road. Trains only account for 6 per cent of passenger miles travelled annually and only 8 per cent of freight tonnage. Buses account for another 6 per cent of passenger miles. There are now more than 33 million vehicles in Britain, an increase of more than 6 million over the past 10 years.

The 1997 Labour government came to power believing that it could create a substantial shift from private vehicles to railways and other public transport; this would, ministers felt, solve the problem of congestion. Unfortunately, their sums did not add up. They planned an increase of some 50 per cent in rail capacity in the first 10 years but did not succeed in increasing capacity by that much, owing to the expensive nationalisation in the middle of the period. Even had they achieved such a 50 per cent capacity increase, the railways would still not have been able to keep up with the total rise in transport demand. There could have been no modal shift based on a mere 50 per cent increase in capacity, given the substantial pressure for more travel and the very narrow base from which the railways started.

Since privatisation of the railways in the early 1990s, there has been a strong upward movement in the number of passenger journeys by train: from 750 million journeys at the time of privatisation to around 1,100 million more recently. Despite this, the overall growth in travel has meant practically no modal shift occurring. Even if rail capacity could be doubled from its present level, this would cater for less than three years of the total traffic growth which would result from the normal growth in the economy overall.

The only policy the government has ever followed in the last 11 years which has succeeded in curbing the appetite for more car travel is the economic policy which plunged the country into credit crunch and sharp slowdown. A combination of surging oil, petrol and diesel prices, the ever-higher tax take on the motorist, and the slowdown in job opportunities and business activity combined to halt the otherwise inexorable growth in road travel. It is probably not the way the government intended to do it, although they have always been ambiguous about the issue of price.

PRICING THE MOTORIST OFF THE ROADS

Throughout the 11-year period of the current administration, some in the government have believed that it is important to price people off the roads and out of their cars. A stunning array of techniques has been developed to do this. First was the introduction of a congestion charge in London and Durham. Bristol, Reading and some other cities are also considering their introduction – but, as the book went to press, Manchester comprehensively rejected the idea. Congestion charges are taxes on the use of the vehicle at certain times in certain areas. You need to be rich to be able to afford, out of net income, the £8 a day that it currently costs to travel on central London roads between 7.00 in the morning and 6.00 in the evening.

Second, local government has been encouraged to make sharp increases in the charges for parking. The government has reinforced this by demanding of planners that they allow fewer parking spaces for each new shop, office and housing estate developed, creating more pressure on the available supply of parking places, and enabling authorities and private owners to increase the charges.

Third, the government has increased vehicle excise duty, the tax on owning a vehicle in the first place. Fourth, the government has allowed VAT on fuel to increase as the price of fuel increases, greatly increasing the tax take over a long period of rising oil prices. Fifth, the government has, from time to time, also increased fuel duty itself with the expressed intention of trying to force people out of their cars or force them to buy more fuel-efficient vehicles.

Under pressure, the government has accepted that there are limits to how much it can use these techniques. It does seem to realise that a policy of trying to tax people off the roads has greater impact on the poor than the rich. It has also managed to grasp the fact that people working for successful and well-financed businesses often have their bills paid for them.

A PROBLEM OF CAPACITY

The simple truth about transport in Britain is that we are chronically short of capacity of all kinds. If we do get people out of their cars, there are not enough trains onto which to put them. There is not enough road space to carry all the lorry freight and passenger vehicles wanting to use it. Our airports are congested, our motorways are congested, our trunk roads are congested, our railways are congested (at least at peak times of the day) and our ports are congested. For any government wishing to restore the British economy and to give it the space and room to grow, the prime task must be to increase the capacity of these networks.

Our strategic motorway network has never been completed. There is no continuous south coast motorway. There is no continuous motorway along the east coast from London to the Scottish border and Edinburgh. There is no motorway link to Britain's biggest container port, Felixstowe, through either the Midlands or London. There is no motorway to Southampton from the Midlands, no motorway to the holiday areas of Devon and Cornwall, no motorway to the important cross channel port of Dover, no motorway serving East Anglia or Lincolnshire. The motorways we do have are often too small for the traffic seeking to use them.

The massively successful M25, the motorway ring around London, acts both as a strategic highway network and as a series of local routes for a highly congested part of the south east. It allows people to get from north and west of the country to the east coast without having to cross the capital, and acts as a series of local routes for a part of the south east which lacks decent road capacity. Even the present government has continued with plans to widen the M25 on its western section, but the motorway ring as a whole is sadly lacking in capacity to handle the huge numbers of vehicles wishing to use it each day. There is insufficient capacity on the M4 out to Reading, on the M3 out to Basingstoke, on much of the M1 to the north, on the M42 ringway around Birmingham, on the M5 and M6, from Exeter to Manchester.

The trunk road network is similarly under siege. The A12 and the A14, the two principal haulage routes from London and from the Midlands to Felixstowe, are far too small for the huge amount of container and other traffic seeking to use them. The A2 to Dover, the A23 to Brighton, some limited sections of the A3 to Portsmouth, the A303 holiday route from the M3 onwards to Exeter, the A40 from Oxford to Gloucester and on to the heads of the Welsh valleys, and the A52 Boston to Nottingham are among the trunk roads that are in great need of improvements and widening.

Britain's leading European competitors have around 50 per cent more motorway capacity than the United Kingdom (when adjusted for the size of the country and the number of people living in it). Of the total road length in England, just 2 per cent carries one-third of all its road traffic and two-thirds of all its road-based freight. In England there are just six main motorways, four of which radiate from London.

Business groups predict growing congestion on the UK network, imposing more costs on business – thus making Britain less competitive. Growing congestion makes the transport system less safe, as well: crowded roads make collisions more likely and add to motoring frustrations. Mistakes and misjudgments are more likely in such conditions. Because, in most cases, there is only one principal route available to drivers, an accident which results in the whole or partial closure of that route for several hours of the day can cause congestion and chaos for many miles around.

TOLL ROADS

Recent governments have experimented with tolling and allowing the private sector to pay for a new road out of the revenues. The main link for the M25 over the river to the east of London is provided by a toll tunnel and a toll bridge. The Dartford river bridge was designed, built and financed by the private sector and financed out of the tolls. It was so successful that, under the terms of the scheme, the builders and owners soon recouped their money plus a suitable profit and the bridge was then made available free to the taxpayer. More recently, a relief road for the M6 running to the north of Birmingham was constructed as a toll route by private enterprise. Here, a completely new alternative road has been provided for those who wish to pay to avoid the congestion on the existing, free, motorway.

In order to give Britain the roads that it needs to be comparable to France and Germany, and to compete more successfully in the global economy, then *additional* routes need to be permitted – financed by the private sector and paid for by tolls on users. Such routes could take the form of additional toll lanes on existing highways or alternative routes such as the M6 toll road. Any franchise period would need to be long enough for private contractors to be able to make reasonable returns on the substantial investment they will have to make, before allowing for the transfer of the route to the taxpayer and government. The private sector could take responsibility for the management of the route and the traffic flows, as well as collecting the tolls.

The government could lay down a regulated maximum tariff, with permitted rates of increase, to different categories of user. This would be a necessary precaution where a monopoly route was being offered. The private contractor should be free to vary the charges downwards at different times of day, in a way that would encourage the maximum spread of use, thus helping to avoid congestion and to maximise smooth journeys on the route. The government should also retain the right to replace the management of the road if it is not meeting safety and other requirements – whilst preserving the right of the owners to be able to repay their capital expenditure. If a franchisee fails to carry out his agreed tasks, the government should have the opportunity to offer the contract or the opportunity to somebody else. Where some of the work involved had already been undertaken, there would have to be rules about repaying the franchisee who was being dismissed – or transferring his interest at fair value.

LOCAL ROADS

The UK is similarly short of capacity on local roads, which are managed by the local district or county council. In many cases, in recent years, these councils have specialised in restricting use and limiting flows of traffic on their local road network, for a variety of safety and environmental reasons. These measures have often proved to be self-defeating, resulting in the creation of less safe roads with more congestion and so, in any number of journeys, increasing the fuel burn for any volume of traffic. There needs to be a review of these traffic restrictions and dangerous junctions, both to increase safety and to improve the average fuel efficiency of the users of the local road network.

AN EXCESS OF SPEED?

The main argument used by experts in recent years has been that safety improves if speed is reduced. This flies in the face of the evidence that road safety is far worse at junctions and at speeds within the speed limit than it is on straight stretches of highway where people can travel faster. Indeed, the safest roads in Britain, by far, are motorways, where speeds are the highest. High speeds are wholly compatible with greater road safety here, owing to the absence of dangerous junctions. Each junction has separate traffic flows onto and off the motorway, with no vehicles needing to cross another to turn right or left.

Conversely, on our local road system, there are endless intersections. Some of these are controlled by traffic lights, others by roundabouts and some simply take the form of junctions with signs indicating where people should give way, or stop, while awaiting a safe passage. Most collisions occur at junctions where drivers make misjudgements or take unreasonable risks when trying to cross other traffic streams; they are not travelling at anything like the speed limit.

Indeed, national traffic statistics indicate that speed is an important factor in only around 5 per cent of all accidents, according to **www.safespeed.org.uk**. It is strange to see safety policy dominated by the reduction of speed, when all the indications are that a strong pro-safety policy requires rather more concentration on better driving – and better design and management of junctions. Some stretches of road are inherently unsafe, allowing (or even encouraging) overtaking on narrow highways; poor sightlines, where an overtaking vehicle can end up on the wrong side of the road, facing an oncoming vehicle (possibly at a high closing speed) are also prevalent. Again, this may occur well within the speed limit of the road concerned, but reaction times have to be fast to avoid a collision: impact speed in a head-on crash is the sum of the speeds of the two vehicles. This type of collision is virtually impossible on motorways or dual carriageways, where people cannot enter the opposite carriageway.

In the name of safety and controlling speed, councils have come up with a wide variety of devices. In some cases, the carriageway is deliberately narrowed, to try to persuade people to travel more carefully, negotiating a very narrow lane. In other cases, traffic lanes are removed, or cycle lanes and bus lanes taken out of the main carriageway width; artificial chicanes and barriers may be created on one lane, to slow or stop vehicles travelling in that direction. Traffic lights are rephased, to reduce the flows of the main routes across junctions; in certain junctions in London and elsewhere, an all-red phase for vehicles has been created at traffic lights to allow pedestrians to cross in both directions at the same time, while all the traffic is stationary.

Another cause of danger and congestion comes through the many places where a railway line crosses a local road. Level crossing gates now are lowered for longer periods prior to a train's arrival, greatly increasing delays, congestion and motorists' frustration. Sometimes this results in motorists taking undue risks, trying to get across level crossing gates before they finally come down.

So what needs to be done? We do want roads which are both safer and capable of sustaining better flows of traffic. Most of our towns and cities have a street layout which is not easy to vary. The public are no longer willing to accept urban motorways on stilts flying past people's windows, so we have to make do with the spaces available on the ground. That requires intelligent highways engineering to maximise the use we can make of the available road space, and to improve the chances of vehicles being able to make smooth passage across junctions and across railway lines at most reasonable times.

Fortunately, in view of all the adverse changes made to local road networks in the last decade or so, it should be quite easy to get 10-15 per cent more capacity. Lanes could be restored, carriageways widened, right-hand turning lanes inserted at junctions, traffic lights rephased to give more priority to main routes and dangerous chicanes and highway reconfigurations changed. The emphasis should be on designing smooth-flowing and safer junctions. Indeed, the two go together. The closer one can get to segregating traffic moving in different directions across a junction, the safer it will be – and the better will be the flows on the main route crossing that junction. Flows improve if traffic proceeding on the main route is not detained by traffic turning to the left or (especially) to the right; if right-hand turning traffic, in particular, can be segregated, and lights phased sensibly, a junction will also be safer.

Safety and congestion would be greatly improved if money were spent on providing bridges and tunnels to allow roads to cross railway lines: there have been too many level-crossing accidents for comfort. The inflexibility of a train and rails means that a collision at a level crossing has the potential to lead to a derailment – risking the lives of large numbers of passengers and reducing the railway network to chaos for a considerable length of time afterwards.

There is a growing desire, on the part of many environmentalists, to limit the amount of pollution coming from road traffic. The main way to achieve this is through further technological developments; in recent years, there has been great progress in eliminating nitrates and sulphur oxides from vehicle exhaust gases and, more recently, curbing the amount of CO_2 emitted by an efficient engine. There have been great leaps forward in fuel efficiency and the environmental cleanliness of saloon cars sold to the private market, but there has not been anything like the same improvement in the efficiency and cleanliness of diesel trains or buses. The average age of these transport fleets is considerably older than the average age of the car fleet – and less attention is given to fuel economy for public transport engines, as they receive favourable tax treatments which keep costs down.

Some environmentalists refuse to accept that all transport creates emissions. There has not been sufficient research on, or proper audit of, the relative contributions to CO_2 emissions and other more noxious emissions of rail, bus and private road transport. The ready assumption, namely that travel by private car is always dirtier than travel by train or bus, simply does not stand up. If you travel on a bus which has very few other passengers on it, and that bus is 10 or more years old with a dirty engine, it would be cleaner to take all the people off the bus and to let them travel in their own private cars. If undertaking a train journey involves, first of all, taking a car through a crowded city to park at a station, and then using an old taxi at the other end, you may end up generating more emissions for your travel than if you had used a modern saloon car to drive from your home, via the motorway network, to your destination – at an efficient cruising speed for the engine. It all depends how many people are on the train, how much emission you create getting to and from the station, how well you drive and how fuel-efficient your car is. It is by no means certain that it is always greener to go by train.

We need to have proper end-to-end journey audits. In practice, people often choose the car rather than the train or the bus because the car journey is shorter – if you take into account *total* journey time. The train would usually be faster between cities, but it can take a long time to get into a city centre, park your car (at an extra cost), buy a ticket and wait for the train; further journey time is added at the other end, if you need to travel somewhere not adjacent to the station. Similarly, if you wish to use a bus, but you do not live near a bus stop and your journey's end is not near a bus stop, that, too, can add substantially to the total journey time. People also may choose to go by car because they are carrying lots of luggage – or samples or equipment for their work. There are sometimes limits to the amount of luggage you are allowed to take on a bus or train – and difficulties in getting substantial amounts of luggage to and from stations or bus stops. And, if it is raining, it is especially tempting to get into the car to keep dry, rather than having to walk through the driving rain to the public transport facility.

USING PUBLIC TRANSPORT

My car is never late for me – but I can be late for my car. Conversely, a bus or a train is often late for me – but I am not allowed to be late for it. If a timetable does not offer frequent services, or you are uncertain about the timing of your return, that could also put you off using public transport. You wish to have some flexibility and do not want to have to spend an hour or more sitting around on a station or standing at a bus stop. Public transport works best where there are many people wishing to use the service on a frequent basis, such as for commuter traffic, when many people travel between similar places at the same time of the day. Public transport works least well outside the busy times of day, at weekends and for less-popular journeys in less-populated areas. In Britain, it is quite possible to have a good mass transit system in the centre of London, where the density of population and the frequency of use can easily sustain a good, regular service by underground and overground train and by buses. It is far more difficult to maintain such a level of service in most of the market towns and smaller cities of Britain, where there are not enough users wishing to go in the same direction, at the same time of day, to sustain it.

Britain's railways were once a marvel of the world. Our Victorian system was a pioneer of the global railway industry: British railway engineers were fabled for their excellence and took their technology and expertise to the four corners of the Empire and to the world market. After the war, the nationalised British railway had a much less satisfactory experience. It fell further and further behind continental railway systems, suffering from a lack of investment, old technology and poor customer service. Throughout the period 1947 to the early 1990s, under nationalisation, we witnessed a decline in the use of the railway and a substantial increase in the cost of using it; a failure to put investment into the highly populated routes that could be successful; and a failure to make the right decisions on the priorities and uses of the limited track space available.

An example of this lack of investment could be seen during the period of the rapid growth of Heathrow as the country's leading airport; the nationalised railway did not bother to put a spur line in from Heathrow to the Great Western Railway (which runs between Wales and London), in order to offer a mainline railway service from what became the world's leading international airport to one of the world's leading cities. It was only the advent of private capital and free enterprise which produced a surface rail link, less than two miles long, from the airport to the main western railway line.

The nationalised railway retreated from much rail freight, dropping single-wagon marshalling which enabled medium-sized companies to use rail to carry their goods around the country. Britain, in the 1920s and 1930s, had many industrial estates built around good railway links, with sidings and branch lines into the estates and factories themselves. The post-war world, however, saw a similar profusion of industrial estates grow up around the main trunk and motorway networks, owing to the unwillingness of the railway to offer a freight service to anything other than the largest companies. For both freight and passengers, rail's market share diminished year after year. The railway had to shed a great deal of labour and, from time to time, undertook bouts of retrenchment, closing lines which were no longer used sufficiently to justify their maintenance.

For a while, in the 1990s, privatisation changed this. By forcing those who wished to run railway trains over the centrally-owned track to compete for franchises, enough competition was introduced to create an atmosphere in which there was more investment in new capacity and new rolling stock – and a renewed emphasis on customer service – to attract people back to the trains. In the early years after privatisation, both freight and passenger use of the railway surged. Many new carriages and trains were delivered and the railway started to look more businesslike. Unfortunately, a couple of tragic crashes occurred on the network which gave the pro-nationalisers in Labour the opportunity they were looking for to move in and bankrupt Railtrack, the privatised monopoly track provider, and transfer the assets to a new body, Network Rail: a company with monopoly control over provision of railway track within the UK. Although it was, theoretically, a private sector body, it was given Treasury guarantees for its very substantial borrowing, and soon started to behave like the old nationalised industry it had replaced.

TROUBLE ON THE TRACKS

Private sector financial discipline was lost and the costs of the railway started to mount very rapidly. Large sums were spent on extra administration, consultancy and management. In the financial year 2000-1 the government provided £1.3 billion for expenditure on the railways, but this had leapt to £5.5 billion, by 2006-7 – in addition to the very substantial sums Network Rail was borrowing with a government guarantee. Much of this money was just absorbed in extra costs. There was no noticeable improvement in rail capacity or acceleration in the growth rate compared to the 1990s, when expenditure had been under much better control.

There is growing frustration with the railway as a result. Despite all the money and the attention it has received from the government, many commuters into the big cities, especially into London, have to depend on inadequate services. Many have to stand as there is insufficient capacity to provide them with a seat. Some services are still very unreliable. Ministers felt that they could set a target only of 85 per cent of trains running 'on time' (that is, arriving within 10 minutes of the scheduled time), since they knew they would not succeed in providing Japanese levels of punctuality – which averages at an 11-second variation from the schedule.

The fact that ownership of the track was split from ownership of the trains has been contentious ever since privatisation. There is nothing inherently wrong with such a system; after all, the very successful and fast-growing aviation industry has flourished with separate owners for airports and for planes – and with different companies responsible for baggage handling, airport services and, in some cases, ticket selling. This fragmentation of ownership and management has not got in the way of improving airline service or frequency, lowering costs or selling many more tickets. However, in the case of the railway, the splitting of track management from train management has caused endless bickering and rows between the more commercial franchise operators who run the trains and the less commercial, publicly owned Network Rail. The train companies cannot get the track spaces they need, in order to run the frequency of service at the times of the day they wish – and between the destinations they wish.

Delays are the cause of endless disputes, with the train operators blaming the track company and the track company implying it is the train operator's fault. Probably the weakest part of the railway structure lies in the fact that the track provider has a monopoly. The lack of competitive pressure means that the train companies have little influence over the level of service they receive, for which the price they pay is often too high. They have to pass on these costs to their customers and it limits their scope for growing the railway.

It is true that the railways are held back by an inherently unsafe technology. Using technology first developed for 18th-century mines, and enhanced for the 19th-century passenger railway, the railway industry has to grapple, daily, with the inadequacy of steel wheels on steel tracks for acceleration and braking. Because there is, deliberately, very little friction between wheel and track, it makes it difficult to run a commuter railway with many stops and starts. A railway is at its best over a long distance, or when used for hauling lots of heavy freight or moving people at great speed in straight lines. There, the lack of friction between wheel and track is an asset: for any given amount of motive power, a load can be hauled either in increased quantities or at a faster speed than using the equivalent engine for road travel – where there is, by design, far more friction between rubber wheels and concrete or tarmac routes. Britain is a relatively small country, with many towns, villages and cities needing a railway service. In these conditions the railway cannot use its natural advantages to best effect.

The commuter railway needs many trains using the track within the two or three busiest hours of morning and evening; it needs the ability to speed those trains up and slow them down rapidly and frequently, so as to serve all the stations along the line. It is not possible to run more than around 27 trains an hour using existing technology: for safety, there need to be large gaps between trains on each track, and allowances made for the long braking distances (and slow acceleration) involved. By contrast, coaches and cars on a tarmac road can run almost bumper to bumper: they are able to brake quickly and accelerate quickly when the road allows. People using trains have to put up with very large gaps between the trains on the track (and, therefore, with a less-than-optimum service) to take account of the lack of friction between wheel and rail.

Some countries have experimented successfully with using rubber-tyred wheels to create greater adhesion to deal with this problem. For example, the Paris Metro uses rubber tyres to enable the trains on some lines to speed up and brake more rapidly, as well as allowing them to undertake gradients which would be difficult for steel on steel. The UK railway has always been reluctant to make such experiments.

Under more recent pressure to do something about the lack of frequency of service – and the poor capacity on the existing route network – the railway industry is now examining the possibility of developing lighter trains. Current UK specifications for trains require substantial weight, which naturally impacts on both braking and acceleration. It is now thought possible that the frequency of trains could be increased to 35 or even 40 an hour, by reducing their weight and improving their acceleration and braking to match.

The old, nationalised, British Rail was often derided for its frequent interruptions to service during periods of bad weather. We were told there was 'the wrong kind of snow' – or even 'the wrong kind of rain' – which could be sufficient to disrupt services. Icy points, frost on the line or other natural phenomena, including falling leaves, could prevent trains from moving or braking, owing to the slipperiness of wheel on rail. These problems could be addressed by introducing new compounds on the wheels and could be ameliorated by lowering the weight of the vehicle. At the moment the technical solution is to drop sand from a sandbox onto the track as the train proceeds, to try to create additional friction or grip between the steel wheel and the steel track.

If Britain is to become competitive, railways need to take more of the strain, moving more people, more frequently, to and from their offices at busy times of the day. They also need to take more of the strain for freight traffic: we need an industry capable of single-wagon marshalling, offering a service to smaller and medium-sized businesses as well as to the very large. Instead, the railway has been mesmerised by the wish to compete over longer distances against both the motor car and the aeroplane. The industry has felt that it can only compete in this way by pursuing greater speed. Instead of looking at *total* journey time, and worrying about why it is so difficult to get into towns at busy times of day and park conveniently at stations, the railway industry has concentrated on trying to lop a few minutes off the journey time between London and Birmingham or London and Manchester. The investment to do this is massive, requiring new signalling, new track and new trains.

Because the UK is trying to run a multi-purpose railway over the same track, it is often extremely difficult to schedule the faster trains. In many cases the same track has to be used for freight trains, commuter trains and cross-country trains – as well as express trains. Clearly, you need to empty the track for a fast train to go through at the required high speed, limiting the ability to use the track for other purposes. Increasingly, the industry is coming to realise that to run efficient, fast trains over long distances requires segregated track, as is the case in France and Japan. This is a luxury Britain finds difficult to afford, both financially and in terms of space for the routes required. If you need to live near one of the tracks, trains are not very environmentally friendly: they are heavy, noisy and vibrate considerably when passing. Our long and democratic planning processes make it difficult to find sufficient routes for the high-speed trains that some in the industry would like to create.

But there are things that can be done to increase the capacity of our railway to allow it to take more of the strain. We should allow and encourage a large number of shorter links from the existing railways into the industrial estates and to ports, to permit more freight on the trains. We ought to improve the technology for the commuter railway. This may include the railway solution of improved signalling and should also include improved traction by one means or another.

It is one of the paradoxes of the transport policy of the last decade that the government has wished to promote the railways – the transport industry least successful at investing and winning new business, and the least popular with the travelling public – at the expense of the roads and the airlines. The roads remain by far and away the most popular with the travelling public, judging by the numbers using them and the miles travelled; airlines, from a smaller base, have been the most popular in terms of growth rates. As they have improved their service and cut their fares so there has been a huge surge in demand.

The paradox does not end with the government's wish to reverse the natural inclinations of the travelling public. The government reinforces this when it seems to think that running trains faster is a good idea with no safety problems – whereas allowing people to drive faster on roads is a bad idea, with safety implications (hence the growth of Safety Partnerships and speed cameras). Similarly, the government believes that people using cars and lorries at faster speeds burns more fuel and is therefore not green – but does not come to the equally sensible conclusion that running trains at faster speeds also burns more fuel and cannot be so green. Ideology has replaced common sense in coming to a judgment on what is the right balance for transport provision in Britain. We have had a government that wishes to override the clearly expressed views of the travelling public; it seems to believe that railways are the answer, whatever the problem.

A sensible transport policy would wish to make considerably more use of the existing railway network and to make selective improvements and increases to capacity, just as we need to do on the roads. The accent should be upon rail freight and commuters – where trains should have a natural advantage compared with the road or airborne competitors. It is difficult to see the commercial case for investing in high-speed rail passenger travel between cities in Britain, given the distances involved and the excellence of the alternatives. Cost, convenience and total travel time are the deciding factors for most people.

AIR TRAVEL – ONWARDS AND UPWARDS

In recent years, the most successful of all of our public transport industries in terms of growth rates has been the aviation industry, one which is almost entirely run and financed by the private sector. The major airports are privately owned; the competing airlines are privately owned by UK or foreign companies or are overseas nationalised industries. Ticket sales, baggage handling, catering, retail and surface transportation are also wholly or primarily private sector owned. The whole industry is subject to enormous competitive pressures at every level and stage.

As a result there has been an explosion in the provision of cheap air travel and a surge in the popularity of cheap air travel for holidays and business. This success has been widely condemned by the green movement and by the government, who see the public airline industry as public enemy number two (after the private motorist), and who wish to divert travel from the fuel-burning airline to the fuel-burning railway.

Over the last 30 years, aviation has seen colossal growth. 32 million passengers in 1970 grew to 228 million passengers in 2005. The form of travel which, only a few decades ago, was reserved for the rich and for the business traveller, is now available to most people; a large expansion in choice has been brought about by low-cost airlines. A quarter, by value, of all UK freight is shipped by air, and this has also grown quickly. Air freight is undertaken both in dedicated freight transport planes and in the holds of the larger passenger jets. The government has studied the problem on several occasions: its 2003 White Paper, *The Future of Air Transport*, provided a strategic framework for the development of airport capacity, whilst highlighting potential large growth over the following two decades. In 2006, the Eddington Report reconfirmed this assessment and identified important international gateway airports as important for the British economy.

Heathrow Airport is more than just an important regional and national airport. It is the complement of the success of the City of London as one of the world's leading financial centres. The complex network of routes into and out of Heathrow is central to the flows of talent, ideas and deals into and out of the City of London. Throughout the last 20 years, London has experienced constraints from insufficient runway and terminal capacity. London's airports are always behind the curve compared with their competitors in Amsterdam, Frankfurt and Paris – where much stronger action has been taken to increase the number of terminals and runways ahead of increases in demand.

The structure of ownership of British airports has been one of the factors contributing to the poor level of service and the high fees which have been the common experience of their users in recent years. The previously nationalised body, British Airports Authority (BAA), was the original owner of Stansted, Gatwick and Heathrow, the three primary airports serving the capital and the wider nation. This business was transferred whole into the private sector, allowing private sector owners to borrow substantial sums against the assets and greatly increasing the bargaining power of those owners with the airlines and other airport users when it came to service levels and fees. As a result, service and quality has fallen below the standards of major competitors on the Continent and has become a very contentious issue.

I, and others, have argued strongly that the competition authority should intervene and demand that the owner of Heathrow should not also own Stansted and Gatwick. The preliminary findings of the Competition Commission, announced in the middle of 2008, confirm this viewpoint. The current Spanish owners of the airports are heavily borrowed. Requiring them to dispose of a couple of successful London airports and a Scottish airport would greatly reduce their borrowing and their financing strain, and allow them to spend more and concentrate more on developing the jewel in their crown, Heathrow Airport itself. In September 2008, the company announced that it was seeking a buyer for Gatwick.

The current government has indicated that it is willing to grant permission for a second runway at Stansted and to consider a third half-runway at Heathrow. These are bitterly contentious environmental and planning decisions, vigorously opposed by those who believe that any provision of new capacity is an incitement to businesses and people to provide more flights and to travel more. The problem with this argument is that it assumes that Britain is an island and that people cannot go elsewhere to undertake their international travel. Instead, observation tells us that with business-hungry airports not very far away in Paris and Amsterdam, it is all too easy for people to hop across the Channel in order to get access to cheaper flights – and more choice of routes – from the big hub airports on the Continent. If Britain refuses to expand her airport capacity, it is unlikely to have much favourable impact on limiting demand for airplane travel – but it is very likely to damage the competitiveness of UK aviation by transferring travel and business to the overseas airports.

How can one make air travel more environmentally friendly? The best way is to find a propulsion system which burns less fuel and generates less CO_2 in the process. It is difficult to put the genie back in the bottle and to tell restless people around the world that they are no longer allowed to travel the world, to trade, to make friends and to see the sights of our glorious planet. Trying to stop British people doing it unilaterally will not work. Seeking to make it more expensive will price some people out of air travel in the short term – but, as people generally get richer, so there will be a resumption of air travel, as it is a luxury or discretionary purchase that more and more people wish to make.

The British economy's strength lies in financial, business and professional services. In recent years the economy's success, such as it has been, has been powered by the growth of London's business, financial and professional services. Crucial to these has been the performance of Heathrow as the leading airport. If Britain wishes to earn her crust and maintain her living standards in the early decades of the 21st century, it is vital that she understands the importance of building, improving and expanding airport capacity to service London's needs.

MARINE TRAVEL – CALM WATERS AHEAD?
Shipping remains the main method of transporting most of the bulky trade that we undertake. 75 per cent of trade by value – and 95 per cent of our international trade by volume – are transported in ships. There has been a big increase in the UK's shipping fleet in the last six years, partly as a result of welcome changes to the tax regime undertaken by the present government. The government has been right to permit increases in capacity at Felixstowe and near Harwich, two of the UK's largest container ports. We will need further expansions at Liverpool, London, Southampton and elsewhere to cater for the increasing flows of goods across frontiers. It would also be good to see more domestic shipping encouraged. In the 18th century the British economy flourished, as a result of coastal-borne goods using local wharves and ships travelling just offshore, backed up by an important network of navigable rivers and canals. Goods could be transhipped from seagoing vessels to river- and canal-travelling barges. The Newcastle coal trade, the movements of clay and finished potteries from Stoke, and the woollen and cotton textile trades all relied heavily upon barge and ship to import raw materials and export finished goods.

There have been substantial debates about how green shipping is. Most greens incline to the view that switching freight from air to ships, or from lorries to ships, is an environmental improvement which they welcome. However, in the green movement there has also been a recent tendency to criticise the shipping industry, as well as the aviation industry, for the fuel it burns and the impact it has on the environment. In green demonology, car, lorry and plane are always bad; train and bus are always good. The ship, barge and boat float (metaphorically and literally) somewhere uneasily between the two. In practice, the carriage of goods by sea and river is necessary to ease the capacity problems of the roads and the air – and can be a greener option if modern vessels are used at full capacity.

In London itself, one of the strange paradoxes of the modern era is that the crucial central highway that goes right through the centre of the City – the Thames – is still virtually unused, other than by tourists wanting to view the sights from the more leisurely environment of a cruiser. In previous centuries, the Thames was a veritable bustle of activity. It was one of the main highways for the transport of people and had steps, quays and wharves all along the river bank. It was the principal commercial artery, with boats and barges delivering building materials, food, finished goods and the other necessities of urban living. Attempts have been made to revive the Thames as a means of travel – but no one has succeeded yet in finding a working business model that delivers goods and the people at a price they can afford, and in a way they find attractive. Maybe part of the problem lies in the complex regulation of the river and riverside, the expense and inadequacy of the modern wharves and steps, and the complications of keeping the river clean enough to avoid fouling propellers.

LIGHT AT THE END OF THE TUNNEL?

The British economy suffered for many years from totally inadequate transport facilities. Our leading continental rivals and partners built much bigger and better motorway networks to take the strain. You can travel further and faster on a German autobahn than on an English motorway. Far more freight moves effortlessly across frontiers on the Continent, thanks to the prevalence of the large truck – and the large road to take the truck. Similarly, in the United States of America, a massive investment in turnpikes and highways has given great access to the cities of that mighty continent.

Britain's early construction of a massive railway network should have placed it in a better position. However, the long era of nationalisation meant that much of the money going into the railways was wasted. There was little enterprise and innovation, and the railway network increasingly reflected a pattern of yesterday's industry and population settlements – not tomorrow's. The railway lines and stations did not shift to where the new housing estates and new industrial estates were rising, so people using and living on those new estates naturally turned to the car and the lorry. Britain has muddled through with aviation and has by accident created one of the world's foremost airports. In recent years it has been a story of pinch, argue and do too little, too late, to keep up with the ever-increasing demand.

Despite all this, Britain has seen phenomenal growth in motor car and lorry ownership, private vehicle use, in the development of cheap airline offerings and air travel. It has been the public sector elements in the equation that have failed or have been very constrained. The publicly owned railway experienced decline for practically all of its life as a nationalised industry. The road network remains nationalised and so is too small, poorly managed and out of date. If Britain is serious about wishing to be prosperous in the next couple of decades of the 21st century, it has to develop more exciting private-sector solutions for the provision of new railway capacity and new road capacity. Both are required to bust congestion. Beating congestion means encouraging greater fuel efficiency and helping safety.

7 | A world government of regulations

INTRODUCTION

The United States of America is, on the whole, hostile to the idea of world government. The world's superpower naturally prefers to act on her own, making her own decisions and pursuing her own interests. Many American policymakers believe that their general views on the desirability of democracy, free trade and free enterprise are good not just for America – but for everyone. They express a certain naive disbelief when others around the world disagree with them; when disagreements are extreme, people tend to confront each other more strongly and even violently.

Smaller countries often like the idea of more things being done collectively. They feel this gives them a chance to have some influence, for at the very least they can sit round the table and see what the more powerful countries are deciding; at best, their views or their proposals may gain some support from the bigger countries and even be adopted.

In practice, the world's leadership gets involved with more and more world government, as do many of the smaller countries. The post-Second World War settlement included the idea of much more international collaboration. In the economics sphere could be found the Bretton Woods Agreements to manage currencies and balance-of-payments deficits; in the political sphere there was the establishment of the General Council of the United Nations, together with its Security Council. Subsequently, the United Nations branched out into more common action in areas such as health and education. More recently, successive rounds of trade talks have extended international reach beyond trade in physical goods, to cover intellectual property, services and investment flows. The United States, in common with other countries, sees the advantage of trying to use international agreement to move the agenda in the direction that America favours.

There are many problems with the idea of 'world government'. Most people do not see themselves as 'citizens of the world': their sense of identity is much more local, even parochial. Various countries have instilled strong feelings of national identity; some religions have engendered great feelings of religious and racial solidarity and identity. In some countries there are a number of regions or city states where the local identity is stronger than the national identity, as noted in Chapter 3. More widely, people may classify themselves by income levels, by skin colour, or by geographical location of their country. People might say they are African, or representatives of developing countries, when they go about their task of forging coalitions and trying to change the world agenda.

COMMUNITIES OF INTEREST

In order to have successful government there first needs to be a 'community of interest'. People have to accept that they belong to a place, region, city, country or world in which they should come together for common organisation, law making and the provision of public services. Very few people feel that 'the world' is the appropriate level for the organisation of public services, for the collection of taxes or even for law making in principal areas.

Ask people in Britain what they think their main governing area should be and most will specify either the United Kingdom or one of its constituent countries – England, Northern Ireland, Scotland or Wales. They are unlikely to say that they think they would best be governed at a European level, by the European Union; very few would suggest the creation of a new world government to take most of the decisions. In the United States of America, most Americans would automatically say that the USA is the correct level for the main thrust of government.

In many smaller countries, people have fought long and hard battles to establish new borders, just so that they can govern themselves together with their neighbours, without a government being imposed from a remote city in another area which they do not regard as part of their identity. The Czechs and the Slovaks decided they needed to be apart to have their own central governments. A host of Eastern European countries extracted themselves from the Soviet Union, each preferring a smaller unit – with its own currency, its own foreign policy and its own right to self-determination.

In a world where, if anything, the trend is for there to be more countries and physically smaller governing areas, it is unlikely that we will soon see a passionate movement for more world government. If you look at Western Europe itself, it seems more likely that we will end up with more countries rather than fewer. Scottish nationalism is on the march. There are two Italys struggling to emerge from the unified Italy of the 19th century. Belgium is close to splitting in two, the Basques and the Catalans are not entirely happy with the Spanish union, and even Bavaria prefers a considerable degree of independence from the German federal state. You need to go to countries as small as Luxembourg to find a state where there are no strong movements to break it up and make it smaller.

So why then write about 'world government' at all? If it is so clearly not the present trend and not the popular will, why does it matter? The irony is that, although the popular mood favours smaller states and in consequence favours smaller governments, in many countries the political elites are furthering a move to increasing global governmental activity. At the global level they govern differently from the way they do at the national level, in order to reflect the popular will. Indeed, governments' approaches to global government are as ambiguous as those of the publics they serve. For, while most people want either to be governed by their own present country or by something smaller, there are also many people around the world who think it would be good if there was more cooperation, collaboration and common government. This is not an easy paradox or contradiction to reconcile. The very thing that impels people to want smaller states and smaller government is damaged or made impossible by the move to global government.

People want politicians who are accountable. They want to feel that they can have some say in decisions that might otherwise go against them. They want to feel that, if they are contributing substantial sums in tax, it will be used to pay neighbours, friends, relatives and fellow citizens who are a bit like them and to whom they can relate. Yet, this wish for more countries and more peoples in the world to get on with each other, and for there to be a more common system and common rules, pushes in exactly the opposite direction. The global rule or the global law will turn out to be the law of the *least* common denominator; this may not serve the interests or meet the wishes of any one particular country or political grouping. It is, by definition, extremely difficult to initiate change: once a policy or law is agreed, nation states are reluctant to seek to overturn, improve or amend it, knowing just how difficult it had been to reach agreement in the first place.

In a way, what is surprising about the world post-1945 is just how much global government has been built up, despite the obvious disagreements and conflicts between the nations of the world; despite the presence of significant ideological differences between the main power blocks; despite the popular mood in many places in favour of the smaller and more accountable.

As the credit crunch unfolded it became obvious just how much it had been influenced and affected by global government and global financial control. In the financial world, there are the Basel Capital Adequacy Regulations, which affect all banks. There is a global agreement on money laundering, which has introduced a cat's cradle of controls and requirements on anyone conducting financial business in any of the main financial centres of the world. There is a growing set of detailed regulations which affect banks, insurance companies and brokers, as well as company listing and company information. While it is true that, in many cases, individual countries and regional trading blocks retain substantial scope to influence, amend or to implement regulations selectively, there has been a surprising amount of agreement on the general framework. This has led to a lot of legislation around the world which bears a family resemblance from one country to another, even if some of the detail is different. But this has also revealed one of the biggest weaknesses of world government. If, collectively, the world makes a mistake, it multiplies the problems through every jurisdiction. When the world makes a mistake, it becomes so difficult to get together enough people with a spirit for change – and so to make the necessary adjustments – before *more* damage is done.

WORLDWIDE FINANCIAL CONTROL

So it proved in the credit crunch in 2007. Worldwide banking regulations laid down the capital requirements for the amount of lending that banks can offer. As we have seen, these requirements encourage banks to lend more and more off balance sheet, where less capital is required under the rules. The regulators worldwide did not merely turn a blind eye to the massive movement into securitisation: in a way they encouraged it and they even created it.

Similarly, the world's banking and monetary authorities collectively decided that, since the Chinese and Indians were capable of producing ever-more goods and services at ever-more competitive prices, there would be no inflationary consequences from keeping interest rates very low – nor from encouraging a huge increase in borrowing in the advanced economies by both public and private sectors. The leading central bank authorities in America, Britain, Europe and elsewhere took interest rates down, and kept them low, despite the growing evidence of a borrowing binge. The authorities reassured each other, both by their actions and sometimes by their conversations, that we were living through an extraordinarily nice period when you could borrow as much as you liked, at very low interest rates, and there would be no inflationary consequences. Even when they started to see commodity prices shooting up, the authorities felt all was well. However, once the boom was well advanced and inflation was starting to become persistent, they all collectively changed their view and precipitated the credit crunch by moving to (relatively) very high interest rates. This immediately put people under pressure and greatly increased the risk of default. In money supply we lurched from boom to bust just as the banking and securities and regulators were reinforcing tendencies to over-lending.

The United States of America responded more swiftly to the second crisis, the sharp fall in activity. US authorities also understood, more quickly, the dangers of pro-cyclical regulation. Collectively, regulators are more likely to be acting to prevent the *last* crisis, long after it has happened, rather than foreseeing the *next* one. Over recent years, this tendency has been all too evident, and the growth of coordinated global responses has greatly increased the pro-cyclicality of the regulatory response. The world, as a whole, is likely now to lurch from being too loose and too lax at one point, to being altogether too tight and too tough at another point. This tendency increased the looseness on the way up to the credit crunch – and is now intensifying the crash on the way down.

This leads us to question what regulation is actually for. We have seen how there is a temptation for smaller countries to want to try to influence the rules and regulations of their neighbours, by coming together globally to reach agreements. We have also seen how, at times, the interests of the largest countries may also point in the same direction, as they believe they will influence the neighbours more readily through cooperation and negotiation than through simple assertion. Politicians and governments love extending their power. One of the main purposes of active bureaucracies is to increase the number of people they employ, increase the amount of money they spend, and increase their influence over the populations they seek to govern. Globally, bureaucracies see great scope to extend their powers jointly through cooperation. Cooperation may help a bureaucracy win an argument with reluctant politicians, if such exists, as the bureaucrats can say that a particular country has to undertake these measures since it does not wish to be isolated. It wishes to be cooperative, it needs to be part of the mainstream of world events.

More often than not, in wishing to augment and extend the powers of government, the politicians are in cahoots with the bureaucrats. Some politicians do this for noble motives; they are persuaded that more regulation would prevent future crises, or would make life fairer or better for consumers and citizens. Some politicians do it for the worst of motives, because it gives them the opportunity to parade their self-importance, appear on the national and international stage, and increase the powers of the department of which, briefly, they are in charge. The question that should be asked more often is 'Do the results of the joint labours of politicians and bureaucrats create a fairer, more just, more prosperous society?'

STATE REGULATION
Much regulation turns out to be self-defeating. Legislators frequently indulge in the triumph of hope over experience. They wish to live in a world where the sweep of the legislative pen can guarantee that the banks never make incautious loans, that people cannot over-borrow, that no one puts their hand into dangerous machinery, that no one slips on a wet pavement and that everyone can send back goods if they change their minds after they have bought them. For many in government, they believe that the mere act of legislating will put everything right. Others understand that the legislation is but the first part of the process; it has to be followed up by education, by training and by enforcement.

Sometimes regulations achieve exactly the opposite of what the legislators were setting out to do. Years ago, when the Bank of England wished to limit the outflow of money over the exchanges, it placed a control on the total amount each person could take out when going abroad. One of the paradoxical effects of this was to tell a lot of people, who did not think they could afford to go abroad, that it was possible to go to a foreign country with surprisingly little money, thus increasing the numbers who wished to do so.

More recently, Home Information Packs (HIPs) have been introduced into the United Kingdom residential property market. Ministers stated that the purpose of this was to make it easier to buy and sell houses. The theory was that the provision of a wide range of information to potential purchasers, paid for by the vendor, could speed up transactions and reassure people by providing authoritative information. Instead, many potential sellers were put off by the idea that, effectively, they had to pay a tax by paying for various bits of information *before* they could put their property on the market. They were worried that, if the property did not sell quickly, they would have to pay all over again to update the information to stay within the law. Instead of increasing the numbers of people selling their property, the market dried up, partly because of the credit crunch but also because the regulation brought in, ostensibly to help, exacerbated the effect.

There is a growing gap between those who do the regulating and those who are regulated. Many people in businesses now believe there is far too much regulation, both nationally and globally. This is encouraging a new kind of 'defensive management', which manages to conform to the requirements of the rules in a box-ticking, form-filling culture – and this can get in the way of true safety, better performance and higher standards of customer service. Some businesses, of course, like regulation. Large businesses often see expensive and complex regulation as a good way of keeping smaller rivals out of the marketplace in the first place. In a regulated business area, start-up costs can be very large, often delaying the ability of a company to get to market quickly, and increasing the number of staff and the amount of legal and regulatory advice they need to take before opening their doors. Some medium-sized and smaller businesses also like regulation because it can endorse a requirement to do things their way. If they were ahead of the game and the regulation endorsed what they were doing, or if they chose to do something which was well within the regulations, they would see the regulation as a useful restraint on trade, preventing innovation and competitive choice emerging.

A great deal of European Union regulation is especially prescriptive. It does not just try to make things safer or to give customers a better deal. It goes into considerable detail on how to achieve these ends, taking an important role by proxy in the management of an individual enterprise, dictating how a service should be delivered or a how a manufactured good should be made. Regulation can become the enemy of innovation just as, so often, it is the enemy of common sense.

In the United Kingdom there is a particular frustration on the part of many with health and safety regulation. Most sensible people agree that we want to minimise accidents at work; we do not think people should have their lives put at risk, or be in fear of serious injury, because they are making something in a factory. Of course we want machines to be guarded, hazardous chemicals to be properly stored and handled, and people to be equipped with protective clothing when appropriate.

On the other hand, it does seem to most of us to be excessive to have to give adults visiting a construction site a briefing on health and safety, which might include telling them the blindingly obvious – that they need to be careful when crossing the road or need to avoid walking under a moving vehicle! There is growing frustration that health and safety requirements, now set out in considerable detail, make it too costly or too difficult to make jam at home to sell at the village fete – or even to hold a village fete at all. There needs to be some common sense and sense of proportion. Indeed, if there were a general 'loose' requirement for safe operation, without detailed prescription on how you might fulfil that requirement, many more people might be happy and many more events might be organised and pass off without incident, without the complications that current regulation seems to create. The search for the best can be the enemy of the good; an over-regulated culture can result in less happening.

Since the United Kingdom government changed in 1997, the British Chambers of Commerce calculate that the government has, so far, added a massive £60 billion of additional regulatory cost to British business. Each year brings thousands of new requirements, which businesses have to know, and with which they have to comply.

The EU is in regulatory overdrive. Thanks to the actions of Brussels there are now 175,000 pages of live legislation. Open Europe (**www.openeurope.org.uk**) has told us that, in printed form, current EU legislation would stretch for 32 miles. Even Günter Verheugen (currently EU Vice-President, and Commissioner for Enterprise and Industry) estimates the total cost at 5.5 per cent of European Union output, a massive £400 billion of cost on businesses. The European Union government, like the current British government, seem to think that without all this regulation banks would steal our money, drinks makers might poison us, builders might build houses that were unstable, and investment managers might put all their clients' money on the 3.30 at Newmarket. This just reveals how little they understand how a competitive market works.

People running businesses generally take pride in their brands and their products. They want to produce a better return for their investors or a tastier drink for their customers. It does not require regulation to tell them to do so, and they do not need detailed law to specify how they should carry out their task. They do so because they want to, and because to do so makes business sense.

If a businessperson were not well-intentioned by nature, he or she would soon be made well-intentioned by the marketplace. An investment manager who started placing unreasonable deals and losing money would soon find other investment managers ringing his or her clients, indicating that they could do a better job for them, and clients would be likely to switch. If a manufacturer started injuring customers due to faulty products, he would soon stop selling his goods – and would undoubtedly also be appearing in the courts on serious charges. You do not need *additional* regulation, since there is already a law which makes it a criminal offence to harm people.

The three bulwarks of the customer interest are these: firstly, most people running businesses want to do a good job and do not set out in business to harm people. Secondly, in a competitive market, if any business does do badly there would soon be plenty of others taking the customer away. Thirdly, in extreme situations, a bad business or a business in error would face prosecution for harm or criminal damage.

Regulation adds extra cost and delay to a product or service. Businesses have to pay extra taxes so that the government can employ staff to draft regulations, keep them up to date, and enforce them. A business may be asked to pay specific fees and charges to a special regulator – who is usually only too keen to increase his or her own staff, and then to increase these fees and charges. The regulator is supplying a monopoly service – adherence to the regulation – which enables the imposition of monopoly charges. Businesses have to hire more people to comply with the details of the regulation, and make sure the right boxes are ticked and the right forms filled in.

Regulation limits innovation. Sometimes regulations are so detailed that a new way of doing something would be against the law. Sometimes it is just the delay and difficulty of getting approval for a new way of doing things which deters business from trying. In the City of London, many businesses now tell me that they will launch their best and newest financial products offshore because it just too slow and expensive to get approval for them in the domestic market.

In Europe there is a particular enthusiasm for employee regulations. Of course, people would like to be able to enjoy much higher wages while working fewer hours. There are those in the government and the union movement who seem to think that simply changing the rules will push wages up and bring hours down – to the benefit of all. Unfortunately, life is not that simple. We can only afford to push up wages and reduce working hours if we are able to compete in the world market, selling the goods and services that we produce at a price that others can afford to pay. That is why there have to be limits on how high a government can push minimum wages, or how low it can take maximum hours, before a country becomes too uncompetitive. If a government's employment legislation is too costly, it will do the opposite of helping people. It will mean fewer jobs in the country regulated in such a way, hitting hardest those with least skill or those on lowest wages, since they are the most likely to lose their jobs or fail to gain employment.

Quite often, regulation sets out to achieve something which happens naturally. We do not need a law or regulation to stop people sending boys up chimneys. We already have laws and regulations requiring boys to attend school up to the age of 16, and mercifully the advent of the vacuum cleaner and the flexible brush have made it quite unnecessary and inappropriate to send boys on dangerous journeys. A huge industry involved in creating and enforcing money laundering regulations has been built up. However, is it likely that without such regulations a reputable bank in Britain would accept £1 million in used £10 notes from a customer making a first deposit, without asking any questions about where the money came from, and without reporting this to the authorities if they were suspicious? Yet, thanks to the suspicion by regulators that reputable banks would fail to ask the obvious questions, we now have an absurd bureaucracy. A client well-known to a bank who wishes to deposit or encash a cheque from another legal, taxed source in Britain, where there is unlikely to be a problem, may well have to brandish a utility bill or passport to meet the tests!

For the politician and the bureaucrat, regulation offers an exciting and cheap (or even free) way of interfering in the market and in the businesses being regulated, without having to spend a lot of money on nationalisation – or without having to accept directorial responsibilities themselves. In a way, the regulator becomes a shadow director, someone who is effectively controlling or manipulating the business from afar. In most cases in British law, the regulator is given immunity from having to take any responsibility – and yet the regulator is often one of the causes of the poor results being achieved.

Pension fund regulations
This is particularly obvious in pension regulation in the United Kingdom. Over the past ten years there has been a collapse in the private pension fund movement. We have moved from being a country where most people in employment were members of pension schemes, saving to provide themselves with a pension related to their final salary when they retired, to being a country where most do not have access to such a fund. A combination of tax and regulation has hit these funds very badly. Quite a lot of funds have been wound up altogether, while the majority of funds have stopped taking on new members and many have stopped accumulating for future earnings of the existing members. The funds have had to take this view because their assets have not been sufficient to cover their liabilities, even though many of their members have been making large contributions to the pension funds.

How has this come about? Well, of course, taking a substantial sum of money from the pension funds each year in tax did not help. It left them short of around £5 billion a year that they otherwise would have enjoyed by way of tax credit. However, and in some ways even worse, there was the impact the regulator has had upon the system. The regulator has effectively created a money-go-round for the government which has undermined the apparent values of the funds. The regulator has said, especially in cases where the funds are closed to new members and which therefore look after people of, or near, retirement age, that the fund should be wholly or largely invested in government securities. The government issues new government securities because it wishes to spend more than it collects in taxes and so it is delighted to be able to borrow from the market. The regulator has created a huge demand from pension funds for government debt, which has enabled the government to raise the money it needs to borrow at very attractive rates. This, in turn, means that the interest on offer to the funds buying the government securities has been disappointingly low. As a result, funds have not made very much money by buying these low-interest investments forced upon them by the regulator. Subsequently, the regulator comes along, provides a valuation method which says that – in the long term – the funds will not be sufficient to pay the bills, adding to the number of funds which then close down altogether.

The regulator has this strange idea that growing liabilities can be matched by fixed income bonds. Most people seem to believe this absurdity, which is self-evidently untrue. Clearly, the liabilities of a typical pension fund rise in line with wages and salaries. Wages and salaries in normal times grow by the trend rate of growth of the economy, which in the UK's case has been around 2 per cent real growth in recent years. That is to say, if average inflation is 3 per cent and real growth is 2 per cent, the liabilities of the fund are growing by 5 per cent per annum. If the fund is required by the regulator to invest all or most of its money in fixed-income lending to the government, then by definition its income does not rise at all over the years ahead. The capital value of the bonds is eroded by the 3 per cent per annum inflation and the income fails to meet the payments. That is why, prior to all this regulation, most pension funds invested in claims on property and company shares, so that they had access to rising income where the rent and the dividend was likely to go up in line with the overall growth in the economy or, in other words, in line with the growth in salaries and wages.

It is quite extraordinary that regulators can believe that funds must buy these fixed-income securities, egged on by a government keen to find a cheap source of funding for its overspending. It is even more bizarre that, to date, there have been no court cases or legal redress against the government for creating such a mess. The government's spin machine has been very active in trying to blame greedy companies for not putting enough into their funds – rather than blaming careless regulators, who have managed to create a system of investment in managing the pension funds which often fails to prevent them meeting their liabilities without ever-larger injections of capital from the sponsoring companies.

CLIMATE CHANGE

From time to time, new subjects come to the top of the political agenda that offer governments and regulators enormous opportunity to greatly expand their empires. In the last three years there has been almost universal fascination by the governing classes in the issue of global warming, now known by many as climate change. Politicians and bureaucrats latched on to the academic thesis that the planet was warming up and that this was caused by too much carbon dioxide being emitted from human-based activity. They drew attention to the big increase in CO_2 being sent into the atmosphere by more cars, lorries, central heating and air-conditioning systems, and other heat-generating and burning processes. They said that CO_2 was a leading greenhouse gas and that the increased human emissions of CO_2, when mixed with the far more substantial and naturally occurring CO_2, was causing the planet to warm up.

There have been a number of challenges to this view. Some have argued that the planet is not warming up at all, basing their case on the figures for the last 10 years. Some have argued that human CO_2, being less than 3 per cent of total CO_2, is unlikely to have caused such a big set of changes as is being claimed, and that if global warming is taking place it may be related to natural phenomena. Some favour the theory that there are more sunspots and flares on the sun; others that, perhaps, there is more natural CO_2 emerging from volcanic and other activity. Within the proponents of global warming itself there are also different groups. Some take a multilateral view that the world can only proceed in tackling human CO_2 if it does so collectively. What is the point, they argue, of Britain – which accounts for a very small proportion of the world's CO_2 – spending a great deal of money to curb its emissions, if that decrease is swamped by the impact of India and China who will naturally be burning a lot more fuel in the years ahead. On the other hand, others say that the rich West has plundered the planet for too long and needs to set an example, and should bring its emissions of CO_2 per person down to a lower level, much closer to that of poorer countries.

Overall, there is a consensus that CO_2 emissions are damaging, that they are too high and rising too quickly, and they need to be brought down. There is a consensus among all nations that the rich West has to do quite a lot to curb its own appetite for fuel, but less of a consensus around what, if any, restraints should apply to emerging economies such as India and China. In the West this has led to a surfeit of law-making and regulation, some increase in green taxation – and to a debate about how far each of these should go. Regulation is being used in a number of areas. Regulators are setting ever-higher hurdles for car manufacturers to leap, demanding less and less emission from new vehicles, and setting high standards for fuel efficiency. Regulators are also turning their attention to aviation emissions, to the output of the domestic boiler, the commercial boiler and the air-conditioning unit. There is general enthusiasm for higher standards of thermal insulation and considerable regulatory interest in requiring or assisting alternative fuels and new ways of generating heat and power. The West, especially the European West, has imposed ever-higher taxes upon energy consumption. These have been particularly high when it comes to taxing diesel and petrol for individuals, cars, lorries and vans. Many countries also impose taxes on energy for heating homes and on business.

Despite all this tax and regulatory activity, the trend of worldwide production of carbon emissions is endlessly upwards, even within some of the richer western countries which are seeking to curb their appetite for fuel. The regulators and the tax specialists can force people to buy or run more fuel-efficient vehicles, but they cannot stop them travelling more miles; they cannot prevent a society which is getting richer from buying more vehicles. Even if the West does eventually find the right policy mix which deters people from more usage, it is certain that, as people in developing countries get richer, the world as a whole will see a huge increase in usage of cars, lorries, vans, air-conditioning units, boilers and other heating systems. Climate change is one of those areas where regulators will never succeed, by regulatory means alone, in achieving their ultimate objective: a huge reduction in human CO_2 emissions worldwide.

INTERNATIONAL TREATIES

The preferred means of getting world leaders to tackle a problem together, as with climate change, money laundering or banking regulations, is to hold a series of talks resulting in an international treaty. In many places treaty law takes precedence over other laws. At the very least, treaty requirements have to be incorporated into domestic national law as part of the process of ratification. The treaty law is drafted on behalf of the international community by technicians and bureaucrats with a lead interest in the subject; negotiations proceed for months or years, until a compromise package or agreement is brokered. The bureaucrats, lawyers, jurists, and administrators then attempt to reproduce, in detailed treaty language, the general agreement that the politicians have reached in the plenary sessions. This, in turn, has to be translated into enforceable regulation, country by country – and perhaps also at the international level. It can lead to private lawsuits in courts in some jurisdictions, as well as to cross-border government action. Once imposed, treaty law is quite difficult to amend or change, since this would require reconvening the dozens of countries that were party to the original treaty and getting their agreement, even to a simple amendment. This builds inflexibility into the system.

THE WAY FORWARD

So what, then, should be done about the growing intrusion of regulation of common world government into the world of business? Does it matter that costs have been increased so much? Does it matter that innovation is damaged, that customer choice is reduced, and that sometimes regulations achieve the opposite of what they set out to do? I believe it does: this is not only limiting our freedom but also reducing our income, and it is diverting some jobs from the more highly regulated to the less-regulated parts of the world. When these effects are combined with failure to achieve the stated aims of the proposals, it is worrying.

What can be done to reverse this tidal flow of new regulation and internationalism? For any individual country it requires, first of all, a group of politicians with the political will and understanding to get on top of the problem. They have to argue – and win the argument – to stop more of these international agreements. Then they have to revisit those agreements signed by previous governments, with a view to renegotiating, improving or abating their impact. In each major western country the regulatory increases now come both from domestic legislative pressures and from global ones. A newly-elected government has, of course, more direct control and ability to influence the domestic legislative programme it has inherited than international agreements, and it is in the domestic arena that governments normally concentrate their deregulatory activities.

REGULATORY BUDGETS

For some time I have favoured for the United Kingdom a government approach based upon regulatory budgets. Each department should draw up a list of the current regulations for which it is responsible. It should include cost estimates: the costs imposed by government on the taxpayer and regulated businesses to create the regulations, to police them, to license the established businesses, to improve them – and also of the costs of compliance imposed upon the individuals, families and businesses.

For many years, each new regulation is meant to have been accompanied by a statement to Parliament of regulatory impact or total cost. Some of these statements were better done than others, but they give each department a starting point from which to establish a base of budgets for the total cost of regulations imposed. Each year, a regulatory budget would be drawn up for each department. A deregulatory government would want to cut the total amount of cost imposed on businesses and individuals by the existing stock of regulation. This would require annual identification of old regulations that could be removed altogether or, for those areas where regulation is still needed, the introduction of better regulations that are less costly for those having to comply.

A government that favoured some increase in regulation could use the regulatory budget structure to accommodate this, by allowing increases in regulatory budgets. It would, however, improve the quality of debate: the fact that the government had to go to Parliament to get approval for any increase in the regulatory budget to put through the regulations would be an additional hurdle that it had to leap over in order to impose the new structure.

After considerable debate, the Conservative Party agreed to adopt this as their official Opposition policy for the 2005 General Election, linking it to a pledge that they would cut the cost of regulation, year after year, over the life of a Parliament. I reviewed this proposal for Conservative policy in the *Economic Competitiveness Review* published in the autumn of 2007, recommending that a Conservative government should pledge itself to cut the total cost of regulation imposed on businesses and individuals by one-fifth over the lifetime of a five-year Parliament, or a reduction of 3.7 per cent in total cost each year.

In 2008, the Labour government decided that they would adopt the idea of regulatory budgets. We have yet to see what they think the base cost is. Using the European Union figure of 5.5 per cent of national output would give us a figure of over £80 billion for the EU component alone. Drawing on the work of the British Chambers of Commerce and others, it seems likely that the total regulatory cost imposed in Britain is nearer 10 per cent of total output, or around £150 billion per annum. The present government has said that it does not believe it can actually cut the cost of regulation each year – but it could use the discipline of regulatory budgets to reduce the rate of increase in the costs, which has been particularly rapid in recent years, owing to the twin pressures of European and domestic requirements. The government expects regulation related to climate change to be increasing quite rapidly, and does not believe it can fully offset this by cutting out other areas of regulation.

If the avowed intention of a move to regulatory budgets is to be anything more than a presentational stunt, several conditions have to be met. Firstly, there has to be greater energy and skill devoted to trying to get to the true costs than has been shown to date. One part of the cost should be relatively easy to prise out of the machine. A government, presumably, knows how many officials are currently involved in drafting and maintaining existing regulations within the central government machine, and how much money and how many people are involved in policing and implementing the regulations through the quangos and regulators responsible. These figures are already in the public accounts and can be extracted quite simply. The more difficult figures to identify are the true costs incurred by businesses. Some will argue that many of the things regulations require business to do are either best practice, or things that the businesses would do naturally for themselves; they should not, therefore, be regarded as an additional cost of the regulation. Others might take a view that they would do things in a very different way, but not necessarily a worse way, were the regulation not in place. Therefore all of the processes connected to the regulation should be deemed part of its cost. Judgments have to be made, and in the bigger or more contentious cases Parliamentary debate is quite a good way of teasing out the advantages and disadvantages of any given levels of established regulatory cost.

Another element arising from turning budgeting into an exercise which will more than cover its own paper-chase cost is to make sure a government identifies and repeals regulations that are excessive or simply unnecessary. It should be quite easy to identify a number of regulations which are achieving the opposite of what they set out to achieve, of regulations that are positively damaging. For example, the present government could repeal compulsory Home Information Packs, as it seems that their introduction has hindered rather than helped the property market that they were meant to assist. If they are found to be desirable or necessary (that is, if the market itself actually requires them) people can still have them prepared for themselves, without it having to be a legal requirement. It should be possible to identify a number of regulations where things are likely to happen anyway without the regulation being in place. We do not need a regulation to stop people taking their elephants into Parliament Square, as observation tells us they don't do so anyway – and very few people have elephants.

Thirdly, it should be possible to identify a range of regulations where the regulatory cost is out of proportion to the alleged, intended or perceived regulatory benefits. There must be many cases of health and safety regulations where the costs are disproportionate to any possible improvements in practice or savings. We can see the effect of this in the number of charitable and voluntary events that are now cancelled or reduced in scale owing to the cost, time and complexity of implementing the full scale of modern regulation which previously did not apply.

A government serious about reducing regulatory costs would need to be bold. It would need to find some substantial areas of regulation that could be reduced or removed altogether. For example, it is difficult to see why extra mortgage regulation was introduced into Britain in recent years. It is one of those ironies of life that, in all the years when we did not have much specific mortgage regulation, we never had a run on a mortgage bank, we never had a nationalisation of a mortgage bank and we never saw the complete collapse of the mortgage market. In recent years, following the introduction of mortgage regulation, this is exactly what was achieved. It demonstrated that expensive regulation introduced into the market was not only unable to protect people from the dreadful spectacle of a run on deposits on a mortgage bank, but also that the regulation was addressing the wrong things. Therefore, by definition, it was unable to protect people from what they might most fear. The failure occurred elsewhere, while people had a false sense of security from the extra regulation.

It is difficult to see why we need all the complicated data protection legislation, with a licensing authority and administrative back up. Would it not be sufficient to have a right in law for people to see data held about them by businesses and government, without having to have an expensive bureaucracy to intervene directly in policing it?

There are a number of small things that could be removed. Why do we need gaming licences for charities holding raffles or offering bingo games at one-off events? Why do we need mandatory horse passports, or substantial regulation of traditional herbal medicines, which used not to be so regulated? Why is venture capital fundraising, an investment for professional investors, regulated at all? Surely the normal framework of contract and banking law, allied to their ability to employ lawyers and sue each other if things go wrong, should be sufficient, without the need to run to the regulator as well? Overall credit extended should be regulated through proper central bank controls.

Amongst the bigger areas we do need to tackle is money-laundering regulation, which is excessive and not necessarily very effective. Of course, we all wish to see the big rings and organisers of drug dealing, terrorist financing and the like tackled vigorously by Customs and other government authorities. I cannot, for the life of me, see how asking you or me to take our passport and utility bill to the bank when we wish to deposit a modest sum makes it any more likely that, as a result, the government will bust a drug ring or find its way into a professional racket based on benefit fraud.

A useful technique which should be deployed more often by legislators is that of the 'sunset' regulation or clause. Quite often, a regulation is introduced for an immediate issue or problem which then becomes less important with the passage of time. Why not put into most regulations a requirement for review at the end of, say, five years? If the government of the day does not wish to renew and is not prepared to make a positive move to seek parliamentary approval for renewal, then the regulation or law should lapse.

STATUTORY INSTRUMENTS

It would be a good idea to encourage more parliamentary debate about much regulation going through. Current parliamentary processes are far from satisfactory. A typical Statutory Instrument, which may involve a very complex new law, receives only 1½ hours of debate in a committee with a limited number of MPs allowed to participate. None of them can amend the proposal. If the government makes a mistake, it either has to leave the mistake on the face of the statutory instrument or remove the whole thing and start again. If the Opposition or backbench MPs have a good idea for improving the effectiveness, reducing the cost or simply improving the language of the proposal, they are unable to do anything about it because the proposal stands or falls as originally written. It makes the 1½-hour debate rather pointless, as in practically every case the government is determined to drive it through and usually has the necessary votes to do so. 'Regulation' has become 'legislation by the bureaucracy', with practically no parliamentary or ministerial supervision, save in a limited number of cases where there are talented and hardworking ministers who provide the parliamentary scrutiny *within* the department before the proposal is tabled.

Parliamentary procedures should allow tabling and discussion of amendments to improve the clarity and expression of the regulation, to minimise the cost of its implementation and to improve its effectiveness. Given that so much detailed legislation is now done by way of a Statutory Instrument, containing all or most of the detail of the underlying Act of Parliament which gives the overall powers, it makes it even more important that procedures should be changed for proper debate of Statutory Instruments. It would also slow ministers down and make them more reluctant to legislate if they felt there was a bigger hurdle to leap, in order to get the new regulations or legislation through.

These days, quite a lot of Statutory Instruments go through in the very long periods of holiday which the government insists on Parliament taking. When Parliament is not in session – and hence public debate is missing for 17 weeks of the year – it gives the government considerable opportunity to put Statutory Instruments onto the statute book. On the return of Parliament it is for the Opposition to call any Statutory Instrument in for a special debate. Again, this will only be for 1½ hours and takes place against the background of the Statutory Instrument already being law. There has been no known occasion in the last 11 years when any of these instruments has been reversed as a result of this procedure.

PROTECTIVE LEGISLATION

Globally, the success of countries that keep regulation under control or to a minimum, will have some impact on persuading other governments that they need to be careful. Exporting excessive regulation is one of the important strategies employed by advanced western governments, as they seek to limit the competitiveness of other countries. Sometimes they do this for the best of reasons; they always do it with a good story to tell about their intentions. If the European Union is experiencing too much competition from Asia, it will seek to engage Asian countries in global discussion and debate, with a view to getting them to accept something more like western standards when it comes to working hours and working conditions. The Americans tackled the Chinese on toy safety when they were experiencing a tidal wave of Chinese imports of all kinds.

Trade disputes escalate between America and Europe over the export of agricultural products in markets which are already very controlled by government subsidies, quotas and other interventions. Each major country or trading block is seeking to export its own standards of safety, employment and environmental protection, ostensibly in the name of improving life, but often with the baser motive of trying to stop people exploiting a lower-cost exporting base elsewhere in order to advance the jobs and prosperity in their own country more rapidly.

The decades ahead are likely to see an escalation of many such disputes, given the growing strength and economic success of China, and of the oil producers of the Middle East, Russia and of India. The United States and the European Union often see these new arrivals on the trading block as disruptive forces – rather than as helpful collaborators and good suppliers of cheaper goods and services. As the Asian, Middle Eastern and Russian economies expand, so there will be more attempts to lasso them in to the world diplomatic and trading framework. An ever-more complex series of international treaties and international regulators will attempt to tie down more of the issues over how they are to compete and how they are to conduct their business. Although the United States may rail and kick and scream about the United Nations and other international organisations when disagreements surface, the USA will also be a keen advocate of higher regulatory standards in fields where she most fears foreign competition.

Democratic electorates are likely to remain in two minds about all this. If you ask the general population if they want to be governed by foreigners, they will say 'No'. If you ask if it would be right to shift government and accountability from the national to the global level, they would also answer in the negative. If, however, you tell them that, through international agreement, their jobs can be made safer, the planet can be made cleaner and products could be made better, they are more likely to be positive. The challenge for those who wish their countries to follow policies that promote more jobs and greater prosperity would be to try to use the international organisations on the side of greater freedom and free trade – rather than on the side of more protection and more restriction. The ever-growing regulatory bureaucracies will prove slow, backward-looking and costly – and will often achieve the opposite of what they set out to do. As we live through the convulsions of the credit crunch, so there will be more discussions about a new framework for banking and financial regulation. We are unlikely to end up with less regulation overall, or with less global regulation than we have today, as a result of these discussions. Indeed, we are likely to end up with more. As I write, there is the deafening sound of the stable door not only being bolted but double-locked, well after the horse has gone.

The regulators are likely to repeat past mistakes in a different guise. They are likely to make banking business too difficult to conduct for a year or two, intensifying the downswing of the cycle. It will take banking businesses and others time to work out new ways of expanding and growing, by exploiting the complex but perfectly drafted regulations which will emerge from this period of soul searching. It was out of the last lot of banking regulations and the attempt to deal with problems of previous crises that the present credit boom emerged. It will be out of the embers of this credit crunch that the next boom also emerges. The extent of global financial regulation and the extent of international government are such that they will slow down a favourable recovery from the present credit crunch. That does not mean they will prevent a future boom getting out of control or even that they will succeed in dampening the future boom. It just means that any future boom will be caused by different mechanisms from the syndicated credits and the off balance sheet financings that characterised the credit boom of the last decade.

8 | Taxation

INTRODUCTION

Taxation is regulation's big bad brother; both impose a great cost on business. Taxation is a strong legal entitlement for government to take certain large sums of money, at times of the government's choosing and to a formula the government lays down. Regulation is a continuous requirement to meet certain standards at the cost of the business, permitting a little flexibility over where and when payments are made.

Most governments are rapacious. They love taking people's money and spending it for them. They believe they are uniquely capable of supplying certain kinds of services, spurning the market to do so. They believe they are the best judge of how to transfer income from certain people in society to others. Above all, they seek sizeable sums of money to ensure that they, the ministers and the advisers in the government, are paid good salaries and have all the money they need to live a comfortable lifestyle. These three functions of the state always take precedence over everything else. If choices are to be made because an economy is performing badly and does not have enough income to sustain itself, it is rarely or never that the government decides to cut back.

The government asserts that it is important that it carries on spending for the delivery of public services, which usually include education, health, transport and, in some societies, energy and communications. Above all else, the government believes it must carry on spending on itself, rarely or never recommending reductions in the number of bureaucrats and ministers as an obvious economy measure. Understandably, when times are hard, it would be difficult for governments to recommend taking less from the rich to give to the poor; similarly, 'social security' budgets are sacrosanct – and, indeed, usually rise in times of hardship, as more people qualify for the benefits on offer.

A lot of democratic politicians believe – wrongly – that the more money you offer to spend on people in the form of dearer public services, the more popular you are going to be. Many of my parliamentary colleagues on both sides of the House, but especially within the Labour Party, take this view. Any suggestion that the government might spend less, or even that the government might increase its spending at a slower rate, is greeted with howls of derision. Vivid language is used to suggest that anyone advocating this believes in massive cuts. Debate is overtaken by name-calling and crude caricature. No one is allowed to recommend reductions in the number of bureaucrats or a cull of quangos or some reduction in government advertising or travel bills. A cut is a cut and always, in British debate, is misrepresented as involving the sacking of people such as teachers or nurses – popular groups with the public.

A combination of the belief that spending other people's money for them buys you votes and the thuggish approach to anyone who suggests prudence or caution in public spending has meant that in Britain, as in many democracies, there is an upwards-only ratchet to public spending. Every government assumes that, year after year, it should increase the amount of public spending on offer. It wishes to increase the public spending not just by an amount sufficient to take care of rising prices – the rising cost of buying in goods for the public sector. It does not even wish just to increase the cost of the public sector in line with wage bills, given the dominance of direct employment and payments in lieu of wages in the public spending mix. The aspiration is always to increase public spending by *more* than both prices and wages, so that the government can truly claim there have been 'real' increases.

PAYING FOR GROWTH

There are two ways of paying for this real growth. All elected politicians understand that if you can pay for the growth in public spending out of the growth in the economy generally, without having to raise tax rates, you will upset fewer people than if you increase taxes. With the exception of a few extreme left-wing politicians who want to tax the rich more heavily – and believe it would be popular to do so – the consensus amongst political classes is that, wherever possible, you should finance growth in public spending out of growth of the economy. As an economy grows, so people earn more and thus more income tax is paid. As an economy grows, more goods and services are traded – and so more value-added tax or other sales tax revenue can be collected. As an economy grows, property values usually rise, enabling governments that use property taxes, such as stamp duty and council tax in the United Kingdom, to increase their take.

In Britain, the surprising thing is how unpopular some governments have become when they embark on too much spending and are forced into borrowing and taxing too much to pay for it. For much of the time the polls in Britain tell the unthinking politician that increased taxes are popular – the polls often say that people want better health and better education, and they accept that more tax should be paid to deliver it. However, any party in power which has tried offering people higher taxes has discovered that when people find out that they have to pay the higher taxes (rather than it being something which their rich neighbours could pay) the reaction is rather different. The Labour government of 1974-79 put taxes up, as well as failing to control the trade union problem. The better-paid industrial workers were amongst the many groups that shifted their vote from Labour to Conservative at the end of the 1970s, as they were very frustrated by controls over income and wages and by the high rate of income tax and national insurance they had to pay.

At the end of the 1980s and in the early 1990s, Conservatives gave people the opportunity to pay more for their local government services by asking all adults to make a contribution through the Community Charge, rather than just householders paying through the rates. Polling suggested that everyone thought they should pay a bit more to have better schools. However, when offered the opportunity in the form of a Community Charge, primarily to be used for payment for schools, by a massive majority they said they did not wish to have to make such a payment. Some of the voters entered the so-called poll tax riots; this led to the government having to dump the tax.

John Major's tax rises in the early 1990s were made legendary by Labour constantly reminding people that the Conservatives had put taxes up. This reinforced the worries people had about the conduct of economic policy in the early 1990s and led to the massive defeat of the Conservatives in 1997. To win the elections of 1997 and 2001, Labour made very reassuring noises about tax. They embarked instead on a series of stealth tax rises, which gradually sapped their popularity.

For British politics, the interesting thing about the credit crunch is that it has transformed voter attitudes as expressed in opinion polls – not just on voting intentions as between the ruling party and the opposition, but also over these sensitive issues of tax and spend. For most of the Conservative years, and for the early years of Labour, voters were still prepared to say that they thought that, if it brought better public services, a bit more tax was no bad thing. Today they all feel that quite enough money is raised and spent in the public sector, and they have no wish to see any further increases in taxation. Indeed, many now favour reductions. As the recession has worsened, so government too has come round to the popular view that tax cuts are needed to stimulate activity, and proposed some in its Pre-Budget Report in November 2008.

The long Labour experiment of increased public spending, some of it paid for out of stealth taxes and the rest out of borrowing, has come to a sticky end. After some seven years of big increases in spending from around 2001, the public has become cynical. What the public wants is better public service. British people do want free access to medical care, with a good general practitioner available for minor matters and a good hospital available for more serious matters if and when they need it. They understand they need to pay taxes as part of this package, but they now feel that they are paying far too much tax and that too little of the money is spent intelligently on making sure the GP and the local hospital is available with the service they might need when they might need it.

Similarly, the public was very ready to accept the Labour proposition that more money needed to be spent in and on our schools. There is plenty of evidence that school buildings were not up to good modern standards and needed improvement. Many bought into the argument that Labour produced, that if you put more teachers into any given school and lowered the pupil-teacher ratios, making the classes smaller, there would be a leap forward in standards. However, after 11 years of hurling large sums of money into a larger and better-paid teaching profession, there is growing cynicism as the gap between the best independent schools on the one hand, and the typical state school on the other, has got ever wider; the gap between the performance of state schools in the richer areas when compared with those in poorer areas has also got wider.

The government points to solid progress in the number of exam passes that the average pupil achieves in the typical state school. The currency for judging educational success is how many pupils get five A-to-C grade GCSEs at around the age of 16 – and how many pupils get any kind of GCSE at all, in the less-academic schools. Judged on these figures there has been progress, although the progress has been more substantial in the richer than the poorer areas. However, there is a growing feeling that the tests are not severe enough and that part of the improvement, if not all of it, has been achieved by degradation of testing standards. It is certainly the case that the very bright pupils today get 10 or 11 A-star grades at GCSE, whereas their equivalent intelligent forerunners 30 or 40 years ago would have had some Bs and Cs as well as As.

Maybe young people today do take their work more seriously, and maybe some do achieve higher standards, but some of those responsible for university entrance report a growing concern that the basic standards of numeracy and literacy are simply not high enough, even from pupils who achieve well at GCSE and A-level.

The government always counters any attempt to explore, honestly and sensibly, what is happening to educational standards, with the jibe that anyone seeking to query what has happened to examination standards is merely trying to undermine the real achievements of pupils. I am the first to accept that there are many clever pupils today, as there were in previous years, and I am willing to accept that many of those pupils work as hard or harder than their equivalents in previous generations. I have met some extremely well-educated and very bright young people in recent years, and some of the changes in curriculum and teaching methods have been for the good. However, there is undoubtedly also an issue about why it is that so many young people from the more expensive public schools get places at our top universities in open competition with many more bright people from the state schools. I am absolutely sure that, if there is any bias amongst the top universities over the allocation of places, it is a bias which sympathises with the state school applicant against the independent school applicant. The unspoken thought amongst those making the allocation decisions is that the university would be doing itself political damage if it appointed too many independent school pupils at the expense of state school pupils, given the general atmosphere. This can be justified in pedagogic terms by saying, through the private inner voice of the examining tutor, that the pupil from the independent school has been taught more intensively to a higher standard and, therefore, on balance the place should go to the person from the state school wherever possible.

We will look in more detail at education and training in the next chapter. All we need to conclude for the sake of this debate is that there is considerable cynicism now about how good the results of all the extra spending are. This is serving to undermine public confidence in the idea that just spending more is the right answer. In so many fields of public endeavour, spending more has not meant a better service or higher standards. It has meant more bureaucrats, more regulations, more guidance notes, more focus groups and polling at public expense, more spin doctors, more ministerial trips and visits, more press releases, more White and Green Papers, more expressions of goodwill and enthusiasm – but all so often a disappointing lack of progress or achievement.

FLOODING – MONEY DOWN THE DRAIN?

Let us take another issue, the response to flooding. In the summer of 2007, large areas of England were damaged badly by flood waters. Prolonged and heavy rainfall swelled brooks and rivers, which in many cases overflowed their banks. The same rainfall also proved too much for the drainage and sewerage system, forcing foul water up into the street or into people's gardens. Although the rains subsided as quickly as they started, for many people it ushered in a year of misery, having to live in temporary accommodation and patiently await success with the insurance claim, the hiring of the builder and the drying out of the property.

Government ministers responded very well – initially. Hilary Benn, the Environment Secretary, and the Prime Minister were well aware how serious this matter was, and both took personal interest in directing the government's media response. They said the right things, made their visits, and expressed sympathy. Over one year later, there has been a complete lack of follow up in many areas. Instead of getting on with cleaning ditches, improving the drains, putting in new ditches or widening and deepening old ones so that future large volumes of water can be handled more easily, the government embarked on a long inquiry under Michael Pitt to find out what went wrong and what could be done next.

It was quite obvious that the main problem the country experienced was the lack of capacity of brooks, rivers, ditches and drains to handle the sudden burst of water. It was also obvious that this problem had been greatly exacerbated by planning decisions in recent years, granting the right to developers and builders to put substantial numbers of new houses, with all the concrete and tarmac that entails, over floodplain land that used to absorb the water, at a slower rate, whenever there was heavy rainfall or when rivers burst their banks. In my own constituency, several of the places worst affected by the floods were relatively recent constructions. In one case a new estate of homes that had only opened three months earlier was badly damaged by substantial flooding – because the drains could not take it and because it had been built on a floodplain.

For all the money the government has now spent on legal advice, on letters explaining why it cannot do things, on Environment Agency planning and memos, on PR and spin, on ministerial visits and on strengthening the bureaucracy at the Environment Agency and in the Environment Department, we could have dug quite a few improved or new ditches by now, which would have taken the floodwaters in future. In my own constituency, the construction of a couple of bunds, or earth mounds, around a couple of fields to act as holding grounds for excess waters on one of the local streams, would protect Wokingham and the village of Winnersh from future flooding. It has now been agreed this might work, but still no one in charge with the budget has got round to ordering the diggers and moving the earth.

It is this kind of experience which makes people despair of their government. As people often say to me, they could just about put up with the tax bill if they felt things which matter to them and which need public action were dealt with promptly and efficiently. Certainly, all those living in flooded houses would feel they were getting better value for their tax, if schemes were now being put in place that offered a reasonable guarantee of no future flooding. Yet in practically every case that is not the position.

A PROBLEM SHARED ...

Problems of taxation and spending are not unique to the United Kingdom. The whole of the European Union is awash with spin doctors, media briefings, additional regulation, clever people sitting in administrative offices feeling self important, seeking to legislate for 300 million people. There is the same difficulty in getting anything done on the ground that might make a difference to people's lives, or giving them any sense that all the money they send to Brussels is well spent. A recent study in Canada, comparing their government with the UK government, demonstrates that there has also been a centralisation of power around the Prime Minister's office and a growing sense of dislocation – between politicians and the electorate, between politicians and officials, and between most politicians and the Prime Minister and his advisers.

In most jurisdictions, the trends are similar – towards more central power, with the president or prime minister seeing the important relationship being his or her relationship with the media, rather than with the wider electorate and based upon what he or she does for them.

Larger, more centralised governments are finding it increasingly difficult to deliver value for money. They still have a natural tendency to think the answer is more money rather than changing the way they run the programmes and administer the government. As a result, governments in most developed countries are now facing a difficult dilemma. They would like to tax more to satisfy their own voracious appetites to spend on themselves and they would like to tax more, so that more visible spending could be seen in each county, district and town. Unfortunately, from their point of view, they also have to keep an eye on what other countries are doing.

In recent years there has been some tax competition between different countries of the advanced world. Any individual country can increase its prosperity very considerably, by lowering the rates of income tax and company profits tax – and thereby attracting more highly paid, entrepreneurial people to work in that country, and by attracting more businesses to locate there. This activity used to be confined to very small jurisdictions, commonly known as tax havens, which offered low corporate taxes and low income taxes to rich individuals, and especially to companies specialising in financial and investment activities. Offshore from the United Kingdom lie the Isle of Man and the States of Jersey and Guernsey, three jurisdictions which have made a good living in recent years by offering lower rates of income tax and corporate tax and a home for those who wish to run investment funds and offshore banking. The Caribbean, Bermuda and the Virgin Islands have followed similar strategies. On the mainland of Europe, Luxembourg has, to some extent, offered the better corporate deal for investment business, while Switzerland has been a magnet for rich individuals' funds, based upon a combination of sensible tax arrangements, a strong domestic currency and discretion about where the money came from and for what it was being used.

The position remained stable for as long as the large centres of the more highly taxed world felt they were not suffering unduly from the growth of this satellite business in the tax havens. The advent of Ireland offering a company tax rate of either 0 per cent or 12.5 per cent certainly made the bigger countries wake up and take notice. The Irish economy exploded into life, and moved rapidly from being considerably poorer in terms of income per head than the United Kingdom to being richer. Over the decade 1997-2007 the Irish economy outgrew the UK economy, growing more than 2.5 times faster than the UK on a sustained basis. Some argued that this was owing to its membership of the European Union and the large amount of subsidy payments made to Irish agriculture through Community funds. However, more careful analysis shows that the agriculture sector was not the main cause of the growth rate, and that the lower tax rates offered by Ireland were crucial in attracting the wide range of businesses to set up offices and facilities in the country. Low tax was important in attracting back to Ireland many talented Irish people who had previously been making their fortune abroad. It is true that, towards the end of the fast-growth period, membership of the euro added a further accelerant to the process, since it gave Ireland a period of lower interest rates than she would have set for herself. This encouraged a credit boom on top of the inward investment boom which lower taxes had triggered.

The first response of the advanced countries with greedy governments has been to try to close down offshore centres, or force them to impose regulations and tax levels similar to those that apply in the advanced countries. The European Union has been especially keen to try to extend its regulatory jurisdiction to the Channel Islands and the Isle of Man. Similarly, Germany, through the EU, has been very keen to change the rules in Luxembourg to prevent so much investment money flowing out to its small neighbour. The EU's case has been twofold. Firstly, it has tried to get the different jurisdictions to impose higher tax rates, as it sees low taxes as 'tax dumping', similar to the dumping of physical goods on export markets by countries who just want to gain market share at any price and are prepared to lose money in doing so. In practice, most businesses operating out of Jersey, Guernsey, the Isle of Man and Luxembourg do not lose money, and in that sense they are not dumping at all. Further, these countries often have much better balances between revenue and expenditure than the higher-spending, higher-deficit countries that are making the 'dumping' allegations.

Secondly, the European authorities are keen to require equivalent regulation of the offshore centres, recognising that regulatory cost too can have a big impact upon where people decide to do business. They claim that their only concern is fair conduct of business for the underlying customers, and they feel that they need to extend EU regulatory protection to the customers who choose to go to businesses which are freer, and often innovate more, based in the differently regulated centres of the so-called tax havens.

The German and EU cases against Luxembourg, and some of the allegations against Switzerland, have centred around the possibility that depositors and investors are using banking and investment services in the offshore centres to avoid paying substantial sums of tax in their home countries. This has fuelled a demand for greater transparency and for the exchange of much more information from the offshore and Swiss banking area, in order to try to close what the EU sees as tax loopholes. However, despite some success in forcing tax rates up and in forcing greater exposure and more regulation upon the offshore centres, the high-spending countries have not been successful enough to solve all of their problems by these means. The problems the UK has faced illustrate exactly how sensitive a business can be to the relative rate of tax in one jurisdiction compared with another. By the end of the 1990s, the UK had a very competitive business tax system compared to the rest of Europe. Reform of the tax structure, removing allowances and lowering rates, alongside better controls over public spending since the 1980s – and reasonable economic growth – had all contributed to producing a better balance between the government's expenditure and the rest of the economy. This allowed tax rates to be set that were lower than in most of the overseas competitor countries.

However, in the last ten years, several of these countries have woken up to the need to cut their own corporate tax rates and have brought their taxes down below the UK level. On the mainland of Europe, Holland has become especially attractive, pursuing both deregulatory policy and offering a relatively low rate of company profit tax. Ireland, as we have seen, has dramatically slashed her rates and has also become a very attractive centre for headquarters, businesses and for service and industrial activity serving the wider European market. For example, Henderson Asset Management decided to transfer its headquarters from London to Dublin as a result of uncertainty over new tax proposals from the British government, and in order to benefit from the lower level of tax. Henderson (a well-respected investment business, with UK headquarters for 74 years) calculated that it would save around £8.5 million a year on its tax bill because its foreign profits would be taxed at 12.5 per cent instead of the 28 per cent in the UK. The engineering company Charter, with large overseas interests, has also announced that it is shifting its tax residence to Ireland to take advantage of the lighter taxation regime there. Regus, a specialist in providing serviced office accommodation, has gone offshore; Brit Insurance is one of many insurance companies going to Bermuda to take advantage of lower taxes for insurance in that jurisdiction. United British Media has shifted to Ireland, and the two Shell companies, one British and one Dutch, have consolidated their headquarters in Holland to take advantage of the better regime there.

At the moment, the movement of companies offshore from Britain is a gentle slide rather than a precipitate stampede. The bigger companies are playing a game of cat and mouse with the British Treasury. As soon as the Treasury starts to make a move into taxing overseas profits in a more penal way, taxing dividend remittances more penally, or taking any other tax action against the UK corporate sector which it does not like, a delegation goes to Downing Street, or emails and letters are sent, until the Treasury backs down. It is a tense situation leading on both sides to gradual attrition – and to the loss of more businesses in due course.

It is not just the UK that is losing business to lower tax jurisdictions elsewhere. European countries as a whole are losing business to Asia and America. The United States of America has kept her taxes relatively light; states such as Delaware have particular advantages for overseas businesses wishing to establish themselves. Caribbean tax havens, Asian tax havens such as Hong Kong and Singapore, and now some of the flat tax countries in Eastern Europe, are providing a much better tax offering to the would-be entrepreneur or to the well-established company than the more traditional advanced country jurisdictions.

The dilemma for the advanced countries is at once apparent. They have tried the strategy of forcing higher taxes and more regulation onto competing jurisdictions, only to be swamped by the number of jurisdictions playing the game. They have then discovered that, in the case of the EU with Ireland, even within their own ranks some are able to play the game as well, forcing others to reconsider the level of their tax rates.

Reconsideration is not as painful as the political establishment and the bureaucracy often think. Most of their tax revenue and economic forecasting models assume that if they cut a tax rate on business they will then collect less revenue. They see the stock of business activity and profits as fixed: the government can increase the tax take from business only by increasing the rate, or it will lose revenue if it cuts the rate. As the dynamism of the world economy increases, and as recent events show, if a country is enthusiastic enough to cut tax rates substantially then, within a period of years, it may well find it collects rather more tax revenue than if it had kept the tax rate high. If you make a tax jurisdiction attractive enough, for example by charging half the standard rate of tax that other jurisdictions charge, then you are likely to more than double your stock of business and business profits – and thus end up with more revenue than you started with. This has been the Irish experience. However it is clearly easier to do this as a relatively small country than to attempt it as a large country.

So what has the role of taxation been in the credit crunch? It has reinforced the difficulties that the high-tax, expensive, jurisdictions have experienced; it has reinforced the trend for more growth and activity to take place in the low-tax countries of Eastern Europe, in the advanced low-tax jurisdictions of the Far East and, more generally, in the Far East in the emerging superstars of India and China – both of which have relatively low tax rates.

Taxation paid a particular role in exacerbating the financial squeeze and difficulties in the United Kingdom. We have seen how the imposition of a tax on dividend income, previously collected in pension funds free of such tax, caused an early collapse of British savings and pension fund activity over the last decade. Big increases in stamp duty since 1998, doubling it to 4 per cent on properties in the highest band, have not been helpful now that the residential property market in the UK is in freefall, with far too little activity to sustain all the jobs of estate agents, surveyors and others dependent upon the market. While the main cause of this is the collapse of mortgages and the credit scarcity in the major banks, high stamp duties have been another reason why people would defer a purchase or refuse to move.

The argument over stamp duty and the British housing market has been a persistent and consistent one, largely because the principal opposition party, the Conservatives, have made it such an issue in debate. The Conservatives said they would offer a reduction or break in stamp duty to help people at the lower end of the market. The Government spent most of its time denying this was necessary, only to give in at the beginning of September 2008 and announce that, for one year only, homes in the value bracket £125,000-£175,000 (previously attracting stamp duty at 1 per cent) would now be exempt. The Government, stretched for cash, decided it could afford to forego what it estimated to be £600 million of revenue for one year, in order to give buyers of the cheaper homes a 'saving' of between £1,250 and £1,750.

Many governments favour deferred taxation rather more than taxation. The principal countries of the world have governments that are able to borrow at quite fine rates for long periods of time. Governments take particular delight in financing things through long-term borrowing; the politician who announces and pushes through the scheme does not have to meet the eventual bills for the repayment of the debt. The danger of too much borrowing is obvious. If a government over-borrows, then the amount of interest it has to pay takes up too much of the tax revenues, year on year. What a government spends on interest payments it cannot also spend on public service provision. In due course the debt has to be repaid or refinanced, leaving a problem for future generations. As far as taxpayers are concerned, heavy borrowing for the long term may make sense for the elderly – but is a bad deal for the young, as at some point in their lives they will face having to repay the debt. Some governments cynically borrow lots on the basis that they will devalue the currency and the money with which they will repay the debts. Inflation eats away at the amount that has to be repaid in real terms, while devaluation of a currency can also have a favourable impact on repayment to foreign holders of the debt.

THE NATIONAL DEBT
The United Kingdom Government states its debt at around £600 billion. This is the money raised from purchases of, mainly, fixed income bonds issued by the Treasury. However, to get the true figure of the underlying indebtedness of the public sector, a number of other items have to be added in. The public sector has made all sorts of pension promises to people, many of which are completely unfunded. The public sector also has some pension funds to pay for future pension provision – but does not have sufficient money in them to meet all of the liabilities. We need to add another £800 billion or so into the public debt to take into account these pension commitments which will have to be paid. There are then all of the borrowings undertaken under public finance initiative (PFI) and public/private partnership (PPP) activities.

Over the last decade there has been a big increase in the amount of this hidden debt, which is not declared as part of the Government's formal borrowings. The system works by the Government inviting in a private consortium or contractor or investor to raise money to finance part of a public service or a public project. For example, the Government may wish to see a new school building. It does not wish to borrow the money directly on its own balance sheet, and it does not wish to pay for the new school building out of taxed revenue. Instead it asks a private company or investment group to raise the money itself, from shareholders or from the banking system, to build the school – and then, in return, receive a stream of payments from the Treasury over a number of years as repayment for the initial debt, for the management of the contract and as the profit of the company or investment group. In practice this is state borrowing since it is taxpayers who have to meet the interest, service and rental payments to maintain the project; much of the risk rests with the taxpayer and not with the private sector investor. We need to add in maybe another £50 billion or more to the figures to take account of this.

There are then the liabilities of the nationalised businesses that the Government has brought into its control. Network Rail has borrowed over £20 billion, with a full Treasury guarantee. This, too, is probably part of the public debt although in the past it has not appeared as such in the figures. Finally, there is the £100 billion liability called Northern Rock where, effectively, the taxpayer is underwriting all of its liabilities; another £40 billion will come in for Bradford and Bingley.

As we can see, a government which advertises its net indebtedness at around £600 billion has, in practice, a net liability and indebtedness almost three times that amount: around £1,600 billion. The British government, like the published figures revealed by the Italian government, has actually borrowed or committed more than the national income for a whole year in the form of promises to repay or to pay flows of payments and bondholder obligations. No wonder some in the government are becoming alarmed by the magnitude of these payments, and are beginning to see that it poses a problem for future public budgeting. The recent addition of shareholdings in RBS and Lloyds to the state adds another staggering £1,000 to £1,500 million to the public debt, according to preliminary figures from the Office for National Statistics (Press release, 19.2.09).

The build up of the UK tax burden is quite dramatic. In 1997, the total UK tax burden was close to the OECD average at around 39 per cent of national income. By 2007, this had risen to over 42.5 per cent – while the OECD average had fallen to below 38 per cent. The OECD itself reckons that, over the last 35 years, there has been an average increase in the tax take of around 10 percentage points in national income in the main countries. This in turn has led to a reduction in the annual growth rates of those economies by around 0.5 per cent per annum. This is a large price to pay. Looked at another way, if the UK tax burden had remained at its 1996 level, the average householder would be paying £1,600 less per year than it does. Furthermore, if the government had managed to keep the real level of UK tax constant at 1996 levels, each family would be paying £5,140 a year less in tax.

It is not just the tax rates but also the tax complications which are adding to the burden. In Britain, the Forsythe Report into tax competitiveness (Tax Reform Commission: *Tax matters: Reforming the Tax System,* 2006) said that there was now an annual cost of £5.1 billion for administering UK tax regulation, over and above that paid in tax itself. A review by the US Congress (Office of Tax Analysis: *Report into 2001-2003 Tax Cuts*) suggested that in the United States it could cost between $0.20 and $0.60 to raise an extra $1 of tax revenue, so expensive were the complications.

The American Office of Tax Analysis was set up to examine the impact of lower taxes. It found that the cuts in income tax between 2001 and 2003 led to the creation of 3 million extra jobs, and an increase in national income and output of some 3.5-4 per cent more than would have been the case if there had been no tax cuts. It found that the most productive tax cuts were those in dividends and capital gains tax rates, followed by reductions in the four higher income tax rates.

President Bush's decision in 2008 to make more tax cuts available also had a desirable effect in stimulating the American economy during the period of the credit crunch. Second-quarter growth in the United States of America pleasantly surprised people, with 3.3 per cent annualised growth being recorded at a time when the Eurozone economy was shrinking and the UK economy was at a standstill. Once again the magic of tax cuts paid off and injected enough spending power and confidence into the credit crunch-ridden American economy to give it a decent rate of growth.

GREEN TAXATION

The latest scheme that governments have devised for taking money off people is to do so in the name of the environment. The introduction of substantial 'green taxes' on fuel and carbon emissions has provided a useful source of revenue. The United States has been more reluctant to join in with the Europeans, ever-conscious that India and China are growing rapidly without imposing such big increases in taxation in the name of reducing carbon burn.

Governments around the world are looking at schemes for so-called carbon trading. The first initiative devised by the European Union was a crazy scheme which ended up helping business rather than reducing the amount of carbon produced. The European Union gave carbon credits or permits to businesses on such a scale that many of them were able to sell on surplus carbon permits. Only in the United Kingdom did the government play the game, and ration the number of carbon permits in the way originally intended. This resulted in British businesses having to export cash in order to import permits from the more permissive countries on the Continent. Future schemes are likely to entail businesses having to purchase carbon permits for burning fossil fuels, providing a ready source of further revenue for the state.

In a global world, at last, there are some constraints on the ability of an individual government to impose ever-higher income taxes and company taxes on people earning and conducting enterprise in their territories. There is now some competition between different countries and tax jurisdictions; this is beginning to establish a downward pressure on the headline rates of both company tax and, to a lesser extent, income tax. The main aggressive jurisdictions, including the European Union and, to some extent, the United States of America, are attempting to combat this pressure by seeking to export more regulation, and in some cases higher tax rates, to those jurisdictions that they think are too successful in competing by choosing much lighter regulation and lower taxes. These jurisdictions are treated as pariahs, are briefed against in the world media and are invited to meetings where increasing pressure is placed upon them to try to get them to drop their tax haven status, and to move into line with the barrage of regulations that are now customary in the advanced, higher-tax countries.

In this respect globalisation is paradoxical. On the one hand, it is encouraging healthy tax and regulatory competition. On the other hand, it is characterised by the addition of global regulation and global taxes on top of the national ones already liberally imposed by many countries.

THE EFFECT OF THE CREDIT CRUNCH

The credit crunch is beginning to change attitudes towards some of this. There is no doubt that the arrival of the credit crunch, constraining incomes and putting pressure on family budgets in American and Europe alike, has changed public attitudes towards how much tax and regulation they will accept. This is very notable in the area of green policy. In 2006 and early 2007 there was considerable popular support for the idea that the polluter should pay more: that the generator of carbon dioxide should have to buy permits or pay higher taxes, and that more regulation was a good way of tackling this global problem. However, as interest rates rose, incomes fell, mortgages dried up, and house prices started to fall on both sides of the Atlantic, popular priorities shifted very noticeably. People were no longer willing to volunteer for a tax rise or an increase in regulation. They wanted governments that were sensitive to their immediate problems: the difficulty of balancing the family budget and the need to find ways of stimulating more growth, jobs and activity.

The bold campaign to use tax and regulation to change people's behaviour and get them to conserve energy, to travel less and to burn less fuel, became unpopular at the very point that it started to succeed. The ballooning of oil prices, the limitation on people's incomes, the fear of unemployment, and the impact of higher tax and regulation all conspired to shift downwards demand for air travel, for road travel and for energy burning generally. Instead of people welcoming this as the arrival of the outcome they had all been seeking through agreed political consensus of a year earlier, people saw this as evidence that their national government's economic policies were failing, leaving them exposed and having to cut back on their important budgets. The truth is that globalisation is primarily a system which the public will tolerate for so long as it delivers greater choice and higher living standards. The attempt by the believers in big government to hijack the globalisation agenda for their own purposes is causing more damage than did the underlying free trade and globalisation in goods and services that started it all. As soon as countries started to prosper by expanding trade in goods, and trading in services on a much more lavish scale than had been possible before, the advocates of big government arrived. They claimed that all this was dreadful unless it was put under global regulation – and unless some taxes were collected from the proceeds. More than the underlying process of expanding trade and choice, it is this process that is causing aggravation amongst the electorates of the western countries.

As 2008 drew to a close, there was not a popular government of any longevity existing in the West. The Republican president in America, the Labour government in Britain, the right-of-centre President in France, and the Chancellor in Germany were all suffering from the same circumstances: the economic system was not delivering. People will turn to blame the domestic national incumbent, the person who is most prominent and best-known on the national and world stage, for the way in which incomes are under pressure. As this book illustrates, there is no evidence that governments' rash of taxes and global regulation, sparked as a result of the more successful globalisation of trade in goods and services, has done anything to prevent the problems. Indeed, in many respects the higher taxes and more intensive regulation have been the problem; they have exacerbated, rather than dampened, the impact of the cycle and encouraged, rather than prevented, the over-enthusiastic build-up of credit which led to the collapse.

9 | Skills & training

INTRODUCTION

The global marketplace is not just a coming together of trading in goods and services across frontiers; it is also a growing marketplace in skills and intellectual property. While the credit crunch was made more difficult because so much money moved around – over national frontiers and between continents, increasing the complexity and the volumes of outstanding credits and transactions – so the arrival of more global trading is beginning to create a global marketplace in skills and management.

Many multinational companies are run by people of very different backgrounds, nationalities and languages. Although the common international business language is English, used for accounts, board meetings and much internal discussion within multinational companies, it is quite common for there to be a multitude of people at the top of big companies who, daily, speak different languages and who come from very different backgrounds. The trade unions are worried about the 'race to the bottom': they see the advent of the global labour market as meaning that there is downward pressure on wages in the high-cost, advanced countries because activities and employment can be switched so readily to lower-wage countries, where people are more willing to accept poorer terms and conditions.

The global market can increase the range of incomes, while at the same time pushing upwards the global average; strong competition for people with the best business skills means superstar salaries for the people at the top of the ever-larger global corporations. Companies can afford these salaries, because they are so much bigger – and with so much more turnover and profit; the superstars are able to attract these salaries, because the elite of senior international business people is still quite small, relative to the ever-growing demand for new multinationals and for management to expand the existing multinationals.

THE FOOTBALL ECONOMY

The extreme movements are clearly visible in the growing globalisation of the so-called 'beautiful game', soccer. Originating in Britain and Western Europe, soccer has spread worldwide. People in the Middle East are keen to train better teams and to buy stakes in the best European clubs. People in Asia, similarly, want not only to have a good local team – but are prepared to spend fantastic sums of money on acquiring interests in western clubs. At a lower level, they spend considerable money on television access to the games and achievements of the best western clubs.

As soon as European clubs realised that they were no longer constrained by the 20-50,000 people they could get into their own grounds each Saturday to watch their principal fixtures, they felt very liberated. Instead of concentrating on the experience of those who attended the stadium, they could concentrate on the television experience which could be sold to, literally, hundreds of millions of viewers around the world, through the TV channels and digital outlets. A new market opened up for the live TV footage, for the TV footage in replay mode, and for the video or DVD of the games for those who wished to watch it at some later date. This new market, in turn, generated many more people wanting to buy football ephemera: match programmes, football kit, magazines and details of the lives of the footballers and their achievements on (and off) the field. Celebrity football grew bigger and bigger, with celebrity magazines following the fashions of the footballers' wives, the details of their romances, their passions, the managerial stories behind the fabulous transfer fees and the attempts to bid and counter-bid to attract the best talent.

The more the best clubs could gain money from a wider world audience for the football matches, the more they could afford to spend on bidding wars to attract the best players. An elite cadre of superstar players emerged, the people who were judged best to play at the highest level in the inter-club competitions in Europe. As managers with big cheque books provided by billionaire backers fought each other in the transfer market, so we moved from a world where £1 million had been a big transfer fee, to a world where £10 million was now a big transfer fee – and on to a world where a payment of £50 million may well be feasible for a single player.

The extremes in football have been exacerbated by the fact that some people funding the businesses are not taking just a business or investment judgment; they see the advantages of the publicity that the celebrity status of club owner can bring. Buying a substantial stake in a western football club, and becoming part of the court that surrounds the glamour and the celebrity, can be an attractive option. It may also not be a poor business decision: while you may not get a good financial return on your investment – you may even end up subsidising the club's losses – you may get enough publicity and benefit out of your association to promote other business interests. And, as with all investments, an investment in players and clubs can prove financially beneficial: although apparently unconnected to much financial reality, their value can rise as well as fall and, with suitable timing, successful business people can make money.

The football case is one of the most difficult for socialist criticism of the global market. While most socialists abhor capitalism in general – and dislike global capitalism in particular because, as they see it, it gives the rich so much more opportunity to get richer – they understand the popular support for the game of soccer. It would be a brave socialist who wished to stop the better-known and richer clubs from attracting the best talent, and an even braver socialist who actually introduced controls over the amount that clubs could spend. Socialist-style controls in one country would clearly not work; any such intervention would soon lead to even more of the talent being attracted offshore, to countries which were not taking such a line. Even if our theoretical socialist could get salary and transfer fee controls placed at a

European Union level, it would simply hasten the day when more talent was drawn away to Asia and the Americas. And this would lead to the reverse process to the present: more and more European viewers would pay substantial sums to watch the best talent playing games in faraway places, instead of people in faraway places paying large sums to watch the games in Europe. For a socialist, the problem with globalisation is that – if you are to fulfil your ambitions to control, plan and prevent extremes of remuneration and reward – you need to do it on a global basis.

THE RIGHT RATE FOR THE JOB

It is conventional now for parties of the left throughout Europe to attack high levels of remuneration by business people, at the same time as accepting high levels of remuneration by sports or entertainment personalities, especially in the over-extended area of soccer. The best business people generally attract less than the best soccer stars – although there have been examples in financial services and elsewhere of people who have reached these levels of remuneration through bonus payments related to measures of achievement, revenue and profit.

One of the interesting questions the market needs to answer, and will do over the years ahead, is whether the talent pool for the best management of global corporations is really as narrow and restricted as many businesses seem to think it is. Is it acceptable that the talent pool for a chief executive of a major corporation comprises that group of people who have already probably failed (or not distinguished themselves very well) at a comparable level in other corporations? Are the headhunters right to concentrate on people who have already done the job with greater or lesser success, or who are making a small step up from doing the job in a smaller company – rather than thinking more laterally, and bringing in new talent which might be good at the job? While the global marketplace is a very big place, and it is possible to find talent from different geographical areas and a wide range of companies, there is still a certain narrowness and reluctance to promote at the top of many of these large corporations.

The typical chief executive is male, in his 40s and has spent all or most of his time in large corporations. This may not always identify the best talent.

The traditional model has been rather colonial in its basis. The great multinationals were established by, primarily, the Americans and the leading European nations. They set up branch activities and new factories in Asia, Africa and Latin America in order to exploit their brands and to bring their design, their innovation, their marketing skills and their abilities as organisers of labour and capital, to places in the world far beyond their origins. Traditionally, they sent out senior management from the home country to organise local management and recruit local labour.

The advent of Japanese success added Japanese management to this approach: senior Japanese managers turning up in European countries, to establish Japanese factories capable of organising labour effectively to produce cars, electrical goods and the other Japanese successes. The Japanese rewrote the books on how to run manufacturing industry.

More recently, the advent of large Indian and Chinese corporations in the global marketplace (thus adding to the variety developed by the Europeans, Americans and Japanese) has meant a further blending of senior management. Meanwhile the Europeans and Americans have got better at picking senior managerial talent from outside the country of the multinational's headquarters. We now see, at the top of multinationals – wherever they may have originated – managers from a wide variety of countries, including senior management recruited from countries that have no great tradition of developing large multinational corporations themselves. These multinational linkages of management can bring their own strengths. It means that the multinational can draw on direct linguistic and cultural experience from a wide range of countries, to avoid faux pas in developing its goods and services and to ensure more empathy with each individual marketplace as it goes about its task of selling worldwide. It means that the multinationals draw on a wider range of cultural understanding, practices and viewpoints.

It also poses new problems and challenges for the governments and peoples of countries responding to multinational investment and seeking to cooperate with, or do deals with, the larger multinationals from outside the host territory. Most countries, these days, welcome inward investment by multinationals – from wherever they may come. The process of joining the global marketplace is one of a host country deciding that it now wishes to be part of the system of global capital and global enterprise organisation; it wishes to be a suitable location for an inward investor to establish sales, offices, to build factories, to recruit service sector professionals and to supply the local market. When a multinational turns from simply selling its product into another country's marketplace, to establishing a proper manufacturing and service centre in that country, it represents a deepening of the relationship. It also means that the host country gets more of the added value for herself: it now pockets the wages, salaries and much of the supply contract value that would otherwise have been paid outside the country, had she only been importing the goods or services.

Those countries which do not welcome inward investment by multinationals are usually planned Marxist or authoritarian regimes; they have decided to stay much poorer because they wish to retain control over the employees and other inhabitants of their country. They do not wish to have to deal with the vagaries and complexities of the global marketplace. When they make their investments in a low-income country, multinationals often attract substantial criticism from left-of-centre parties and interests in the West, who argue that the multinational is arriving in order to exploit the local labour force. The very people who would otherwise promote more, and better, jobs for that country become critics of the multinational for daring to come into the country in the first place: although they are offering good wages by that country's standards, the wages are clearly below the level that would be offered in an advanced country.

Those on the left pose two moral dilemmas about this process. The traditional trade union objects to the multinational hiring people in the, say, African country: they see it as undercutting employment and wage rates in a first-world country. They oppose it for selfish reasons. Why, they reason, should the multinational be allowed to sack (or not employ) people in, say, Britain in order to hire people in, say, Nigeria – just because Nigerians are prepared to do a similar job for lower wages than British? Isn't this social dumping? Doesn't this negate or nullify much of the work western progressive parties of right, left and centre have done to ensure higher wages and better protection for employees in the West?

The other left-wing criticism is almost the opposite. While they welcome the advent of jobs in the new country, they condemn the multinational for not paying 'enough' to the local workforce, compared with the wages being paid in the more advanced world.

Both these arguments betray economic naivety, as well as some selfishness. In a way they are advancing the same cause: the cause that the multinational should not practice or intervene in the African country's market at all. If the multinational did what the second set of critics are implying – offer western level wages in the African country – it would be a very strange intervention indeed. A relatively few people in a poor African country would, suddenly, be paid wages beyond the dreams of avarice, giving them enormous spending power and riches in that country. Because there is a much bigger pool of available talent than necessary for the low-level – but now (relatively) well-paid – activities in the multinational corporation, there would be great anger and competition between those who wanted the jobs. The jobs would become valuable items, probably traded on the African market itself as local people developed systems for sharing the super incomes that only the privileged few managed to obtain. It would be quite difficult for the multinational to police this sensibly and ensure that all of the income they were paying went to the operative or administrator concerned, without some leakage.

The sensible thing for the multinational to do when it arrives is to offer wages slightly above the local market rate. It needs to do this to attract sufficient talent and demonstrate that it is making a contribution to making people better off. If it offers them pay which is significantly higher, it creates jealousy and artificial scarcity of those jobs and makes policing the system extremely difficult.

The global marketplace delivers raised living standards in all the areas where multinationals operate, with their superior technology, strong brands, good training and good labour organisation. It gives individuals the opportunity to learn, to grow and to move to other countries to increase their pay. Whilst the shop floor or administrative staff may receive wages on a par with the local labour market, those who make the grade to more senior management leapfrog to much better pay rates, based upon the global market rates for middle and senior management. At this level, differences in remuneration compared to the poorer country can become significant, but very often the footloose and fancy-free multinational executives need the higher pay because they are living all or part of the time in more expensive countries. However, as this process continues, living standards will tend to rise more rapidly in the poorer countries than they do in the richer countries. The intensity of Chinese development has seen an explosion in salaries and wages for millions of Chinese (in the larger cities) who have joined the global marketplace by being recruited by large foreign companies and the Chinese multinationals which are plugged into this wider market.

THE SPREAD OF KNOWLEDGE

The same is true of the more entrepreneurial people who come up with business ideas. Until quite recently, business people were prevented from disseminating their ideas too widely, by the barriers of transport and language. Indeed, entrepreneurs used to be constrained just to their own town or county: travelling was expensive, long-winded and arduous. Advertising beyond the local area was either prohibitively expensive or impossible – and buying goods or services from a distant town or county would also have been problematic. In pre-industrial England, businesses were more likely to be county- or town-based than they were to be national.

The industrial revolution produced better transport and more of a national market, with national media to communicate messages and to spread the word about goods and services. More, and bigger, national companies emerged. Similarly, globalisation has enabled more direct access to the world market than ever before. Whereas, 30 years ago, only the biggest multinational with huge budgets could hope to make its presence felt throughout the world, today access through the Internet (using the English language) gives even the smallest of businesses immediate access to hundreds of millions of people who could be potential contributors, consumers or suppliers.

Before the advent of the Internet, a business seeking a world market, or wanting to buy in from the best in the world, needed to have a physical presence in every national area. It needed to brief newspapers, buy television advertisements and communicate locally through offices, agents and local advertising media. Today, even the humblest of businesses can put their offering on the web and, with some modest expenditure, buy good links. If they choose the right keywords and the right language they may get picked up by the increasing array of people hunting the Internet, worldwide, for the best offerings and the most interesting services. It is possible now to rapidly grow a business from very humble beginnings by web-based, global, communication. Some of the previous constraints have been removed from the entrepreneur, who now has a choice of home base location, with a wider window onto (or from) the global world.

While governments, particularly in the advanced world, are busily trying to make it more difficult and more expensive for entrepreneurs to develop their services and produce their goods by regulating and making life much more complicated, the digital revolution is driving things in the opposite direction: making it easier for entrepreneurs, people with good ideas, to set up in the cheapest jurisdictions and to promote themselves using simple and inexpensive technology.

We can see the speeding up which the digital age has achieved by looking at the colossal and rapid growth of modern multinationals. 15 years ago, no one had any idea that companies such as Google and Yahoo would come to dominate Internet global communication. Just as Microsoft emerged rapidly and dramatically as a huge player on the world stage, by developing crucial software to extend the range and improve the accessibility of computing to hundreds of millions of new people, so the great search engines made the Internet accessible and useful for those same hundreds of millions of people, now linked into the global market directly – from their bedroom, their study, their office or, on the move, from their laptops.

The power of the digital revolution and the speed at which ideas can travel has also affected the way that markets in individual countries respond to international and global financial events. Today, news of a banking problem in New York or Newcastle or Frankfurt can spread instantaneously through Internet and television communication. More and more people come to see that they are part of a plugged in and wired world. The digital age means that events in New York and London are relevant in Beijing and Singapore and can be heard about as they happen. Because there is much common ground in the actions of governments, regulators and large corporations in the major centres of the world, a shock administered to the system in one jurisdiction quickly transmits to others. Indeed, worse than that: if New York discovers that it has weak banks and too much credit extended through American actions, it is almost certain that London, Frankfurt, Singapore, Beijing and Mumbai would soon discover very similar problems. The old diversification of the world, based upon national and regional segregation in the markets, different languages and different cultures, has been changed to a system where, so often, the regulators, governments and leading corporations reinforce their mistakes by duplicating them from jurisdiction to jurisdiction.

As the credit crunch unfolded, it became more difficult for the European administrations to maintain that this was a credit crunch made in America by Americans, with very little implication for European banks and markets. It soon became obvious that the American sub-prime market had collapsed. It also became obvious that American sub-prime mortgages had been packaged up and sold on the security markets of the world. These packages, 'assets' of rapidly falling value, were just as likely to turn up in the balance sheets of European or Asian banks as in the balance sheets of the originating American providers. Worse still, it soon emerged that, far from the over-extension of credit being a phenomenon just of the American mortgage market, it was also apparent in the Spanish mortgage market, the British mortgage market and the German banking system.

Low interest rates and easy credit had been the norm around the world. Central banks had followed each other's lead in driving interest rates down and keeping them low. Banking regulators around the world had followed the lead of America and others in turning a blind eye to the creation of massive credit through securitised vehicles; they had been relaxed about the very favourable terms offered to borrowers, on the grounds that we were living through a non-inflationary, risk-free era. This was a collective folly of governments and regulators, driven by a collective greed or passion by the world's banks to write more business that knew no boundaries; it was drawing on the digital revolution, the communication of information and the rapid spread of ideas that the global marketplace facilitated.

This has made some say that the process of spreading ideas and innovation around the world has now gone too far; it is creating problems where its advocates had been claiming that it would produce a better world. What has happened is not just that the process of transmission has evolved where there was none before – but that the process of transmission has become faster and more enthusiastically followed. It is difficult to say that it is a fundamental weakness of western capitalism that it is now able to export its bad ideas around the world as quickly and easily as its good ideas. Overall, the impact of the arrival of new technology, new ideas, better organisation and more money in poorer countries is positive rather than negative.

Clearly, training people in local, poorer, communities to perform to higher standards and to earn more money is the way to get them out of poverty. At the same time, if this means importing mistakes from the governments and regulators of the western world, and if it means the multinationals of the world reinforcing the mistakes they are making elsewhere in the first world, it is difficult to see how this can be prevented. Those who dislike it do so ideologically; they do not like the idea of free choice and free enterprise. However, they never really explain to us how you can prevent it: after all, the Internet cannot be removed or disinvented. You cannot stop people in poor countries wanting access to the best ideas and technology available in the west, and you cannot stop people in the poorer countries replicating and reproducing the mistakes or the bad ideas that do, from time to time, get made in the west as part of the market process. It is probably best to say that what we need is intelligent government and intelligent regulation of a counter-cyclical nature, instead of unintelligent central banking and central regulation which has characterised the violent swings of the last cycle.

EDUCATION AND TRAINING

Just as there is now a global market in senior management and a global market in football players, just as there is now a global market in commercial ideas and regulatory ideas which speeds their transmission, so there is an emerging global market in education and training. As in so much else, the educational field is dominated by the Americans. The United States has most of the top-ten, best-ranked, universities in the world. The rankings are based upon the number of times the research papers and writings of the faculty members are cited and used by other academics, on the amount of money and resource backing the educational institution, on the educational attainment of their students and the student-lecturer ratios. The gap between the best in America and the rest is actually growing, as the American universities at the top of the table prove superior in raising more money from their alumni and in investing their endowments more successfully, so that their funds grow more quickly.

As in much of business life and in top sporting activity, money is power. If you are a leading institution with more endowment funds and more income than rival institutions around the world, you are the institution which can attract the top talent to the faculties. You can pay more to secure the Nobel Prize winners and the leading researchers in your field. Once you have done so you then naturally attract the best students in the field – and the virtuous circle is completed: best faculty, leading to best students, best fund-raising opportunities, best faculty, best students, and so on.

The United Kingdom has demonstrated, with Oxford and Cambridge universities, that it is possible to stay in the international top 10, operating from a more modest capital base. Even over the last decade, when the United Kingdom government has been at best lacklustre and at worst positively hostile in its approach to our leading universities, Oxford and Cambridge have managed to maintain their positions in the league tables, a bit below Harvard. They have shown that excellence can also be based upon long traditions and upon the romance and history of a great university as well as upon their innate abilities as fundraisers and modern managers.

Nonetheless, the world is getting more competitive by the day and there is a danger that many of the European institutions, including the two leaders, Oxford and Cambridge, will fall behind. It is going to require ever-bigger sums of money to compete for the best talent. The same pressures, of digitalisation and the Internet circulating ideas ever-more quickly and creating ever-bigger markets for the successful, are having their impact on education. Top faculty members will command ever-bigger salaries – just as top soccer or baseball stars do. Universities which do not have the money or the will to pay these salaries will gradually fall behind in reputation and esteem.

While at the moment many in China and India are still very happy to come to Harvard, Yale, Princeton, Oxford and Cambridge for the education of their top talent, the leading universities of India and China are on the rise and are busily trying to emulate and supplant the excellence that they see in the western academies. Indian and Chinese students are diligent and keen to learn. They find some of the caricatured antics of western students difficult to grasp, as they see the joy of a place at a leading world university as a great opportunity, a meal ticket for life, the chance to earn fabulous money (by the standards of their home countries), based upon the skills and the confidence that a top education can impart to them.

When the Vice-Chancellor of Cambridge University recently visited China to give a lecture on her university, one of the first questions she was asked came from someone who rattled off the achievements and scientific breakthroughs of many Cambridge University's alumnae, and then asked how the Chinese could establish a university which could match that record for finding and nurturing talent. Needless to say, the Vice-Chancellor of Cambridge courteously declined to give a long and too-informative answer on how to do it. The very fact that this is a recurring Chinese question, and they are keen to engage in conversation with top universities from the West, should alert us to the fact that, just as in the commercial world, India and China are now intending to become serious forces to be reckoned with in the academic world as well.

Some western schools and universities are waking up to this New World reality. A recent visit to Harrow informed me that Harrow now has two Harrow schools in Asia, using the brand, skills and the tradition to make an offering relevant to the Asian conditions – but still based upon the excellence of the home product. English universities have, for some years, been setting up outposts or satellite universities in leading Asian centres, aware that there are many talented Asians who would like the advantage of an English-style degree but would prefer to have it in a modern institution based nearer to their home than Nottingham or London.

The success of both the New World universities gradually recruiting more talent and learning from the best in the West, and the success of the western universities in raising the numbers they can educate to a higher standard and extending their doors to new premises in Asia, is crucial to avoiding too many shortages of talent and skill as the world economic revolution continues.

Globalisation is bringing 2,500 million Indians and Chinese to the western party. Although there will be bumps along the way – the credit crunch being a good example – the trend is clearly onwards and upwards. The advent of so many people on the verge of higher incomes is creating a huge demand for more graduate-level, talented people capable of providing the engineering, financial, legal and management skills to power the new wave of large corporations and smaller entrepreneurial businesses which will be generating the action and the growth that their new host economies are needing.

THE RISE AND FALL OF JAPAN

In the 1960s, when Japan emerged from middle-income to higher-income status, there were many in the West quite dismissive about what they were doing. We were told that the Japanese simply copied western designs and plans. Silly jokes were circulating that if we designed articles that didn't work and sent the blueprint to Japan they would end up making them. We were told that the Japanese would never develop an independent capacity to change or improve technology and product, and would never develop blue skies research in their universities.

How wrong all those critics were. Japan rapidly rose to the position where it was supreme in automotive and consumer electricals and electronics. Its brands had more lustre than many of the western brands with which they were competing. The Japanese started using their own Japanese names to sell the product instead of trying to 'disguise' their product with western-sounding names. They showed that they were masters of incremental innovation, launching and relaunching a product in subtly modified ways, such that each version was an improvement on the previous one – without huge revolutionary change worrying customers or entailing too much risk for the company making it. Over a decade or more, by incremental innovation, Japanese products moved effortlessly into top-selling and top technical slots, demonstrating a great firmness of purpose. Japanese university education also rose in stature and excellence.

It is true that, when the great advance of the digital revolution came, America left not just the Soviet Union standing, unable to compete with this completely new way of looking at things, but also left Japan standing. The Japan of 1989 was at the top of its game. People were making unfavourable comparisons between America and Japan, saying that Japan was the new economic giant, strong at exporting, with strong reserves and a well-run economy – compared with what people thought was a weakening, credit-ridden and debt-ridden US performance.

Instead, it turned out that 1989-90 was the peak of an enormous credit bubble in Japan. This had inflated property and share prices beyond recognition, with an economy based upon a rather narrow industrial base subject to cheaper and more aggressive competition from lower-wage countries, and subject to a huge backlash from American competition as the US powered ahead with the digital revolution. The all-conquering microchip from Silicon Valley was soon turning all kinds of machines on and off, making possible all sorts of new word processors, computers, telecommunications equipment, and fitting together the world of the computer, the world of the television and the world of the telephone in a way in which engineers and electronics specialists from Japan to Europe had scarcely dreamt about, let alone been able to do.

The excellence of America's science base, academic university base and entrepreneurial base came to the fore. American digital supremacy swept all before it. The mighty Soviet Union was humbled and broke up, unable to compete with the military implications of American technology. Japan was put into her place and entered a long period of little or no growth, attempting to sort out the mess created in her banking system and her general financial system by over-inflated property and share prices and too little collateral for loans. Europe was left floundering, wedded to a project of political and economic union which seemed to have little or no relevance to the real challenge of matching and competing with the American achievement in service, industry and technology.

In the modern global world, new centres will arise that will be capable of innovation and enterprise. In the transitional period for China and India, as for Japan, much of the process will be transferring technology that Europe and America has already established, effortlessly and smoothly, to Chinese and Indian conditions and demands. We should not, however, think that China and India will, in perpetuity, merely wish to emulate or copy technology made elsewhere. China and India will be looking to rival and to contribute to the technology already in existence in the West and will be reinforcing the growing excellence, breadth and scale of their university offering in order to do so.

THE RISE OF LONDON

The United Kingdom has earned a good living in recent years through specialising in business, professional and financial services, and through reinforcing the success of London, its leading global city. As we have seen, much of the growth of the United Kingdom as a whole has come from London and the South East; within that, it has come from heavily concentrated areas of London, populated by a growing international class of senior financial executives, professional service people and entrepreneurs from around the world. London has become a great metropolis of ideas, a meeting place for moneyed people from around the world, a place where new services, new financial and business technology, and new administrative systems can be tested out and developed. It has produced its own version of the Japanese property boom, with more and more money concentrated in the hands of rich people and businesses chasing fewer and fewer properties in a narrow number of postal districts around SW1, SW6 and W1. The giddy prices of one, two or even three thousand pounds per square foot have been happily paid to purchase larger flats and houses in Belgravia, in Kensington and Chelsea, in Notting Hill and in Mayfair. People just needed to be in London because, like New York, it was one of the big, buzzing cities of the world where people of enterprise and skill met and dealt with each other.

The United Kingdom has experienced its own version of the growing gap between the haves and the have-nots; between the skilled, enterprising and well-trained on the one hand, and people lacking in skill, good training and energy on the other. In Britain, a strong welfare net has made sure that no one goes without food, shelter, clothing or other basic necessities of modern living. The benefit system is generous by world standards and the administrative hassle of claiming benefits not normally too great an impediment to the millions who need or wish to do so.

EDUCATION, EDUCATION, EDUCATION

The Labour government came to power repeating Conservative language about wishing to have opportunity for all, adding some Labour flavour to the effect that it wished to remove inequalities from Britain. It went on a crusade to tackle what it called child poverty, the fact that too many children were born to single parents or to couples who were not at work and had only benefits to live on. Studies showed that children from financially deprived backgrounds tended to do worse at school, tended to live in areas clustered around poorer performing schools and tended to inherit a sense of helplessness from their local community. Many of these children felt that good grade GCSEs and A-levels were not attainable and that, therefore, university or higher skills training was out of reach.

There were no political objections to Labour's wish to spend more on education and to see if doing so might break this cycle of depravation. Conservative and Labour, Liberal Democrat and most others were united in wishing to see opportunity extended to every district and council estate in the country. There was also unity across the political spectrum in agreeing that it was worth trying out the proposition that spending more overall (and spending even more in targeted areas of relative deprivation) would be the way forward. Eleven years into the experiment, the sad truth is that, if anything, educational opportunities have grown less equal – with the examination-intensive systems liked by Labour apparently favouring middle-class areas more than lower-income areas. Certainly, the gap between the best independent schools and the best-performing state schools has grown very much in favour of the former. The more that Labour has railed and ranted in trying to stop the independent schools doing so well, the more they have succeeded. Labour has set the Charity Commissioners onto the private schools, setting them ever-higher hurdles in order to maintain charitable status. The schools have met these hurdles with ease, making ever-bigger contributions to their local communities and extending more scholarships to people on low income, giving the Charity Commissioners no opportunity to take away their favoured tax status.

The government has complained to Oxford, Cambridge and other leading universities that they are recruiting too many students from the independent school sector, and has told them to address this inequality. The major universities have responded magnificently, with active promotion to state schools, encouraging pupils to get the grades and to apply to the better universities. Despite this, and despite every effort made by those undertaking university selection, the independent schools are capable of regularly achieving half of the places at Oxford and Cambridge – even though they only account for under 10 per cent of the total pupils in secondary education, and under 20 per cent of the pupils undertaking A-level work.

There is now a growing awareness across the political spectrum that money is not the only answer. Of course, it is true that the leading independent schools still spend far more per pupil than the state schools. It is also true that part of the reason for the expenditure difference is that many of the independent schools are boarding establishments and have to provide entertainment, lodging and food which would otherwise be supplied at home. These costs are not included in the expenditure for state school pupils. It is also true that, even allowing for this, the expenditure per pupil remains considerably higher in the leading independent schools than even in the best-funded state schools in the poorest areas.

However, it is also true that there is no closing of the achievement gap between the best-funded state schools in the poorer areas and the worst-funded state schools in the middle class areas. If anything, the gap has grown in favour of the latter despite the growing disproportion of funding in favour of the former. This has led people to realise that educational achievement is driven not just by the amount of money that is spent, but also by how that money is spent. It is not just about budgets – but also about leadership, expectations and ambitions for pupils.

There is a growing sense of fear in some of the more advanced western nations when they see the excellence of the schools and universities now emerging within Asia. We have to earn our living largely by our wits. Many people in our country now earn their living slaving over a word processor, behind a desk or using a computer. They need to be computer-literate, as well as generally literate and numerate. We are now living by having better investment funds, organising better companies, arranging better contracts, offering better engineering advice, designing better buildings, designing better marketing strategies and designing better commercial products. We no longer primarily make our way in the world by being the workshop of the world – nor even by being the shopkeepers of the world. We are now, mainly, the financial and professional advisers to the world. This requires the training and recruitment of ever-more talented people capable of serving an ever-faster growing world market in these skills. To be able to do so, many more people are going to have to join the educational party in Britain. Labour are right to say there should be no artificial ceiling on the numbers that can go to university, no attempt to ration or to provide quotas which militate against children from poorer backgrounds. Labour are wrong, however, to say that we must just set a target for an increasing number of young people to go to university when they have not met the standards required to go, nor have acquired the basic skills that enable them to get most benefit out of a university education.

I do not favour a quota or target – and I am certainly strongly against restricting opportunity. For a country such as Britain, one that will depend on the future skills of its population, the answer must be that we encourage more young people to achieve the grades at A-level. More importantly, they must also achieve those skills at English and mathematics, at research and computing, that are necessary to be able to get the fullest benefit from a university education. It is no good fooling ourselves into believing that we have enough well-educated people if people no longer have confidence in the tests they have passed – or if the tests have been dumbed-down sufficiently such that candidates get the grades without having the understanding.

The world now has a global market in ideas, in talent, in management, in sporting ability, as well as in capital, credit, mortgages, property, goods and services. Countries, individuals, regions, towns, and cities are getting more prosperous where they specialise, where they plug into the global market and where they are capable of trading with the best. In the last couple of decades, Britain has been remarkably successful at exploiting a crucial market niche in financial and professional services. To sustain this we need to do better at education. It is good that some of our educational institutions are at last exporting and understanding the opportunities of the world market – but the scale of their activity is still tiny compared to the opportunity. If they are not to fall behind, they need to speed up before others around the world have grasped the opportunity and are providing the excellence in education through their own universities.

The world market in talent, skill, academic achievement and enterprise cannot be stopped, however much some critics of capitalism might like to. Much of this market for talent is benign, allowing more people to lead more interesting lives, with better jobs and higher incomes. There are problems with it, as the credit crunch is showing. It will mean growing gaps between rich and poor – not because the poor are getting poorer, but because the rich are getting richer. It is simply much easier to earn fabulous money if your target market is 3 billion people worldwide rather than a target market of, say, 60 million relatively well-off people in a single country such as the United Kingdom.

10 | Conclusions

INTRODUCTION

The credit crunch has provided a battleground for the warring factions on both sides of the globalisation campaign, to argue again over the wisdom and success of global capitalism. There is nothing the Left likes better than a crisis in global capitalism. It reminds them why they dislike it, gives them a cause to complain about and an opportunity to demand more regulation and more government control. The Left have certainly enjoyed the credit crunch so far – in a macabre sort of a way.

THE CASE AGAINST ...

They have argued that the simultaneous problems in banks in different parts of the world illustrate just how foolish it is to allow worldwide capitalist enterprises to link arms. While they want workers of the world to unite and create worker solidarity on a cross-national basis, they find it altogether more harmful and worrying when big businesses do the same themselves. They have argued that the credit crunch is the result of greedy bankers, greedy mortgage brokers and other greedy businesses that seek to lend too much to unsuspecting victims amongst the poor. These critics highlight the way in which certain mortgage brokers peddled mortgages to those on low income in the United States of America, daring to offer them the chance of owning their own home when the wiser Left knew that such workers were not ready for it, and might not be able to sustain the mortgage. They point to the growing greed of lenders in banks around the world, offering ever-higher multiples of earnings and ever-larger valuations of the assets against which the lending was made.

Advocates of the case against global capitalism think the credit crunch is typical of what they most dislike. It's all greed and competitive excess, leading to some people getting hurt and to many others beginning to worry about the whole process that underlay it. What is the Left's remedy? They believe the answer is simple: national governments should play a bigger role. More businesses should be nationalised, allowing wise and altruistic left-wing politicians to run them – instead of executives committed to free enterprise, seeking better returns for shareholders. They believe that central banks and regulators should take a much tougher line, limiting the amount of lending that banks and other financial institutions can offer to individuals and companies at every stage of the cycle. They see the credit crunch as a failure to regulate enough, as a failure to curb the excessive animal spirits of the free enterprise market, and a sign that things go wrong when national governments lose power and allow international companies more sway.

THE CASE FOR ...

Proponents of enterprise capitalism see it rather differently. In some senses this was not a failure of an unregulated, Wild West, cowboy industry but one that was all too excessively regulated. In many senses the failures of the western banks were the failures of the regulators themselves. It was, after all, the Basel I system of regulation which encouraged the banks and bank managers to put more and more business beyond the balance sheet. It was the regulators themselves who laid down how much capital the banks needed to sustain any given amount of loan. It was the regulators who watched benignly as the banks lent ever-larger multiples of earnings against ever-larger asset valuations. They did not demur, but rubber-stamped the loans.

Furthermore, the biggest regulators of them all, the regulators of the money markets – the central governments, the treasuries and the central banks – lay behind the whole process. The credit crunch was born of the aftermath of the hi-tech bubble. Many regulators, governments and central bankers put in place new regulations and new systems for curbing market excess as they saw the cost and damage done by the hi-tech bubble of 2000-1. At the turn of the century, sluggish performances of the economies coming out of the punctured bubble encouraged the central banks and the governments to drive interest rates down and to keep them low for a long time. In one sense this credit crunch is just another example of a very normal cycle. Central banks have interest rates too high; they push defeated economies down too low, as they did in 2001; they regret their decisions and drive interest rates low, keeping them there for too long – so inflationary pressures build up. Then, once again, the central banks raise the interest rates too high, for too long – and the whole sorry process reverses. This credit crunch may look different, it may be on a much bigger scale, it may have hit more countries simultaneously, but it has many of the similar, simple characteristics of all the credit cycles of the last 50 years. Central banks overdo the loose money – and then they overdo the tight money.

SO WHO IS AT FAULT?

These errors in central banking and regulation do not, of course, mean that all the private sector banks and mortgage brokers are blameless. Of course, it is true that the banks and the mortgage brokers did not have to respond as dramatically as they did to the ever-looser monetary conditions on offer from the central authorities. Of course, wise bankers could still have decided to require bigger deposits, to be cautious about the valuations of the properties that secured their mortgages, and to counsel caution over the multiples of income that people were allowed to borrow. Indeed, some did just that and were happy to see their market share decline as others, with vaunting ambition, took advantage of the easy-money conditions.

It would, however, have been very surprising if all the banks had effectively gone on strike and told the central bank that they were making things too easy for them; that they should be reined in and not allowed to grow their businesses as quickly as possible. It is more natural for banks and bank managers to respond positively in the upswing of the cycle when the central bank and the governing authorities are giving the green light to the expansion of balance sheets and the lending of more money.

Nor should we see what was going on as an entirely unfriendly process. The flip-side of what the Left sees – too many poor people with too much debt – is the success that was experienced in the credit upswing, with many more lower-paid and lower-income people being able to afford their own house. They will not all struggle to maintain it and they will not all lose it in the downswing.

The biggest weakness in the left-wing critique of global capitalism and the credit crunch is in believing that there is a better system on offer. The credit crunch itself has produced some governmental and regulatory answers of the kind the Left desires. It is extremely unlikely that these proposals will stop a future credit cycle. Indeed, it is much more likely that the authorities have overdone the gloom and doom in the downswing so they will, at the same time, nurture the seeds of the next upswing. Who is to say that governments have learnt any more this time around than they did in previous cycles? Indeed, so late and so vigorous is the response of the US and UK authorities to the recession, they may well be sowing the seeds of future inflation, as I write. I have never seen such a huge injection of cash, nor such low interest rates before. All the time the banks remain weak, the money will simply be lent back to governments; once the banks are stable, there is huge liquidity in the system on which they can lend – and restart the inflationary engines.

It is difficult to see why it should be the case that nationalised banks, allied to stronger regulatory controls over the amount that banks could lend, would be any better at getting things right. If, universally, we moved over to such a system in one or more countries as a result of the credit crunch, it is more likely that we would create an unpleasant austerity. In a democracy there would, in due course, be growing pressure against the nationalised banks and the nationalised regulator for being too mean with the number of advances they were prepared to make. As political pressure mounted and as General Elections came closer, it is quite conceivable that a nationalised, regulated system of rationing or credit control would, in its turn, usher in much looser money and much more lending in response to political pressures. Worst still, any such system would replace the judgments of many groups of shareholders and many different chief executives at different banks by the judgment of just one or two people at the top of the political and financial establishment. Who is to say that they would be any better at getting it right than central banks have proved in recent years? Why should we think that, suddenly, central banks and banking regulators would be able to make wise judgments when in the past they have been part of the problem? Maybe it is better to carry on with the multitude of decision makers in a free-enterprise, competitive market, as that way some will get it right and only some will get it wrong.

More importantly, any country that wishes to remain part of the global network would be quite unable to follow such a policy. Let us suppose that a strongly socialist government was elected to office in the United Kingdom and decided to place the principal UK-based banks under public ownership and decided to ration credit to agreed levels. Unless it simultaneously created a siege economy, broke many of the rules of international and European Union trade – and imposed strict limits on the amount of money that could come into and out of the country – it would find its task all but impossible. In the modern, footloose world where money passes across frontiers at the press of a mouse button and a click of a computer key, it would soon discover that its plans to ration credit within the UK system were thwarted by the ideas of many commercial banks from abroad capable of lending and transferring money into the United Kingdom from outside. The only countries that truly ration credit are the poorest countries of the world, those under communist regimes which use a range of techniques, from the brutal to the simply stupid, to make sure that their citizens do not have access to the advantages of the global marketplace. As it is, the UK government has nationalised one complete mortgage bank, Northern Rock; the mortgage book of another, Bradford and Bingley; has taken a majority shareholding in RBS – and a large stake in Lloyds/HBOS, whose merger it also permitted.

A NATIONALISED BANKING INDUSTRY

The UK will find itself with substantial financial problems as a result of its recent nationalisations. The strategy being pursued is piecemeal, born of the 24-hour news cycle to which government is slave, and of its wish to be seen to be doing something at each twist of the crisis. The policy towards the two mortgage banks appears to be to put them into run-off. They are not allowed to make attractive offers of new mortgages in the market. The government wants its cash back from both, so it encourages repayment of outstanding mortgages without replacement business. The government is less the owner, more the administrator of the wind up. More recently the government has changed its mind on Northern Rock, and now wants the bank to undertake some new lending.

Its approach to RBS is altogether different. It sees it as a going concern, and claims it wishes the bank to be managed by professional bankers, at arm's length. A holding company structure mediates between government and the board of the bank, where the directors and chief executive of UK Financial Investments Ltd are to supervise the conduct of the RBS board. RBS has to compete, as before, against the private sector UK and overseas banks. It will be interesting to see if the government can resist the obvious pressures which will develop: to intervene more directly in how much RBS lends – and to whom – as the recession deepens, and to see if the board structures in place act as any kind of buffer against political interference. Given the scale of the potential losses on a bank with £2 trillion of assets, it is important that the government does keep a close eye on how its independent directors and managers are doing; RBS alone could lose the country the equivalent of a medium-sized government department's entire budget in a year.

Any sensible person recognises that globalisation is here to stay. It is obvious that more and more skilled people around the world wish to offer their goods and services to the world market. It is clear, also, that the digital revolution, instant communications and the use of the Internet as an artery of commerce, all point in the direction of more trade in goods and services flowing across national borders. The sensible person understands that this requires big international banks; it also requires wisdom and common sense by the competing jurisdictions and monetary authorities of the world in trying to create a reasonably stable framework.

STABLE FRAMEWORKS

It is to the question of how we create a more stable national and global framework for the future that we must now turn. What lessons can we draw from the difficult experiences of both the boom years in the middle of the first decade of the 21st century and the bust years at the end of that decade?

The first conclusion we have to draw is that central banks need to get better at judging the cycle. All too often they exaggerate the cycle by being slow to respond in each direction. Although the Monetary Policy Committee of the Bank of England, for example, employs (at considerable salaries) very talented people with a great deal of economic wisdom and acumen, the collective result of their deliberations in recent years has been to aggravate the cycle rather than dampen it. During the period when too much credit was building up (with the threat of subsequent inflation) they were quite sure there was no danger – because the actual inflation being recorded was quite low. When there was far too little credit being created, and high interest rates were making the problem even worse, they were quite sure that there remained a large inflation threat because the inflation figures coming through were still high. Talented and experienced economists seem to have forgotten the leads and lags. In the good years they were unable to see that, at a certain point, too much credit chasing too few goods and services is inflationary and will create price increases somewhere. They ignored the warning signs that were obvious for anyone to see: property prices in the United Kingdom were going through the roof; commodity prices worldwide were starting their giddy climb. Still they felt there was nothing inflationary – or even speculative – in those figures. In a rather wooden way, they claimed that Britain was short of houses and the world was short of oil, and that all that was taking place was a shift in relative prices. Instead, it should have been obvious to them that there was excess credit sloshing into markets such as property and commodities, with a great deal of speculation on top.

In the downswing these same people were, apparently, unable to see that we were extremely short of credit: interest rates were high and banking regulations were forcing banks to raise more money before they could lend more money. When an economy is short of credit then, at a certain point, that shortage affects markets for goods and services. The volume of demand falls and the price can collapse. We saw the oil price fall from $147 a barrel to under $110 a barrel in a couple of months. The Bank of England's Monetary Policy Committee saw nothing wrong with this, and did not think in any way that it indicated there was too little credit in the world, and that maybe the inflationary problem was going away. Three months later, the collapse of the oil price to under $40 a barrel helped persuade them how wrong they had been. Property prices in the commercial UK market fell by more than a fifth in the first year of the crash. Again, the MPC looked on and felt this was just an adjustment in relative prices and did not see that it was a harbinger of wider price deflation or evidence that there was too little credit.

There is no guarantee that future members of the MPC or of the governing court of the European Central Bank will be wiser than recent incumbents. However, more public discussion about what has happened in the past and what has gone wrong might help inform them. Senior politicians, such as the Chancellor of the Exchequer in the United Kingdom and the other European Finance Ministers, should remember the problems of 2001-9, and should cross-examine the central banks more accurately if it looks as if they are going to make exactly the same kind of mistake again.

Those responsible for making appointments to the central banking committees which settle interest rates should concentrate on exploring just these issues. Maybe new candidates for office on a monetary policy committee should have to produce a paper on what they think went wrong over the last cycle, and on how they think they might avoid making similar mistakes in the future. Their attention needs to be drawn to this by those in authority, to try to prevent the same thing happening again. There is always the danger that these experts are fighting the last war, always facing in the wrong direction.

There is then the issue of what to do with the banking regulators. Banking regulation is, to some extent, global. In a way, this is a good thing. Because we have a global or widely international banking marketplace, it does make sense to agree common rules across frontiers for monitoring banks, indicating how much they can lend and how much capital they need to remain both liquid and solvent. However, there are drawbacks in these international forums and agreements, as elements of politics, gamesmanship and negotiation overlap with the minutiae of very technical discussions. Decisions based upon sensible compromises may end up being very easy for bankers and other finance houses to circumvent or outwit when they come into operation. In the first decade of the 21st century, the banking regulators were clearly asleep on the watch. With Basel I in their pocket, they felt that there was a series of quantifiable rules which could be applied to banks and which would take care of any potential problem. The presence of the international agreement and the complicated formulae gave the regulators more confidence than was justified that things would be right. If common sense and experience had been applied to the situation, more sensible decisions would almost certainly have been made.

It was, however, an understandable mistake: that it was safe to allow banks to accept all sorts of loans and business, to package these loans up into market-traded instruments and then to sell them on around the marketplace. In one sense, this is a very good thing to do. It did allow the banks to lend more money when they had securitised the last lot of loans. It also meant that large amounts of money from around the market could be used, sensibly, to lend to people with good schemes and good projects.

However, it also meant that some non-bank institutions could start to behave like banks. It meant that quite a lot of banks could get away with arranging loans – maybe to a lower standard than they would have arranged if they were going onto their own balance sheets – safe in the knowledge that they were selling them on. Many people have come to the view that, perhaps, the worst feature of the credit explosion of recent years was the rating agencies' decision to give high ratings to so much of the securitised paper (the packages of loans bundled up and sold around the marketplace). In their defence, the rating agencies say that at the time that they gave those ratings, they were correct. They, too, had some kind of quantified formula which they applied to these instruments – and these instruments met it. The rating agencies have never said that they are in the business of forecasting: a piece of AAA paper today is not guaranteed to be a piece of AAA paper tomorrow. The rating agency reserves the right to change the rating of the paper downwards, if it discovers things that have deteriorated in the trading circumstances and in the balance sheets of the underlying assets of companies. The rating agencies are validating the past – not forecasting the future. All too many people trading their bits of paper came to think that the AAA rating meant that this item would be guaranteed for the future as well as the past. Those buying the bits of paper also fell down on the job, failing to apply their own experience and judgment and their own risk appraisals to the paper they were buying.

The credit crunch became severe when the banks decided that the bits of paper they had been selling each other were not as valuable as they thought. Market trading dried up; banks could no longer play the game of making loans to people, bundling them up and selling them on – so the amount of new debt fell dramatically. Worse still, as banks and others realised that the market loans in these packages were not as strong as they had at once thought, the rating agencies started to downgrade the bits of paper. The result was that all the bits of paper owned by the different banks around the world were no longer worth what they thought they were worth. This accelerated the credit crunch more. Banks had to mark down the value of all these bits of paper, which meant they had less capital; this, in turn, meant they could lend less money to new borrowers. In some cases their capital position was so dire that they needed both to raise substantial new capital from new shareholders in the marketplace – and they needed to reduce the amount of lending they had been making.

It would be a pity if, as a result of this unfortunate era, any kind of ban was placed on the principle of securitisation. The basic concept – that banks can lend money to individuals or companies, and then sell on the loans to others in the marketplace before making new loans – is a very good one. What went wrong was that too many people in the market suspended their disbelief and bought too many of these loans at too high a price for their own comfort. What went wrong was banks took in each other's loans with a less-critical eye to their value than they should have had. The ideal outcome from this credit binge is that, at least for the next few years, banks and market makers in credit-based paper will be more circumspect; they will apply more prudent checks. The market *will* be able to resume – but at lower prices, and with a better spread of risk.

THE LOSERS

Has the world suffered from this credit crunch? Yes, clearly it has. Unfortunately there will be all too many people who suffer. Many made wrong decisions. They decided to borrow too much money or to pay too much to buy a property or to buy an investment. In one sense they only have themselves to blame for making the error. They will have to adjust their own positions, by selling the asset and repaying the loan, or by working harder so that they have enough income to pay the interest to see them through the difficult period. Many of those who bought properties at high prices will be able to carry on living in the properties and, in due course, will have the pleasurable experience of the property value exceeding the mortgage. The less-fortunate minority will be those who cease paying the loan off and have their home repossessed – or who sell at a loss and have to pay off the loss over the years ahead. There will be similar stories in the business world. Some people bought companies at too high a price – and with too much borrowing. As the world goes into a downturn, so they will struggle to pay the interest to keep the company going. Some will fail. As a result, some people will lose their jobs, some people will see their savings wiped out, and shareholders will have a miserable time. In the cases where the underlying business was sound, new shareholders and bankers may step forward, take on the company and save the jobs. The losers will be the shareholders and (probably) the original lenders. In other cases, companies will go under and stay under. The general drop in consumer demand, as disposable income reduces, means we need fewer companies and less capacity, so there will be a reduction in the number of jobs available – which in turn leads to even less disposable income and a further lowering of demand...

... AND THE WINNERS

In another sense, the credit binge leaves us a better legacy. Out of all the credit advanced, many new homes have been built. They will remain with us and will be used either by their original buyers or by others; furnishing and fittings have been made and purchased, ensuring full order books. Many great public projects have been, or will be, completed at considerable expense. Many companies have constructed new factories, new refineries, new mines and bought new computer systems which will continue to function in the years ahead. A credit binge does command real resources, pays people for working, and gets things done. Not all of it is wrong and there is a favourable legacy as well as heartache amongst those who are its casualties.

The credit crunch will not break the process of globalisation and free enterprise capitalism. The problems that the western banks have experienced, and through which many of the world's economies are now living, are not suddenly going to turn away the Indians or the Chinese from seeking western living standards. The difficulties of some people with their mortgages and their shares in the West are not suddenly going to persuade the electors of the United States of America or of Germany that they wish to turn their back upon the free enterprise system which has, by and large, delivered huge improvements in living standards over the last 50 years. The credit crunch does not suddenly prove the communists right or imply that, if only we had had a system of state planning, we would all have been richer and lived happily ever after.

The decisive experiment of the post-war period, from 1945, was won conclusively by the free enterprise system. In the East, state planning reared its ugly head. After 50 years of state planning in Eastern Europe and the former Soviet Union, people were much poorer, the economy was much weaker, the environment was suffering much more damage, and the state subverted the production process in a desperate attempt to keep up with the technology and arms of the free-enterprise West. Across the borders, in Western Europe and the United States of America, where more free enterprise was allowed, people were freer, they had more choice, their living standards were higher, less of their income was spent on weaponry and state purposes, and far more was spent by individuals and families on higher standards of food, household appliances, transport, holidays, clothing and all the other things that make life acceptable. This lesson will not be unlearned, nor will politics suddenly reverse the message from it as a result of the misfortune of the credit crunch and the damaged banks.

LESSONS FROM JAPAN

A bigger worry that some have is how long it will take to work our way through the results of the credit crunch. When Japan lived through an inflationary bubble and blow off at the end of the 1980s, she settled into a period lasting more than 10 years, with weaker banks, low credit expansion, deflation and no inflation – and found it extremely difficult to grow. However, despite the apparent poor performance throughout the 1990s, Japan remained one of the richest and most powerful economic forces in the world and, more recently, had been able to resume some low or non-inflationary growth. Those who studied Japan carefully at the time felt that she took too long to write down all of the inflated assets in the banks and took too long to try to create, within the banking system, the additional stimulus that might get the economy moving again. Japan is now suffering from the collapse of western demand for her goods.

The question for the West is whether it has done enough to avoid similar errors. In the United States of America, there has certainly been much more positive action to slash interest rates, make liquidity available to the American banking system and at the same time encourage American banks to make large write-offs to create honest balance sheets that people can believe in again. Reactions have been somewhat slower and less dramatic in the United Kingdom and Europe, but the direction of travel is similar: banks have been confessing substantial write-offs, seeking large new capital injections, with central banks taking difficult loans and assets from them in exchange for better quality paper and cash, to try to get the credit creation process underway again. Some of the lessons appear to have been learnt from the Japanese experience. There has also been a dash to reflate in every conceivable way.

In the UK, public money has been committed to loans to banks, guarantees for banks, new share capital for banks, for a cut in value-added tax and for extra public spending. In the USA, public money has been committed to provide loans and banking capital, with the new President elected on a ticket promising to increase public spending and borrowing. The system is now awash with money – but the banks remain too weak to lend it on, and the regulators are still demanding better capital ratios at a time of large bank write-offs.

It is going to take some time for property values to find a new base on either side of the Atlantic. At the time of writing, American residential property has fallen further and faster than most European residential property. Commercial property, especially in Britain, has fallen quickly but may well have further to fall. The sooner the property adjustment is made, the better. It will then be easier for banks to work out how much they have lost on lending against property, which was the main source of collateral and at the heart of much of the credit crunch problem.

Experts who felt that, maybe, the overall downturn might not be too bad have been regularly revising their views downwards as 2008 advanced. In the United States of America, concerted action by the administration in cutting taxes and the central bank in cutting interest rates produced good second-quarter figures. However, as the effect of those started to wear off, there was the need to become more pessimistic; there was the realisation that the damage done to property prices, and the continuing difficulties of the banks in producing enough credit, would have a substantial impact on the level of US output. The bigger the falls in output, the bigger the losses in the banks – and the longer it will take to get the credit mechanism well-oiled and functioning properly again.

LESSONS FOR GOVERNMENTS

So what should governments do on the back of this sorry tale? They should look to themselves. Governments should get better at managing the cycle in their role as central bankers. They need to get cleverer in their role as regulators, trying to break the pro-cyclical regulation of banks which they currently indulge in by creating some counter-cyclicality in their actions. They should be panicking about the riskiness of banks when they are lending a lot – and they should be worrying about the inadequacy of the amount of lending they are doing when times are hard. Instead they do it the other way round. Governments should, above all, seek to borrow less themselves towards the top of a cycle. The United Kingdom government was particularly poor in this respect. As the boom continued, so it was the government that was up to additional tricks, borrowing increasing amounts of money under the Private Finance Initiative and Public Private Partnerships – which it felt it could keep off its own balance sheet. The biggest off-balance sheet borrower in the United Kingdom was the British government itself, shortly before it started lecturing others on how foolish this course of action was. If government started repaying debt as the boom advanced it would dampen the cycle. It would take some of the pressure out of the system. When the private sector is at full throttle, the government sector should reduce its claim on resources; when the private sector is weakening, that is the time for the public sector to borrow more and spend more, to provide some counter-cyclical activity.

LESSONS FOR BANKS

And what should the banks learn? The banks should learn that, even when the central banks and regulators are giving them the green light, they should be more careful. Bank directors should see that they need to give equal weight to the risk assessors and the people charged with being cautious in the bank on the one hand, as to the salespeople trying to put new loans on the balance sheet, on the other. They should understand that it is not always a good thing to maximise the use of the bank's capital and to push the banking ratios to the extreme permitted by the regulator. The banks, too, have to learn to be more counter-cyclical. Some banks, in some sectors of the banking market, understood this and did well; others reinforced the dangers of the cycle.

A bank in the mortgage business, for example, should be asking for bigger deposits and advancing smaller multiples of income when house prices climb giddily. Instead, valuers often get looser in a surging market. Conversely, as prices fall, then banks should be expecting less by way of deposit – and should be prepared to make bigger advances in relation to income. The valuers, instead of reinforcing the cycle by being ever-gloomier on the way down, should start to say that the values of houses are now realistic or even cheap – and facilitate lending against them.

LESSONS FOR BORROWERS

And what should individual borrowers do? They, too, need more economic awareness than many seem to have. If you are thinking of committing £250,000 to a single purchase of a property when your own income is only £50,000 a year, you should ask yourself some hard questions as to the time period you propose to repay all this borrowing and how (or whether) you are going to afford it. People should not just think about the interest payments they are going to have to make, but they should also think about the need to repay the capital one way or another. When they are considering the interest payments, they should not just look at the sums based on today's interest rates – but they should ask themselves *'Could I still afford this mortgage and still carry on living in my new home if interest rates have doubled?'* We need more financial awareness, so that more people look after themselves and make better decisions.

NEW REGULATIONS?

There is no simple regulatory answer to any of this. If there were I would, of course, support it. There is no all-seeing, all-wise regulator who can be hired at a reasonable salary to make judgments on behalf of the rest of us. There is no small group of people who know better than the banks how to lend money to people; there is no small group of people influential enough to stop people borrowing too much when they get carried away. The system can only be made better as a large number of all those involved begin to understand more about it. Public debate can help. The salutary impact of the credit crunch on the lives of many families on both sides of the Atlantic will have some short-term impact. It is important we draw a crucial lesson out of these personal tragedies and this wider drama: the lesson that, in every area of financial activity, central banking, regulation, banking and the customer base, we need to get better at dampening the cycle rather than reinforcing it.

In the months ahead the American and British authorities are going to discover, to their cost, that owning mortgage banks and general banks is not a wise course of action. The US had the large obligations of Freddie and Fannie to handle. The UK has to work through its problems at RBS and Lloyds/HBOS. They have to get those institutions onto a more commercial footing as quickly as possible. Both authorities have to recognise that there is no permanent fountain of taxpayer largesse that can provide for their mistakes and their generous costs. They need to be told to cut costs, price services intelligently and write off bad loans quickly. The government needs to get out of the business of banking as soon as possible. These banks are too big for the state to own and handle – the taxpayer needs protecting from these huge financial risks, not exposing more.

If we learn just one thing from this crisis, it is that the actions of too many people and too many institutions throughout the last 10 years have reinforced the craziness of the cycle instead of seeking to abate it. We need wiser central bankers who put interest rates up when the going is good and who put interest rates down when the going is tough; bankers who see ahead, rather than reacting after the event. We need banking regulators who sense when the banks are lending too much (whatever the ratios and the sums may say) and start to rein them in early. We need more bankers who say to their shareholders *'I'm not going to maximise my book of loans at the current stage of the cycle because I think things are going too far and too fast.'* And we need more people wanting to borrow to build a business or buy a house who understand that, if credit is too easy and prices are too high, that is a warning sign – not an invitation to come to the party. If you come to the party late, when the prices are already sky high and everyone else already has a mortgage, you will find the party is close to a sticky end and will end in great disappointment.

I would like to think lessons will be learned from this crisis – but experience tells me otherwise. In many ways this is an old-fashioned cycle. Far from abolishing boom and bust, the United Kingdom government of the last 11 years has reinforced it. Instead of taking the action necessary as the boom was in its upswing, to rein back government spending and borrowing and to create some space for the buoyant private sector, the government did the opposite. Instead of choosing people in their central bank who would raise interest rates as the upswing got underway, the government instead changed the target, allowing and encouraging the central bank to keep interest rates too low for too long. It is no wonder that we have had boom and bust again. When will they ever learn? If we are not careful, their late and wild actions to reflate will start up yet another boom and bust cycle. No more boom and bust? I fear not.